1989

University of St. Francis
GEN 823.809 S818
Steig, Michael,
Stories of reading

S0-BRL-503

STORIES OF READING

Stories of Reading

SUBJECTIVITY AND LITERARY UNDERSTANDING

Michael Steig

The Johns Hopkins University Press

Baltimore and London

LIBRARY
College of St. Francis
JOLIET, ILLINOIS

© 1989 The Johns Hopkins University Press
All rights reserved
Printed in the United States of America

The Johns Hopkins University Press
701 West 40th Street, Baltimore, Maryland 21211
The Johns Hopkins Press Ltd., London

The paper used in this publication meets the
minimum requirements of American National
Standard for Information Sciences—Permanence
of Paper for Printed Library Materials,
ANSI Z39.48-1984.

Library of Congress Cataloging-in-Publication Data

Steig, Michael, 1936–
    Stories of reading : subjectivity and literary under-
standing / Michael Steig.
        p. cm.
    Bibliography: p.
    Includes index.
    ISBN 0-8018-3723-5 (alk. paper)
    ISBN 0-8018-3804-5 (pbk.)
    1. English fiction—History and criticism—Theory,
etc.   2. English fiction—History and criticism.
3. Reader-response criticism.   I. Title.
PR826.S725   1989
801'.953—dc19   88-22599
                                             CIP

823.809
S 818

To my wife, Katharine,
and to the memory of our friend, Branwen Bailey Pratt

134,523

· Contents

· Acknowledgments

My deepest debts are to David Bleich and Jared Curtis, mentors and collaborators in reader response, and to my students at Simon Fraser University. Bernard J. Paris has always given a sympathetic ear to my ideas, and Professor Peter J. Rabinowitz, who read the book in manuscript, made very valuable suggestions as well as giving great encouragement. I am also grateful to Ann Campbell and Monique Salmon for extended discussions of some of the texts and issues treated in this study.

Special thanks are due Maurice Sendak for his helpful replies to my letters, and for permission to reproduce a passage from one of his to me.

A Leave Fellowship from the Social Sciences and Humanities Research Council of Canada made it possible for me to take the sabbatical leave during which I began work on this book; the year was spent in Monk's House, Rodmell, East Sussex, and I shall not make the excuse that the Bloomsbury ghosts were what caused me to require another sabbatical year for its completion. I owe thanks for both sabbatical leaves to Simon Fraser University.

Earlier and now much revised versions of portions of this book have been published as articles in scholarly journals or chapters in books. Two paragraphs of chapter 1 appeared in "'Evasive' Narrative and Authorial Intention, or, Do Critics Make Style?" *Language and Style* 10 (1977), copyright 1978 by Edmund L. Epstein; parts of chapters 2 and 9 appeared in "Motives for Interpretation: Intention, Response, and Psychoanalysis in Literary Criticism," *American Critics at Work: Examinations of Contemporary Literary Theories,* ed. Victor A. Kramer (Troy, N.Y.: Whitston, 1984); part of chapter 5 in "At the Back of *The Wind in the Willows:* An Experiment in Biographical and Autobiographical Interpretation," *Victorian Studies* 24 (1981); part of chapter 6 in "Alice as Self and Other: Experiences of Reading *Alice's Adventures in Wonderland,*" copyright 1986 by the Association of Canadian University Teachers of English, reprinted from *English Studies in Canada,* Vol. XII, No. 2, June 1986, by permission of the Association; half of chapter 7 in "*David Copperfield* and Shared Reader-Response," *Approaches to Teaching Dickens' David Copperfield,* edited by Richard J. Dunn (New York: MLA, 1984); part of chapter 8 in "The Intentional Phallus: Determining Verbal Meaning in Literature," *The Journal of Aesthetics and Art Criticism* 36 (1977); a small portion of chapter 9 in "Psychological Realism and Fantasy in Jane Austen: *Emma* and *Mansfield Park,*" *Hartford Studies in Literature* 5 (1973); part of chapter 10 in "Fantasy and Mimesis in Literary Character: Shelley, Hardy, and Lawrence," copyright 1975 by the Association of Canadian University Teachers of English, reprinted from *English Studies in Canada,* Vol. I, No. 2, Summer 1975, by permission of the Association; and part of chapter 11 in "Reading *Outside Over There,*" *Children's Literature* 13 (1985), edited by Margaret Higonnet, published by Yale University Press. I wish to thank the editors and publishers for permission to use this material.

· Introduction

My main title, *Stories of Reading,* is taken from a chapter of the same name in Jonathan Culler's *On Deconstruction.* Although he is not an advocate of reader-response criticism, Culler makes a point about the impossibility of locating meaning exclusively in either the text or the reader which has been of help in my attempt to create a model of how response and interpretation can be considered to be connected.

The initial motivation for writing this book arose not so much from a perceived need to connect response and interpretation, as from resistance to what has been for years the dismissal by the dominant critical schools—from the New Critics to varieties of structuralists and poststructuralists—of the author as a matter suitable to be considered in the study of literature.[1] My first plan was to demonstrate how, in interpretation, the use of some concept of "intention" is unavoidable; but in trying to develop a model of the role of conceptualized intention in the interpretive process, I recognized that a complex aspect of reading was involved, and thus that I could not consider authorial intention without placing it within the larger category of the "extrinsic," and under the general topic of the relation between individual readers' experiences and the meanings of literary texts. Not being able to relinquish a belief in my own and other readers' need to understand literary works as other than ourselves, and yet having become convinced that to a considerable extent readers do "make meaning,"[2] I was faced with the problem of constructing a model of reading that could satisfactorily connect readers' experiences and associations not only with interpretation and intention but more broadly with the intrinsic and extrinsic aspects of texts.

If one takes "meaning" to be an aspect of texts which exists exclusively in a social domain of shared language and culture, then the reported personal experience (or "response") and associations of the individual reader would seem to be irrelevant, based as they presumably are on the idiosyncrasies of the informant—irrelevant especially if initially perceived as "wrong" by the other members of a group of readers (literature classroom, community of critics), that is, as an experience they do not share. Considered this way, individual readers' subjectivity could have nothing to do with textual meaning. If, as E. D. Hirsch has been insisting for more than two decades, literary "meaning" must be both determinate and sharable, then there is no connection between the unique aspects of individual reading experience and the meaning of a text. One purpose of this study is to propose a way of considering the sharable that does not require determinacy in Hirsch's sense.[3]

The strongest influences on my way of dealing with these questions have been the theory and classroom practices of David Bleich, but I have developed both a theory and practice with a somewhat different focus. Bleich's writings about reader response have not seemed adequate to my purpose because of their primary focus on the reader and the processes of "negotiation" among readers of the same text, a focus that ignores readers' needs to come to at least temporary understanding of a text. One of Bleich's recent articles argues for investigating the development of knowledge within a social context and suggests that not only so-called objective interpretation, but also the concentration of some reader-response critics on the text and their own responses to it, or on analyzing other individuals (students) and their responses, reflects "the masculine hegemony in formal scholarship" and ignores the social aspects of the reading process ("Intersubjective Reading," 419).

This book is an attempt both to talk about how readers read—on the basis of my own and my students' personal reading experiences—and to demonstrate the social role of the communication of personal responses in the understanding of literature on the basis of classroom experiences. Emphasized are individuals' and groups' endeavors to understand texts (however temporary and open to modification that understanding may be), and the way extrinsic factors enter into literary understanding. If I spend more time on the process of my own coming to understand works of literature than on others', it is not because of egotism or because I am a part of the "masculine hegemony," but rather because, like any reader, I know my own reading processes best and can describe them most fully, especially where matters of affect and association are concerned.

My choice of the term *literary understanding* rather than *knowledge* to designate the goal of reading and interpretation stems from a feeling that *knowledge* implies a conclusive interpretation. *Understanding,* as I use it, refers to an inward relationship to a text, a relationship that may be communicated to others and yet is also open to change through the communication of others' understandings.[4] My main argument regarding the relation between response and interpretation is based on the premise that an attempt to make sense out of what one reads is a normal motivation, and that in the case of imaginative literature "sense" involves the affective as well as the cognitive, the unconscious as well as the conscious. What I attempt to demonstrate is that, while there are essential intersubjective ways of making sense based on the *prior* shared assumptions in a particular group—whether the members of a literature class or published critics—there are also personal modes of understanding literary texts based on individual experience, which, when communicated, can enrich others' understanding and can move from the state of subjectivity for the individual to that of a gained, rather than prior, intersubjectivity for the social group. (The predominant usage of *intersubjectivity* refers to prior shared assumptions, and the general restriction in literary theory of the word to this meaning suggests a rejection both of the individual—as distinct from the hypothetical, implied, or ideal—reader and of dialectical social processes as important to criticism.) Because this study focuses on the process of reading by real readers, its concerns are unavoidably personal, and much of it is cast in autobiographical terms—in discussions of experiences as a teacher, a reader, and a critic trying to make sense of texts in terms of the affects they evoke and the particular relation of such evoked feelings to my own and others' lives.

I have found it necessary to address two separate questions. First, how is it possible that individual response has anything to do with understanding a literary work as "other"? Second, how can the "extrinsic" (authorial intention, literary influence, the multiple versions of a text) be a part of a model of reading based on individual response, and of the critical and pedagogical approach generated by such a model? To some extent both issues are discussed in most of the chapters, the role of the extrinsic especially from chapter 5 onwards. And because in considerations of the reading process these two issues frequently overlap, I open with two introductory chapters on, respectively, response and interpretation, and response, interpretation, and the extrinsic (authorial intention in particular).

Without offering any concrete evidential basis for it at this point,

I here present a summary of the model of reading and interpretation developed in this book, in the form of six premises, to which it is the purpose of the book to give substance:

1. A literary text places constraints upon what a given reader may take from it in meaning, feeling, and understanding, and upon the extent to which that reading, when communicated, is likely to obtain assent from other readers. But with many texts the range of variation in response and interpretation may be as great as or greater than the range of textual constraints. Furthermore, the function of constraints is relative, not absolute, as for different readers the constraints found to be important may be different.

2. Works of mimesis or "representation" (narrative or dramatic), or "expression" (narrative, dramatic, lyric, or, in some cases, expository), typically arouse conflicting and to some extent disturbing emotions, as well as confusion as to how to understand the world represented in the work in relation to one's own world and sense of self. Such conflicts and confusion are among the primary motives for interpretation.

3. Understanding, in the act of reading literature, is a temporary condition of satisfaction arrived at subjectively and, in the dialectical sense of the term, intersubjectively; it is not directly related to "meaning" in its narrowest sense—the signification of small language units, such as words and sentences, or the propositional "message" of a text.

4. Because of personality and experience, some readers are capable of more original and deeper understanding of emotionally puzzling aspects of particular literary works than are others; and such understanding can be conceptualized by such a reader through a reflection upon the emotions experienced and upon personal associations with those emotions.

5. Further, such seemingly idiosyncratic understanding can be communicated to other readers of the "same" text so that those readers may absorb the account of that individual experience and make it part of their own understanding, thereby reducing the degree of what may previously have been a feeling of the text's opacity, as well as initial reactions of confusion and incredulity at another's reading of it. Thus the subjective state of understanding may, under the right conditions for communicating it, be made intersubjective.[5]

6. Conceptualization of many kinds of knowledge extrinsic to the text, including, but not limited to, the author and his or her intentions, is for some readers an important aspect of literary understanding. For an individual reader, such conceptualization in aid of understanding functions, like the understanding of the intrinsic text, through that reader's individuality and subjectivity. Furthermore, the boundaries of signification for any given reading of a text may be placed by the individual reader according to his or her assumptions about what is possible for authors, or for a particular author at a particular historical time.

The readers in this text include myself, some of my students, and some critics. I chose the student papers that I quote or summarize on several grounds: in the discussion of *Wuthering Heights* (chap. 3), in which I use such papers at greatest length, I selected them partly on grounds of variety, to demonstrate the range of responses, but the one I quote fully seems to me simply the most remarkable and enlightening one—enlightening for the class as well as for me. For *Bleak House* (chap. 4), however, I limited my selection to three papers that address a very specific matter—how one responds to the character of Esther Summerson—as this became the main subject of heated discussion and has implications for possible differences between "male" and "female" reading. In regard to *Alice's Adventures in Wonderland* (chap. 6), I was again guided by variety, using two very disturbed responses (one incoherent and the other coherent), and one very positive response; but I also chose the latter because of the ways in which it enabled me to come to terms with my own response to the book. And in chapter 7, the papers on *David Copperfield* were selected primarily for their contribution to the classroom dialogue about Dickens's handling of female characters, although one other is used in order to demonstrate how a response paper with relatively few details can in discussion lead to new insights. Whether the reader-response approach described here does in fact convey new ways of looking at and understanding texts is something only the readers of this volume can ultimately decide.

The literary works chosen for discussion may seem to have few interconnections that would justify grouping chapters on them in a single volume, but all these texts do have something in common: they present challenges to understanding. As a group they are useful for demonstrating the relation between an author's text, his life, and the life of the reader; the effect upon a reader of an author/narrator who arouses hostility by seeming to manipulate the reader; the relation between individual or cultural phantasy and the "realistic" in supposedly realist works;[6] how a reader may place limits on the range of a text's signification, specifically in the nineteenth-century novel; and the effect an awareness of literary influence has upon a reader's understanding. But all of these problems are subsumed under the more general one of how the communication and discussion of individual affect and associations can lead to new literary understanding, and as well in some cases to new understanding of oneself and of others. It is from students' responses to literature that I have received new ways of seeing as a result of experiencing through others' experiences, and feeling through their feelings; and it is students who perennially renew my belief that literature has a value for individuals' lives.

Behind my accounts of the stories of reading (and the stories of my responding to others' stories of reading) there lie some convictions that I do not address directly in the following chapters. One is that literature can be subversive of fixed, "normal" modes of thinking, and that it is the teacher's and critic's function, if not to stress this quality directly, then to help make what seems familiar unfamiliar by showing it from new points of view. That it then becomes familiar in time does not mean that such familiarity need be permanent—rereading, especially in a new context (which may mean no more than at a different age), can again make unfamiliar what we thought we had pinned down for good and could thus ignore. I am perhaps in danger of sounding as though I judge texts that are difficult, confusing, or even anxiety-producing to be most valuable as literary works. But they are most valuable from my point of view only in a relative way— that is, they tend to evoke the strongest responses; and without the experience of my students' responses to works so frequently discussed by critics, I almost certainly would have had difficulty in "defamiliarizing" *Alice in Wonderland, Wuthering Heights, David Copperfield, Bleak House,* or *Mansfield Park* for myself. Students' puzzlement at and in some cases revulsion at these novels provided some of the greatest surprises in my study of variation in literary response, sometimes prompting me to try to rethink my own often long-rigidified understanding of them; and in certain response papers (some of which I quote or summarize here), these students' attempts at grappling with their own reading experiences and their personal associations provided fresh outlooks on the texts and caused me to reconsider the bases of my own responses.

I want to conclude this introduction by mentioning two ways in which I hope I offend against both the traditional canon of English literature and the concept of "great" literature: first, by rejecting the assumption—when teaching or writing about literature—that *any* work is unquestionably a masterpiece, and second, by including so many children's books in a serious discussion of the theory and practice of reading. For I consider the assumption about masterpieces to be one that inhibits new thoughts and, especially for students, honest reactions (I take this up especially in chaps. 3 and 7). Furthermore, I regard the exclusion of certain texts and types of texts from the canon of "great works" to be purely arbitrary and, more specifically, the distinction between children's and adult books to be primarily a matter of intellectual snobbery—when it is not simply a matter of marketing and library classification. On the one hand, not only have the Brontës, Austen, and Dickens in my lifetime been considered writers suitable primarily for children (and many Canadian students today have read these authors in early adolescence or even in childhood), but Carroll seems now to be read mainly by adults, Grahame did not think of *The Wind in the Willows* as being for children, and Maurice Sendak intended his most recent book for both adults and children.

As it happens, books (whether "children's" or not) that have been read in childhood or adolescence can provide comparisons between early, spontaneous impressions and more reflective later ones, which can be a fascinating process revealing how a person's "readings" vary with experience and situation. And the fullest and most elaborate story herein of an individual's reading of a literary work at two stages of life (in chap. 3) begins with a young woman's account of her reading at seventeen of *Wuthering Heights*—earlier in this century, if not now, considered a "children's," indeed a "girls'," book.

I · SUBJECTIVITY AND INTERPRETATION

for identifying exactly what the possible explanations are. The reader is not permitted to go outside the text to make up other possible explanations of his own. The indeterminacy lies in the multiplicity of possible incompatible explanations given by the novel and in the lack of evidence justifying a choice of one over the others. The reader cannot logically have them all, and yet nothing he is given determines a choice among them.
—J. Hillis Miller, *Fiction and Repetition*

Two central theoretical questions in literary studies today are those of the determinacy or indeterminacy of meaning and the autonomy or contingency of texts. These questions can be subsumed under another: How does interpretation (or reading) work, and what if anything gives interpretations (or "readings") authority? For those who become influential in the modern discourse on interpretation, as well as the majority of academics who are influential mainly in their own classrooms, the question of authority inevitably takes on ethical and existential dimensions. How one believes meaning to be authorized (or if one believes it not authorizable) may support for the person whose life work is either interpretation or its theory a substantial portion of the sense of self and self-worth. When Stanley Fish insists that meaning is created by "interpretive strategies" and authorized by "interpretive communities"; when E. D. Hirsch argues that it is ethically correct to consider only the "author's meaning" or the "original meaning" (*The Aims of Interpretation,* 77–92); when David Bleich supports the individual, affective, and subjective nature of meaning; or when Hillis Miller says that one is not permitted to go outside a text that itself authorizes a multiplicity of possible meanings—each of these theorist-critics is claiming to have uttered a truth about literary meaning. But each is also revealing his conception of himself and his role within the total community of interpreters and theorists.

Paradoxically, claims for interpretive validity, on the one hand, and for the indeterminacy of meaning, on the other, often carry with them an acknowledgment of, or even a preoccupation with, their seeming contraries. Thus Norman Holland argues for "transaction" between the reader and the text, yet he is obviously proud of the correlation between the objective psychological tests administered to his "five readers" and the personality profiles (Holland's term is "identity themes") inferred by him from their reported responses to literary texts (*Five Readers,* 51–52). David Bleich painstakingly attempts in the first four chapters of *Subjective Criticism* to establish the philosophical and psychological—that is, objective—bases for the subjectivity of meaning. And E. D. Hirsch not only concedes but insists that "meaning is simply meaning-for-an-interpreter" (*Aims,* 79). Related paradoxes or contradictions (discussed below) can be detected in the works of Fish, Miller, and Wolfgang Iser.

The aspect of the debates on these questions in recent years which gives this chapter its title is the way in which some theorists, themselves once literary critics, express strong doubts about the value of continuing to interpret individual works and authors; this implies, ultimately, doubts about the value of the activity in most literature classrooms and of the preponderance of academic literary journals that began publishing before the recent upsurge in theory. This is not true, however, of the author of one of my epigraphs, J. Hillis Miller, who allows the literary text a kind of autonomy, an un-Derridean "presence" as a rhetorical structure that, if it does not yield a *single* correct meaning, provides all one needs in order to identify "exactly what the possible" meanings are. What the reader brings to the text apart from a set of techniques for interpretation evidently does not interest Miller, and he seems to overlook the possibility that even when one takes into account the textual constraints that limit interpretation, the (not fully conscious) decision as to which constraints are to count may depend radically on the experiences, previous reading, expectations, and beliefs of the reader.[1] There is also a seeming contradiction in Miller's not permitting (the word is used in the passive voice—"one is not permitted"—as though some transcendent authority were involved) the reader to go outside the text and yet himself choosing to go at least as far outside as Freud's *Beyond the Pleasure Principle.* Miller uses that text, more metapsychological (and metaphysical) than psychological, in which the highly controversial theories of "repetition-compulsion" and the death instinct are introduced, to help authorize his claim that "repetition" is a key element in the rhetorical construction of meaning. Indeed, Miller as critic has gone outside the text in a number of ways, including references to the author;[2] but the one thing "outside" the text he cannot acknowledge is that which in the reading process is also an inside—the reader. (Miller has retained an enthusiasm for the practice of criticism, for solving problems in ways that will satisfy at least for a time, and in this respect he differs from the other authors of my epigraphs, although all four share a belief in the impossibility of finding the one "correct" meaning.)

Stanley Fish originally became known, both as teacher and seventeenth-century scholar, as the closest of close readers, one of whose early theoretical contributions was to equate the meaning of the text with the immediate and retrospective experience of reading the text line by line or sentence by sentence.[3] But in recent years he has substituted "interpretive strategies" for experience as constitutive of meaning, while he sees interpretations as being authorized only by the existence of an "interpretive community" whose members conform to particular strategies (and presumably agree that a given strategy produces a given meaning in any particular case—though this potentially raises a new problem). Fish developed his theory of interpretive strategies when he recognized that his earlier concept of "the informed reader" was, in fact, "designed to take account of, by stigmatizing, all those readers whose experiences were not as [he] described them" (*Text*, 22). Although he has frequently elaborated on this theory, Fish has not deviated much from its first formulation (published in a 1976 essay, "Interpreting the Variorum," and summarized in the passage quoted as one of my epigraphs). Once the theory of interpretive strategies making meanings and interpretive communities authorizing them has been formulated, only study of the motivation and assumptions of those who use particular strategies or of the nature of a variety of interpretive communities can take things further.

Although Fish has devoted some pages to demonstrating why "interpretation is the only game in town" (*Text*, 355)—that is, how literary critics and theorists are always interpreting *some* text, even if it is a student's or another critic's response to or interpretation of a literary text rather than a literary text per se—it is difficult to predict where this position will ultimately take him. Fish frequently, both in person and in print, assures others that they should not be afraid of his theories, and a comment by Steven Mailloux suggests why this may be sound advice to those who would hold to the idea of meaning grounded in the text:

For Fish, "what is really there" is always produced by the procedures used to describe it. This theory of interpretation is both revolutionary and inconsequential. It is revolutionary because it completely changes the way we understand the activities of literary study. But it is inconsequential in that it actually changes nothing in critical practice: critics will continue to use their habitual interpretive strategies in practical criticism (as Fish has done) and will continue to erect metacritical justifications for their criticism. [63]

Jane Tompkins perhaps gives us a glimpse of the possibilities of Fish's position in calling for a shift of theoretical emphasis to the politics of interpretation, the power-relationships that determine the prevalence of a particular critical strategy at any given time. This metacritical focus would seem to offer the possibility of taking Fish's notion of interpretive communities into the social context he often refers to but never really describes. But Tompkins's proposal to concentrate on "power" is not developed at any length.

Jonathan Culler seems, like Tompkins, to dismiss the interpretation of literary texts as a fit practice for present-day literary study, and he has also expressed hostility to any consideration of individual readers. Culler claims that "there is a central axiom which modern research has established: that the individuality of the individual cannot function as a principle of explanation, for it is itself a highly complex cultural construct, a result rather than a cause," and, he continues, "a first priority, then, if one is to study reading rather than readers, is to avoid experimental situations that seek free associations and to focus rather on public interpretive processes" ("Prolegomena," 56). But the notion that individuals are "caused" by their culture in no way makes the study of individuals' reports of their responses and associations irrelevant; indeed, it is from those very accounts that culturally shared assumptions as well as what we might "deviant" ones emerge clearly—much more vividly than in the typical article by a professional critic. Culler's hostility to studying readers derives in part from his strong doubts about two aspects of Norman Holland's *Five Readers Reading:* Holland's claim to be doing objective, scientifically verifiable studies of individual readers, and his theory of each individual's having an "identity theme" that will be detectable in all of his behavior.[4] However, Culler in a later book has less dismissive and more interesting things to say about what he calls "stories of reading" (see below).

One well-known reader-response theorist who had not yet abandoned interpretation by the early 1970s is Wolfgang Iser. For Iser, the text is constructed by the reader, but this is done by the reader's following the implicit instructions of the "strategies" of the text—that is, the way the text juxtaposes norms, systems, and allusions to create the potentiality for meanings not contained within those "background" elements themselves. Iser distinguishes between the "implied reader" and any actual reader. But on the same page he can say both that "the implied reader as a concept has his roots firmly planted in the structure of the text; he is a construct and in no way to be identified with any real reader," and that the concept "designates a network of response-inviting structures, which impel the reader to grasp the text" (*The Act of Reading: A Theory of Aesthetic Response,* 34). Which of these "readers" is a construct and which is real—and who is the constructor? For the second of these statements implies that it is a *real* reader who is "impelled" by the text to construct a particular meaning. Although Iser frequently distinguishes between the process of the reader following the text's instructions in order to create determinate meaning out of what appears indeterminate in the text, and how each individual reader will "decipher [the text] in his own way" (*Act*, 93), when it comes down to the specifics of such variation Iser has nothing to say. It would seem that by insisting that the "implied reader" is only a construct, Iser is skirting the issue of individual variation, and when he applies his theory of reading to specific texts, as in *The Implied Reader*, what comes out is that all readers in fact construct meaning from indeterminacy in the same way. It is as though in theorizing about a subjective process, Iser is at the same time holding on to the idea of meaning-in-texts and taking no account of how such factors as cultural background or experience may affect a reader's construction of meaning.[5]

Because of his concentration on individual response, one may infer a lack of interest in interpretation as such in the work of David Bleich. And it has become for me a serious question whether a concern with either readers or reading inevitably leads away from a concern with individual works of literature and their interpretation. If it does, the term *reader-response criticism*[6] is self-contradictory if we understand *criticism* to refer to interpretation.[7] In order to develop this question further I must now turn to a subject with whom Miller, Tompkins, Culler, Fish, and Iser will have little or nothing to do: the actual reader.

Even as an apprentice New Critic in the 1950s and early 1960s I noticed that critics frequently referred to the "effect" that a work had on "the reader," and for some years believed that texts contain identifiable properties that create relatively uniform effects for readers. Norman Holland's psychoanalytically based *Dynamics of Literary Response* (1968) seemed to present a coherent methodology for dealing with "the reader's" response, and I adapted it to my use in several articles. Yet I felt uneasy from the outset about Holland's confidence in talking about *the* reader's response, in part because the responses he described often were totally different from mine. A further difficulty for me with Holland's approach stemmed from his assertion that because one could know neither a character's nor an author's "mind," the only mind left was that of the reader;[8] and yet the sense of an author who lived at a certain time in a particular society and whose voice seemed to be trying to communicate was a part of my experience in reading; nor could I dismiss the wish of my students to "know" the author's meaning.

Holland was in 1972 convinced by his former student David Bleich that it is theoretically unsound to speak of "the reader," since readers' responses (including supposedly objective interpretations by professional critics) differ strikingly,[9] but because at that time I was involved in a research project (eventually resulting in *Dickens and Phiz*) that seemed to require an assumption of the presence of determinate meanings and thus "correct" readings, it was several years before I could acknowledge how profoundly my approach to literature would have to change. It was above all David Bleich's principle that individual motivation, response, and personal association largely determine interpretations that seemed indisputable, and still does so (but see the qualification at the end of this chapter). The "de-centering" of meaning and its supposed ground in the text as demonstrated by Derrida and others has had a far-ranging effect on literary studies, resulting in an outpouring of literary theory both asserting and denying the determinacy of meaning. But deconstruction, along with Holland's, Bleich's, and Fish's work, has also caused a general malaise among more traditionally oriented academics, a malaise whose motto might well be the often-spoken words, "So, you mean one interpretation is as good as any other?" Even such an avowed deconstructionist as Hillis Miller has been affected by a sense of the danger of individualism and anarchy in interpretation, or that is how I take "the reader is not permitted to go outside the text to make up possible explanations of his own." Twenty years ago Miller would surely have found no need to issue such a caveat.

Bleich's work more than that of any other recent theorist seems to threaten the very practice of interpretation (not to treat it as a lower activity, as Culler and Tompkins do); and the threat stems in part from the fact that his primary research tools have been the classroom and the response paper, in which, some seem to think, any interpretation goes. On the most basic level the threat of Fish, Holland, and Bleich that some perceive is that the interpretive authority of the teacher and critic will have to be given up, that there will no longer be any distinct methodology for students to learn by imbibing the wisdom of their elders. I have heard this fear, though it was not intended to be understood as such, expressed by a well-known critic who simply dismissed the possibility of there being any value in collecting and discussing student responses, averring that what was needed was for students to learn "mastery" of the craft of criticism. The implicit privileging of the male (the master) as teacher was not, I think, an accident, though it was surely not consciously intended.

My teaching in the past decade has been most fruitful—in students' participation and enthusiasm and in arriving at new understandings—when I have followed a rigorous response approach, requiring students to relate the way they understand meaning to their emotions and those in turn to personal associations. Papers, including my own, are duplicated and distributed to all members of the class, a practice that is indispensable for the exchange of responses and the reducing of competitive one-upmanship. Culler suggests that the spontaneity of a reader's written response is illusory, because the form and content that emerge are controlled by the instructions put or the questions asked by the teacher, as well as the consciousness that one is engaged in the formal process of writing (*On Deconstruction: Theory and Criticism after Structuralism*, 64–67). And I agree that spontaneity is not to be looked for in any kind of writing; but nonetheless the kind of questions set and the kind of papers written in a response classroom involve doing something different from what is done in other pedagogical contexts, and they usually produce a different kind of result.[10] There should be no illusion that we are getting the whole story from any reader, in part because, as Culler suggests, writers, including literature students, inevitably function in certain conventional ways. Yet the process of considering one's responses and trying to communicate them to others is a process distinct from other kinds of literary analysis.[11]

Early on in teaching through response, however, a problem arose. In a graduate seminar in children's literature, I discovered that although the students found the reader-response approach enlightening and stimulating, as potential professional academics they also wondered what one could do with material of the kind we had gathered among ourselves, or what any individual could do with his own responses. They asked how a paper describing affects and associations could ever be made into publishable criticism, unless one were to follow Bleich in deriving metacritical principles from the responses quoted and analyzed. It was a question that faced me all the more immediately, for since I was ultimately more interested in discussing literary texts than developing a theory of reading I had doubts about how to bring personal feelings and autobiographical associations into writing intended to become public.[12] Behind that question lay a concern that something one felt as a committed reader to be of the utmost importance was being downplayed if not ignored by staying with response alone: the urge to understand something "about" the work, and to have some notion of "its" or even "the author's" meaning. Neither my students nor I wanted to give up our interpretive impulses to become pure literary or pedagogical theorists, nor did we want to limit our goal to self-knowledge. A nagging question arose for me: If reader-response procedures (in Bleich's sense) feel liberating to students and teachers alike, what do they liberate us for? It seems clear enough what they liberate us from: for the teacher, from the uneasy sense of spurious authority in what had been a master-pupil relationship, through the partial elimination of the principle that the teacher always has the last word;[13] for the students, from some of the typical feelings of inadequacy, inferiority, and competitiveness, allowing them to gain a new sense of personal authority, a conviction that their own contributions matter. And if the mix of students is right, the classroom can be a mutually participatory milieu rather than one in which there is only a one-to-one relationship between each individual student and the teacher.[14] But again, what do the procedures liberate us *for*? Self-knowledge and increased understanding of the ordinarily opaque other person are for me bonuses, but not the main goal, of an approach that stresses individual factors in reading. As Culler asks regarding Stanley Fish's interpretive strategies that construct the literary work, "What are interpretive acts interpretations *of*?" (*On Deconstruction*, 75), one could similarly ask, "What does subjective criticism criticize?"

One might say that such procedures open up for us more of an awareness of the nature of our interaction, as readers, with the text, thus taking us into a realm where the actual human being, the individual reader, achieves literary understanding and communicates it to others. David Bleich rejects the notions of "interaction" or "transaction" between the reader and the text, insisting that such concepts overlook the fact that only the reader, not the text, can "act."[15] Taken literally, reader-text interaction, in which *both* sides act, is impossible for just the reason Bleich gives. But although the entire process of reading, reflecting, judging, and interpreting does take place within the reader's mind, there still may be a phenomenologically sound use for a term like interaction or transaction: to designate a process between the reader and his perceptions of and responses to the text from moment to moment, whether this be linear (relating each additional perception to what has preceded it) or reflective (relating a number of perceptions that have already taken place to form a new perception—an interpretation). For even if the text does not really "act," reading often feels like interaction simply because as one's perceptions change, the text itself seems to change.[16] In all such processes the text is perceived as an "other," no matter how strongly one may be committed to the principle of meaning-in-the-reader. In developing the model underlying the descriptions of reading in this study I shall suggest how other factors also seem to interact with the reader: the reported perceptions of other readers, the inferred intention of the author and information about his life and times, and knowledge about an author's other works, and of the literary influences he has absorbed.

The main objection to this endeavor might be that it is illogical to claim that what resides in the mind of the reader can have any relation to an external object. How is it possible to interpret a text if one claims that it truly exists only in subjectivity? Culler's later critique of what he calls "stories of reading" suggests an answer, although he might not accept the way I use his argument. According to Culler, Bleich's insistence on meaning-making readers, Fish's on interpretive strategies, as well as combinatory models of reading such as Louise Rosenblatt's or Holland's versions of "transaction," are misleading, because in practice there are "two absolute perspectives" inherent in the reading process—the reader's dominance and the text's dominance (*On Deconstruction,* 73)—and Culler demonstrates that statements implying the latter crop up again and again in reader-response theorists' writings. He points out how paradoxical it is that in stories of reading, "the more a theory stresses the reader's freedom, control, and constitutive activity, the more likely it is to lead to stories of dramatic encounters and surprises which portray reading as a process of discovery" (72). So, does one "create," or does one "discover"? Culler says that such dualisms as creation and discovery are unavoidable "in our dealings with texts and the world," and, along with the underlying question of subjectivity and objectivity, are among the "variable and ungrounded concepts" that "our stories [of reading] require" (77).

Although I agree that terms like *text* and *reader* and related dualisms are necessary in the discussion of reading and unavoidably use such dualisms in the chapters to follow, I do assume that no aspect of reading or interpretation really takes place outside of the reader's thoughts and feelings, except in their communication and discussion. Yet it is also my experience, and that of my students, that attention to one's own or reports of another's reading experiences and associations *does* frequently lead to "dramatic encounters," "surprises," and a sense of "discovery" of something that seems to be *in* the text. Thus it is one of the absolute but also challenging limitations to literary criticism that we can never be certain whether we have, in that aspect of the reading process which feels like discovery, found something "outside over there" or "inside in here."[17]

From another perspective, Susan R. Horton has outlined lucidly the basic problem with the idea of authoritative interpretation: that among various theorists and critics, no matter how much they use the same set of terms such as *meaning, unity, part, whole, context, theme,* or *symbol* in the discussion of what interpretation *should* be, there is no general agreement as to how these terms should be applied (as can be seen in the variety of ways they do apply these terms); and this is especially the case when one deals with large, complex structures such as novels (*Interpreting Interpreting: Interpreting Dickens's Dombey,* 1–21 and passim). Yet Horton begins her final chapter by saying that she has become convinced that "we really do need to put some constraints on the process of interpretation," because "without at least the fiction of a stable entity somewhere in the interpretive process it spins off into outer space" (128). I am not sure what "putting constraints" on interpretation means, unless it means setting up rules to be followed; nor can I understand the cosmic metaphor except as an expression of anxiety. There always seem to be constraints in the text, but confusingly enough it also seems that not every reader is constrained by the same elements. And if there are any such things as *unavoidable* constraints, their nature is likely to be fairly elementary. For example, if an author says a character is wearing a red dress, it is incorrect to report that it is blue, although the reasons for any mistake may be of interest. And that possibility of error goes beyond the single word: if it is stated in a narrative that one character has murdered another, within any group of readers who communicate with one another it will seem to most an interpretive error to deny it (although again, the reasons for denial can be interesting). But even at the level of simple actions, authors, and thus their texts' constraints on understanding, are not always clear—not even about murders: witness Thackeray's ambiguity in *Vanity Fair* about whether Becky Sharp has really poisoned Jos Sedley.[18] Ultimately, the only test of unavoidable textual constraints may be a matter of consensus among readers.

Susan Horton's final sentence, "What a relief it is to know that the complexities inherent in the process of interpretation itself and in Dickens's text have cooperated to ensure that we shall never fully interpret that text" (144), suggests that the critic has proven to herself that the challenging engagement in interpretation is not inevitably entropic, because the text feels vividly alive and the process of repeatedly reinterpreting it natural and necessary; and this suggests that what constraints count in determining understanding is a perennially shifting matter. The report of the death of interpretation has probably been exaggerated. Culler and Tompkins in the passages I have quoted do seem comfortable with the prospect of that death, or at least with the possibility that interpretation may lie dormant while literary theorists investigate how it works. But readers' motives for interpretation are strong and various, and there is much to learn "about" the text, as well as about reading, from responses to it.

I conclude this chapter by offering two examples of varying interpretation that may illustrate the relativity of textual constraints. *The Mill on the Floss* is a text that seems to be, if anything, overburdened with constraints: the narrator's frequent comments on the significance of events and her evaluations of characters' behavior; the presence of river-imagery in the reflective first chapter and the role of the river in the apocalyptic conclusion; the presentation of the Tulliver, Dean, and Glegg families and their roles in a community; and the very shape of Maggie's story—alternating between self-effacement and aggressive self-assertion. Among other ways of reading the novel, critics have argued for Eliot's success in presenting an ideal of family and duty, with brother and sister reconciled to one another and to the community in death; alternatively, for a gap between Eliot's intentions and her achievement, in her failure to recognize overtly the motivations—shifting between neurotic compliance and neurotic aggressiveness—that determine Maggie's behavior; and for Eliot's prophetic representation in Maggie's relatives and in the novel's imagery (and to some extent in Maggie herself) of the "anal character" that was to be delineated by Freud, and the relation of such a character-type to a middle-class, commercial, and Protestant society.[19] Many other examples could be adduced, but my point here is that each of these essays represents the critic's sense of particular constraints in the text which generate the interpretation, constraints that seem important at a particular point in the critic's life and career.[20] My second illustration comes from one of David Bleich's attempts to demonstrate, on the basis of classroom evidence, that meaning resides in the reader. The paradoxical implications of this attempt seem to me to substantiate Culler's emphasis on irresolvable dualisms in thinking about reading, and my own thoughts, throughout this book, about the curious ways in which the "subjective" approach seems to result in new understandings, and that extrinsic knowledge becomes part of the reader's subjectivity. Bleich in this instance depends for evidence not on varied individual readings, but rather on a teaching situation in which the students were a relatively homogeneous group as to age and background and whose responses tended to be similar. The paradox and the further implications of Bleich's actual argument were one key motivation for my decision to attempt to deal with the problem of the text as other as well as self. Assigning Thackeray's *Vanity Fair* to a class of first-year students, Bleich collected fourteen sets of responses among which eleven "explicitly complain about the lack of overt sexuality in the novel" (*Readings,* 88), and because no "Victorian would even see the novel as having omitted something," we "can only ascribe the collective responses to shared personal and cultural values," and not to any "prurient material" in *Vanity Fair* (89). Thus the "meaning" here must come from the readers, not the text.

Bleich's argument, first of all, is based on a preconception of what it means to be a nineteenth-century novelist or reader (a question I take up further in chapters 4, 5, 8, and 9). While it is true that, as one student complained, there is not "one good sex scene" in *Vanity Fair* (*Readings,* 84), the main aspect of this complaint which derives from shared twentieth-century values is the students' awareness of literature that *does* have such scenes. An alternative explanation to Bleich's one of cultural homogeneity (plausible as a partial explanation) as the basis for the consistency of the those eleven students' complaints about the lack of explicit sexuality is that they are all responding to the same thing "in" the text—that is to say, they all find the same textual constraints to be important for them. For the novel's action is repeatedly concerned with sexual frustration: the desire for Becky Sharp of Rawdon Crawley, Sir Pitt Crawley the elder and the younger, George Osborne, and Lord Steyne, fulfilled only for Rawdon and that only intermittently and for a limited time; the pathetic and misplaced love Amelia feels for George, and Dobbin's long frustration in his love for Amelia; and Jos Sedley's desire for Becky, which virtually frames the novel's plot, and is ultimately self-destructive whether or not she actually poisons him. The narrator is at one point quite clear about his own inability to deal directly and in detail with sexual matters, using the metaphor of the mermaid's green and slimy tail, concealed beneath the waters, as a way of not discussing—while pruriently alluding to—Becky's disreputable behavior (beginning of chap. 64).

Although Bleich's students complained about the absence of sex, when one sees Thackeray's novel in the way I have just described (and this description is, like any other of my interpretive statements, not only open to question, but in a sense subjective), it seems likely that they were motivated to do this by its strong implicit presence—that is, while enabled to *make* such complaints because they are late twentieth-century readers, these students were not anachronistically imposing something on the novel's text, but rather were all responding to a particular constraint within the novel—a constraint that may not operate for other readers in other contexts. That a Victorian novelist is evasive and duplicitous in his or her presentation of sexual themes does not mean that there is no sexual content; and Victorian reviewers were often quite astute in sniffing out such content, whether or not they approved of it (in this connection, see my discussion in chap. 3 of a contemporary American review of *Wuthering Heights*). It seems crucially significant that, in the course of attempting to demonstrate that meaning is "in the reader," Bleich had to make a certain assumption about what constraints there could or could not be in the text of a Victorian novel, which is already a recognition on his part of the text as "other." And juxtaposing the students' responses with the interpersonal situations represented in *Vanity Fair* leads me to infer that an aspect of the novel's content has been perceived by readers who lack an adequate vocabulary to describe what they are perceiving. Their complaints about the absence of sex thus become an affirmation of its affective presence for them.[21] If interpretation results from reflection upon response, what happened when Bleich's students wrote on *Vanity Fair* seems to demonstrate that however culture-bound, personal, or even encouraged by the teacher the verbalization of their responses was, they were responding to something "out there," as well as to something "in here." This is perhaps the most cogent illustration I can find of the rightness of Culler's remark about the unavoidable duality of self and other in the process of reading. In various ways the chapters to follow represent attempts to deal with that duality and its implications for the understanding of literature.

2 · Response, Intention, and Motives for Interpretation

I propose that to interpret is to explain some semantic or semiotic structure about whose meaning there is a question, even if it is just a matter of how to think about it. It is a pragmatic task motivated at a basic psychosomatic level by the curiosity and anxiety that uncertainty creates.[1] And because literary texts characteristically deal with human situations, and embody indirection, duplicity, metaphor, and symbol, and because such texts may originate in a past or an alien culture, readers feel a special need to interpret them.[2] But the matter is complicated by the fact that interpretation involves the creating of a new text in addition to the one being interpreted: even the exhortation, "Read it again," is a brief but nonetheless interpretive text that implies, "This work requires at least two readings." Most of the time a second reading will produce a different experience, one that is for the reader a new text. The interpretation of literary texts is, moreover, fundamentally problematic, as Susan Horton suggests, because there is no general agreement as to the nature of the process or its attainable goals.

E. D. Hirsch tries to resolve the latter problem in *Validity in Interpretation* by distinguishing between *meaning,* which is what the author has willed (consciously or unconsciously—which already creates a problem when talking about "will"), and *significance,* which is how one relates a text to something outside itself. To find the first is the task of interpretation, whereas the second is the work of criticism. But how difficult it is to maintain this distinction is shown by Hirsch himself in his later book, *The Aims of Interpretation.* In the earlier study he generally seems to be talking about propositional meanings that can be paraphrased; but in the later he grants that meaning cannot be restricted to "conceptual meaning" but "embraces not only a content of mind represented by written speech but also the affects and values that are necessarily correlative to such a content." In fact, "one cannot *have* a meaning without having its necessarily correlative affect or value" (*Aims,* 8).[3]

But as soon as affects and values are allowed into his model of meaning, Hirsch has put himself in a position similar to that of Murray Krieger, who argues that "it should . . . be the object rather than the reader who is responsible for the aesthetic character of the experience" of reading literature, and that it is the job of the critic to distinguish "between actual responses to the object and what responses the object *ought* to provoke" (*Theory of Criticism: A Tradition and Its System,* 14, 9). These "shoulds" sound, if anything, more authoritarian than Hirsch's dicta, but actually Krieger seems more troubled than Hirsch is by the uncertainty of what "should be." Affects, values, and responses are slippery concepts because they are, like meanings (but more obviously so), mediated by the individual reader's perceptions, associations, and preconceptions, and it is difficult to imagine what the rules might be for deciding what is a "necessarily correlative affect" or an obligatory aesthetic response. Hirsch seems to have become more aware of this as a genuine problem than *Validity in Interpretation* might lead us to expect. For in *The Aims of Interpretation* he makes it clear that meaning is not something in a text, but must always be "meaning for-an-interpreter" (79). That is, "the nature of a text is to mean whatever we construe it to mean" (75), and the choice of the author's intention—his "original meaning," as Hirsch sometimes calls it—as the norm of legitimate interpretation is primarily an ethical one, for failure to respect an author's intention violates the "ethics of language" (90) and is equivalent to using another person as an instrument for one's own purposes. Further, as "professional interpreters" we have an "obligation of shared knowledge" which in turn "implies a shared norm of interpretation" (92). Thus it now appears that the author as the norm of correctness in interpretation is no longer logically imperative, but instead must be justified on the basis of ethics and the role of the members of a profession.

The focus of Hirsch's campaign for "objective interpretation" has changed in another sense, looking quite different in 1976 than it did in 1967 or 1960.[4] *Validity in Interpretation* takes the New Critical proponents of intrinsic interpretation to task for their dismissal of the author as in any way relevant to literary understanding. But in the later book Hirsch seems to be fighting a desperate holding operation against critical relativism and "cognitive atheism," a plague that has spread from France to North America, the "doctrine that since genuine knowledge of an author's meaning is impossible, all textual commentary is therefore really fiction or poetry" (*Aims,* 147). Despite the plain style of Hirsch's writing, I get the feeling of a prophecy of chaos, a world where anything goes, where critics are elevated to the status of poets and where real communication and shared standards of genuine knowledge have been abandoned. And thus one is liable to forget just how much Hirsch has already conceded to the ultimate uncertainty of meaning, and implicitly to the subjective aspects of both meaning and significance, in stressing that we can hope only to find the *most probable* meaning, which ultimately must be construed by an interpreter.

The ongoing attack on the author, against which Hirsch has tried to put up several kinds of defense, brings New Criticism and deconstruction surprisingly close together—surprisingly because the New Critics seemed generally to support the principle of the intrinsic meanings of texts, and thus of objective interpretation, while today's poststructuralists insist on the de-centering or deferral of meaning and allow the critic a kind of autonomy that goes far beyond anything John Crowe Ransom or Wellek and Warren could have countenanced. Where the two schools of thought intersect is perhaps in the importance to both of the idea that language transcends the individual. Michel Foucault, whose view of the transcendence of language is rooted in a concept of historical and cultural change, particularly in the loci of power, has deemed the author a mere "function" within reading, becoming dominant in a culture in which "we fear the proliferation of meaning," and in which the polysemous dangers posed by literature therefore need to be reduced by limiting meaning to the author's ("What is an Author?" 158–59). The rejection of the author by the New Critics, on the other hand, seems to have followed from a reification, a quasi-religious idealization, of literary language, and a denial of historical specificity insofar as history was seen to threaten literature's transcendental status. For poststructuralists, the rejection of the author follows from a rejection of the belief that language is usefully viewed as either expressive or referential; language, or *écriture,* transcends both individual utterance and the illusion of a stable "presence" in texts of meaning.

As one might not expect from an avowed subjectivist, a full chapter in Bleich's *Subjective Criticism* is devoted to the importance of the author in the reading process. Bleich observes that "when language is perceived it is almost always associated with the person who originated it" (238). While he sees the extent of such an association as a variable among readers, he considers it to be something natural to the act of reading. The Prague School theorist Jan Mukařovský had made a similar point forty years earlier.

The creator's personality is . . . always felt to be behind the work even if we do not have the slightest information about the concrete creator and his actual mental life. It is a mere projection of the perceiver's mental act. . . . behind each work of art the perceiving subject intensely feels the subject providing the sign (the artist) to be responsible for the mental state which the work has aroused in him. From here it is only a step to the involuntary hypostasis of the concrete creative subject, constructed only on the basis of the premises given by the work. It is clear that this hypostatized personality, which we shall call the author's personality, need not coincide with the artist's actual psychophysical personality. ["The Individual and Literary Development," 163]

Mukařovský's insistence that readers "always" conceptualize an author is more absolute than either Bleich's or mine, but we concur in seeing it as a normal aspect of reading, and it is interesting to note just how long ago this claim was being made by an advanced literary theorist, more or less contemporaneously with the rise of the New Criticism.

Like many of my students today, I was as an undergraduate virtually indoctrinated with the principle of the irrelevance of the author, for the academy is often, like Dr. Blimber's forcing-house, an artificial context in which some teachers see it as their responsibility to change students' bad habits. Although a teacher cannot be totally free of this tendency, my sense of what constitutes bad habits has changed. It seems that many students normally experience the language of literature as utterance and connect that utterance with the author, and frequently those who have been told that the author is not to be discussed feel great relief when I tell them that it is not forbidden in my class. In particular, post-Renaissance, premodernist literature is often experienced by readers as having a propositional content that an historical author is trying to communicate. Yet I did not always admit this and only began to think that it might be I who had the bad habits some years ago when a student asked in the first lecture session in a Dickens course whether it shouldn't be our object to find out just "what Dickens had in mind." At first judging him to be naive, I hemmed and hawed, trying to brush this off with New Critical clichés about the author not controlling the work, but I eventually recognized that this question might be an expression of a general tendency in reading which I had suppressed in myself.

It is possible to formulate a way of taking into account the "author" (whom I am using here as a stand-in for all types of extrinsic material, whether factual or conceptualized), without at the same time claiming that we can know the author's intention directly (and even Hirsch does not claim that) or allowing to that author total external control over his text's meanings. Although the classic anti-intentionalist argument is "The Intentional Fallacy," a clearer statement and application of the anti-intentionalist position is Monroe Beardsley's discussion of A. E. Housman's poem, "1887." At issue are the closing lines, "Get you the sons your fathers got, / and God will save the Queen." According to Frank Harris, Housman angrily denied that these lines had any ironic intent and insisted that he meant them "sincerely; if Englishmen breed as good men as their fathers, then God will save the Queen" (quoted by Beardsley, *Aesthetics: Problems in the Philosophy of Criticism*, 26). Although his sympathies become clear, Beardsley does not take a definite position on the correct intrinsic reading of these lines, but uses this example to illustrate the difference between an author's conscious intention and the meaning of a text. Thus the poet is "not necessarily the best reader of his poem. . . . And if his report of what the poem is intended to mean conflicts with the evidence of the poem itself, we cannot allow him to *make* the poem mean what he wants it to mean, just by fiat." Beardsley "would have the poem read by competent critics, and if they found irony in it, we should conclude that it is ironical, no matter what Housman says" (26). Yet at the time and in the intellectual context in which Beardsley's *Aesthetics* was written, his "competent critics" would likely have been such as William K. Wimsatt and Cleanth Brooks; and as, in the era of New Critical dominance in North America, complexity, ambiguity, tension, and irony were especially valued in poetry, such critics would most likely have found irony in Housman's lines and a conflict of tone within the poem as a whole.

But can we decide whether irony is present in the lines or is "found" there primarily as a result of attitudes that include an aesthetic preference for irony? If any particular kind of interpretation implies an attribution of authorial intention, surely it is the claim to have found irony—for it is a claim that assumes a double meaning introduced by a conscious agent, while truly unintended irony usually suggests a degree of failure by the author. A reader may well suddenly find it difficult to continue to see irony in Housman's lines once he or she has learned of the poet's disavowal; yet although the lines need mean no more than what Housman reportedly said they did, for some readers such a straight interpretation patently ignores both diction and structure. To me the use of "get" and "got" in Housman's poem still suggests the animalistic breeding of faceless hordes of "fathers" (with even more anonymous hordes of women), while the syntactical separation between what the masses can thus do and what God will do for the Queen connotes a special divine care for the Queen alone, which depends on the breeding of sons who will die on the battlefield in great numbers, apparently bereft of God's favor.

My reading the poem this way has, however, been influenced before the fact by Beardsley's pointing out that the lines sound ironic, and by my attraction to the idea of a patriotic author undercutting himself. But my present understanding has also been influenced after the fact by Housman's reported disavowal of irony. Once having read the lines as ironic I cannot divest them of such a connotation in subsequent readings; but the awareness (assuming that Frank Harris was reporting an actual event—never a certainty) of Housman's statement still affects my reading. As utterance, the poem becomes more ambiguous and the "author" whom I construct in my rereading more devious; ultimately, the poem no longer seems to contain unequivocal constraints that lead one in either direction. Certain correlative affects and values, in Hirsch's terms, may be evoked, but they may be different for different readers. It is possible to imagine a reader of "1887" who would have no trouble with the literal surface meaning of the final lines, would find no irony, and would consider Frank Harris's report of Housman's self-interpretation to confirm such a reading.[5] Such a reader would be constructing his own poet, a different poet from my devious one: his tells the simple truth, while mine lies, unconsciously to himself if not consciously to Harris. In either case a reader's construction of the author becomes a part of the interpretation of the poem in the sense that it is incorporated into that reader's (and interpreter's) total understanding of it.

In saying this, I am not disputing William K. Wimsatt's 1968 reconsideration of "The Intentional Fallacy," at least not within the restrictive model of texts and meaning he seems to be using:

What we meant in 1946, and what in effect I think we managed to say, was that the closest one could ever get to the artist's intending or meaning mind, outside his work, would be still short of his *effective* intention or *operative* mind as it appears in the work itself and can be read from the work. Such is the concrete and fully answerable character of words as aesthetic medium. The intention outside the poem is always subject to the corroboration of the poem itself. No better evidence, in the nature of things, can be adduced than the poem itself. ["Genesis: A Fallacy Revisited," 136]

This strikes me as an obvious epistemological truth, but only *within* the ontological assumption that the words of a poem objectively carry, are "evidence" of, its entire meaning, and that we can somehow experience "the poem itself." Wimsatt and Beardsley also wrote a classic attack on the relevance of the reader's feelings well before reader-response criticism was ever heard of ("The Affective Fallacy" in 1949), and thus it is interesting that Wimsatt here describes with contempt the type of critic for whom an asseveration such as Housman's "will settle the question" of the poem's meaning. Such a critic "prefer[s] to talk, not about the meaning of a poem but about his own 'responses' to it, which may be 'conditioned' by his knowledge of the author's intention, as these create a kind of field of force around the work' or a 'web of associations' " ("Genesis," 118). Surely this describes a variety of reader-response critic.

The target here is the philosopher Frank Cioffi, whom Wimsatt also accuses of yearning for "the flux, the gossip, the muddle, and the 'motley' " of biographical data ("Genesis," 137). Cioffi has, however, made some interesting observations about problems with the concept of the "intentional fallacy," which Wimsatt does not take up. He points out that since Wimsatt and Beardsley claim to admit the relevance of such external evidence as an author's private, idiosyncratic use of words, and apparently also of certain kinds of biographical facts, as well as the historical facts of language and culture, there does not seem to be much "left to commit fallacies with," although Cioffi notes that their demonstrations are much more restrictive than their formulations seem to be. He also suggests that "if a critical remark is one which has the power to modify our apprehension of a work, then biographical remarks can be critical"—for example, in apprising us of whether a presumed allusion was possible for the author at the time he wrote a particular work (Cioffi, 59, 60). And he points out something in regard to "1887" that neither Beardsley nor Wimsatt mentions: Frank Harris reported that, revolted by Housman's jingoism, he himself could never again confidently read the poem as ironic (62). Although I haven't lost my sense of "1887" as ironic, that sense certainly has changed and become more complex, because as Cioffi says, "A reader's response to a work will vary with what he *knows*; one of the things which he knows and with which his responses will vary is what the author had in mind, or what he intended" (63)—I should add, "or what he said about the work."

Wimsatt's and Cioffi's conceptions of what a literary text is are radically different: A critic who holds to the doctrine of meaning as intrinsic and objective, something to be extracted from the text, has a fundamentally different view of literature than does someone who takes into account the relation between what a reader "knows," externally to the text, and the "meaning" of that text. The first position has to do with what Stanley Fish has called a belief in interpretation as "decoding," while the second implies something much closer to my concept of understanding. The former expresses intolerance of, perhaps even anxiety at, the feeling of "flux," while the second implies a recognition and acceptance of the changeability of a reader's relationship to a text. But Cioffi goes even further. Fourteen years before Bleich's *Subjective Criticism,* he saw that readers tend to conceptualize authorial intention. In the essay already referred to, Cioffi remarks that "the notion of the author's intention is logically tied to the interpretation we give to his work. It's not just that our language works this way; but that our minds do" (65). And, using as an example the change in Edmund Wilson's understanding of *The Turn of the Screw* after he found in Henry James's notebooks that James had intended a straight ghost story and not a story about hallucination, Cioffi remarks that "there is an implicit biographical reference in our response to literature. It is . . . part of our concept of literature" (66).

It may sometimes seem possible to understand a short poem or a short story without mentally constructing an author or actually considering the historical one, but reading anything much larger or more complex frequently makes at least a conceptualization of an author, if not the consideration of biographical facts, essential for many readers. But length and complexity are not explanatory in themselves, so given a reader who does not typically refuse to think about an author, what factors might tend to prompt this kind of conceptualization? A rather unusual example of a short narrative, seemingly easy to grasp as a whole, yet confusing for many readers, is Maurice Sendak's *Higglety Pigglety Pop! or There Must Be More to Life,* which I have taught several times and introduce here in order to demonstrate how a particular text may strongly demand from some readers a consideration of the author (though not necessarily the "real" one). The experience of teaching this book has been in some ways frustrating, but is always enlightening. Although many readers have found Sendak's later book, *Outside Over There,* more difficult either to accept or understand (see chap. 11), the earlier work provides enough difficulties of its own, although children possibly have less trouble with it than adults. It is the illustrated fantasy tale of a Sealyham terrier named Jennie who, even though she has "everything," including a master who loves her, is "discontented," and feels that "there must be more to life than having everything!" (5). So she goes out to see the world, and during each of her adventures manages to eat a tremendous amount. She is told by a friendly pig with a sandwich-board (whose actual "sandwiches" she pilfers and devours) that she can be the "leading lady for The World Mother Goose Theatre," but that first she must have some "experience" (8).

Jennie's subsequent "experience" is as a nurse whose job it is to make a particularly defiant and bratty infant, Baby, eat (although in Sendak's illustrations Baby looks anything but undernourished, suggesting that her "NO EAT" has to do with power struggles between children and adults rather than with anorexia). But Jennie's enormous appetite leads her to eat up all of Baby's food, and as the penalty for thus failing to make Baby eat, Jennie is supposed to be eaten by a lion unless she can say Baby's name; but the lion is tired of eating nurses, and decides to eat the baby instead. Jennie bravely puts her head in the lion's mouth to save Baby, and in the process of doing so unknowingly speaks Baby's name, "Mother Goose." After an interlude in the woods, Jennie is taken across a river (indicated only in an illustration) by the lion to "Castle Yonder," where Baby's parents reside, and given the starring role in the Mother Goose World Theatre as the dog in performances of "Higglety Pigglety Pop! / The dog has swallowed the mop." The mop being made of salami, Jennie's great appetite is eternally gratified.

The story seems less silly as Sendak tells and illustrates it than it may in my flat summary, and from the first time I read it I felt that there was something very serious along with all the delightful nonsense and word-play. For the crossing of the river to Castle Yonder, if not Jennie's leaving home at the beginning, seems to symbolize death, and Jennie's ultimate fate some kind of afterlife. The first time I used the book in a course I did so in part to see whether my students could, in their individual responses, come up with anything additional about its meanings. I felt, on the one hand, stumped by some details in the book, but also amused, moved, and disturbed by it, and eager to compare my response with those of other readers. I did assume from the dedication, "To Jennie," that there was some connection between the author's own experiences and the tale, but could get no further than the likelihood that he had owned a dog who had died.

In any event, all three times I have taught the book most of the students have had surprisingly negative reactions. Two common responses, though not the only ones, have been, "I can't make any

134,523

College of St. Francis Library
Joliet, Illinois

sense of this," and "I hated Jennie because she didn't care about her master or anyone else except herself, and was disgustingly piggish about food." The first of these responses was no surprise, but the second, and particularly the vehemence with which it was expressed, really caught me off guard.[6] When I protested that Jennie was only behaving like a dog, students countered by pointing out that as she and the other animal characters speak English and, except for the lion, walk upright, they as readers experienced Jennie as human.[7] Another surprising thing was that very few students in those classes picked up the implications of death and an eternal afterlife in Jennie's leaving home, crossing a river, and ultimately performing in The World Mother Goose Theatre "every day and twice on Saturday" (69). I think it very likely that as the idea of gluttony raised a strongly negative response, so the thought of death was disturbing enough not to be allowed into consciousness. It is even possible that a repressed awareness of the death motif negatively colored their reaction to Jennie's eating, a reaction that initially amazed me because I had thought her gluttony very funny.

There appeared in 1980 a coffee-table book, *The Art of Maurice Sendak*, which, although in many ways a piece of hagiography, contains pertinent details about Sendak's life and accounts of talks with him regarding the whole range of his work, both writing and illustration. The chapter titled "Jennie: 'The Love of My Life'" reveals what one might have suspected—that for Sendak *Higglety Pigglety Pop!* was a "memorial" to his aging pet, who had been his "best friend" for fourteen years, in anticipation of her death (she died in 1967, one month after the book was published [Lanes, 154]). As significant, however, is that in the year 1967 not only did Jennie die, but Sendak, aged 39, suffered a severe heart attack, and his mother was slowly dying of cancer. Most startling, however, is the revelation that the second depiction of Baby is virtually a direct copy of a photograph of Sendak himself as an infant held in his mother's arms (24). Selma Lanes develops an elaborate biographical-allegorical reading of the book, which may or may not be "correct." Like any interpreter Lanes selects the details she considers important, and she does not tackle the question of why Sendak portrays himself as a bratty female child. The relevant point for present purposes is that, although it is intended to be a book readable by children without special knowledge, the way one understands *Higglety Pigglety Pop!* depends partly on whether or not one knows that Jennie is a tribute to a real dog and that during the year of the book's creation Sendak was triply preoccupied with the possibility of death.[8]

I can anticipate an objection to any claim that one can generalize from this example to some larger principle about the kinds of texts that require readers to make a link between the author and the understanding of his work. First of all, it could be argued that a work of literature should be complete in itself—that we should not have had to wait for Selma Lanes's book before understanding and appreciating Sendak's, and that if the biographical facts are truly essential the work itself is an artistic failure. But considering that we need external knowledge fully to understand many sorts of literature, this point doesn't carry much weight—consider, in the twentieth century, the amount of external knowledge required for coming to any comprehension of many of Yeats's and most of Pound's poems.

My teaching method might also be questioned, on the ground that I pulled a trick on the students by not letting them know all that I knew before they read the book. But the effect of my letting them in on that knowledge after their papers have been read and discussed has not been a simple one, effecting a general change in response. For the most part students have said that it does help them to make sense of the book, and some have been contrite about their recoil from Jennie's "selfishness" once they can see her as the product of a real person's attempt to cope with the anticipated death of his beloved pet and that of his mother, as well as the possibility of his own. In this respect Cioffi's remark that the response of a reader to a text (and thus the meaning of that text for the reader) is affected by how much the reader knows about the author seems to be borne out. Yet some of the students whose first reported responses were strongly negative have said that such knowledge didn't really change their view of Sendak's book, because their initial responses were so strong that there was no possibility of change; even if they could understand the difference intellectually, it did not effect an emotional transformation. There is a possible explanation for these responses in relation to certain aspects of my students' social class and gender: at my university students are predominantly working-class or lower middle-class, and in a children's literature course usually mostly female. Both these facts might explain the revulsion at gluttony, because of the necessity for thrift in their families, but especially because of the pressures on women in our society to remain slender. Stray remarks suggested that the revulsion expressed a dislike by some students of their own inability to control their eating as they saw that inability mirrored in Jennie. But I and the students whose response to and understanding of *Higglety Pigglety Pop!* did change with the acquisition of biographical information were, in effect, now reading a "different" text; of course, the text as external object did not change, but the text as a structure of experience and understanding did.

It is likely that within any group of readers there will be variables as to the extent to which a conceptualization of the author feels necessary or even acceptable, and this could be another explanation of why some students felt their response unchanged even after learning about the author; that is, typically in their reading the author was unimportant and did not become more important when they had the relevant biographical information. A general source of such variables among readers independent of any particular text is something about which I cannot conjecture, except to say that on the basis of my own experience as a reader the tendency to read "for the author" may be present or absent at various stages in one's life. Adequate explanation for such a range of variations could come only from a carefully planned empirical study.[9] But can we say what kind of text tends to prompt conceptualization of an author? I'm afraid that I can offer no answer that will serve as a reliable predictor. For me "1887" and *Higglety Pigglety Pop!* require such conceptualization as much because there is biographical information available as that the texts are inherently ambiguous or puzzling. Again, if we imagine trying to understand Yeats's or Pound's poems without any of the historical and biographical information available, it should be clear that the entire process of reading and achieving a sense of understanding can be vastly different with and without such information.

To return to the larger question of why and how we interpret: for an "objective" interpreter a short poem or short story has the advantage of seeming to constitute a single, even if ambiguous, utterance. How meaning is construed from or constructed in the reading of a larger text such as a novel is a much more complex matter. If the tendency of the New Critics or those who wittingly or unwittingly still carry their banner is to view literary works as autonomous and unified entities, with such large, sprawling works as nineteenth-century novels unity can be demonstrated only by a very selective treatment of the text's figurative language, with what are perceived as the dominant symbols carrying the burden of meaning (as if a novel were a lyric poem), or by an abstracting out of the work its "themes"—and the critic always chooses and names the themes. Thus, the calm of Thrushcross Grange and the storm of Wuthering Heights may be taken to embody the central conflicts in Emily Brontë's novel (this is how I was taught *Wuthering Heights* as an undergraduate); the river as connecting Maggie Tulliver's childhood to her ultimate apotheosis; or the railway in *Dombey and Son* as linking the destructive tendencies of merchant capitalism to the death of Paul, Dombey's own destructiveness, and Carker the manager's self-destruction. As Susan R. Horton points out in her study of interpretation, which centers on *Dombey,* such symbolic interpretations relinquish the sequential experience of reading a novel and the immediate contexts of the uses of apparently figurative language for a highly abstract structure of meanings; and one result is that the special textural and affective qualities of an author's work may be largely passed over in favor of a monolithic reading dependent upon a preconceived notion of unity as essential to literary value. It would seem, indeed, that symbolic and thematic readings of narrative are not substantially different, and that interpretations based on a concept of pervasive and connected symbols carrying the narrative's meaning will produce generalized thematic meanings. Because it is impossible to discuss every detail, a critic chooses those that will fit into a unified pattern, and what results at times is a statement of moral meaning either self-evidently true and thus trivial, or sometimes new, and at least temporarily enlightening. Such overly abstract, sometimes moralistic readings can be arrived at whether one's assumptions are Freudian, Jungian, Marxist, Christian, or whatever. The other side of the problem of interpreting large literary structures is like a distorted mirror-image of the first: a tendency to concentrate on local detail so that the work as a whole is lost from view (though it is doubtful that one *ever* sees such a massive work "as a whole"). There is something of this tendency in Horton's reading of *Dombey and Son,* which can be explained both as the result of her reaction against the large-scale "symbolic" readings that miss so much, and the fact that any treatment of details in a nine hundred–page novel must be selective.

The drive to interpret what we read is probably overdetermined, but it seems to depend first of all on an emotional reaction—itself likely overdetermined. As in my first reading of Sendak's little book, that initial reaction is usually inchoate, and for some readers so private that they feel threatened by any attempt at or request for detailed analysis. Most teachers of literature have had the experience of students protesting that it spoils a poem to analyze it; this may reflect intellectual laziness, but I think more often it is an expression of genuine anxiety, as though one might find out something one is afraid of knowing. Typically, the professional interpreter suffers from no such block and works out his or her impulse to understand the feelings aroused in the form of an impersonal discussion of structure, style, theme, plural symbolic meanings, unifying structures, or analogies to myth, or to any number of system-derived categories. The deconstructionist deferral of meaning may have its benefits, but it is no less than other approaches a way of coming to terms with something emotionally inchoate and likely troubling.

If the professional critic refers to response at all, it is likely to be in a generalized, distancing fashion: the "effect" of the text on "the reader" is, or at least used to be, discussed as though there is a single correct way to respond. A need to come to terms with the affective impact of literature is evident even in the *Anatomy of Criticism*, which, despite Northrop Frye's claim to have developed an objective, nonevaluative approach, a systematic study of categories of literature rather than actual interpretation, seems perhaps the most elaborate structure ever created for both distancing and justifying one critic's responses. By *distancing*, I mean projecting one's responses onto ostensibly external objects. While Frye insists that we must read literature *as* literature and not as something else, his discourse repeatedly moves toward a "something else" by rationalizing literature into myth, a process informed by a blend of anthropology with Christian, Freudian, and Jungian concepts. Frye is unusual in that few interpreters of literature are as ambitiously creative; on the other hand, few if any are as pure as that fiction of the wholly intrinsic critic who remains within the text and from that stance analyzes it in its totality. Most of us appropriate limited areas of literature and limited areas of individual texts within those areas—those aspects capable of arousing our curiosity, wonder, anxiety, and passion—by using the most congenial mix of methodologies without worrying too much about combining the intrinsic and extrinsic, in order to reach our desired goal. We seek to still questions, to reduce anxiety, to stabilize our relationship to the literary work, even if we feel compelled to demonstrate that a text always "deconstructs" itself by contradicting its apparent meaning, and that our treatment of it can never be complete. And because there is something fulfilling in the very activity of seeking and solving (or demonstrating that a solution is impossible), of confronting ourselves in works of literature, we continue to look for new areas to conquer and control, new puzzles to solve or to prove insoluble.[10]

No matter how aware a critic is that interpretations are constructed and that their nature is strongly dependent on the assumptions, experiences, previous reading, and personality one brings to the text, the objects of interpretation will to some extent be experienced as other, as separate from oneself. One way to conceive of the other that is nonetheless a part of ourselves is suggested by Frederic Jameson's 1971 essay, "Metacommentary." Jameson describes the role of criticism as "not so much an interpretation of content as . . . a revealing of it, a laying bare, a restoration of the original method, the original experience, beneath the distortions of the censor" (16). He thus assumes that literature always both elaborates and disguises an originating ideological, emotional, and situational (historical) content, which he calls "the object forbidden" (17).[11] Yet we can "reveal" meaning only by writing a new text to set in juxtaposition to the object or experience we are investigating; and if we must at every stage examine our "perceptual instruments," as Jameson argues, it is hard to see how an infinite regress is avoidable, unless we simply choose to stop at a particular point—such as Jameson's version of Marxism.

It seems likely that the fear of just such a regress is one source of the impulse to ground one's interpretations in some system of ideas, and it is even possible that the fear of eternal indeterminacy motivates the deconstructionist embrace of that feared thing, as if one is saying, "Look, I'm not afraid of the absence of meaning or self; they even make me feel good" (granted that this is a gross oversimplification of deconstruction).[12] To say this is not to deny the value of the insights that interpretations based on various systems provide, but only to question the value of an exclusive commitment to a particular system of ideas in interpretation. A regress in the continual questioning of the basis of one's interpretive methods need not (and surely cannot) be carried on infinitely, but for me it is more a matter of consciously leaving the original questions still open at the conclusion of an act of interpretation. My insistence on the process of construction in reading, including the construction of a conceptualized author, represents my own way of trying to deal with the inadequacies of "intrinsic" interpretation or approaches that are restricted in other ways, as for example by the belief that one must, and can, find the exact historical conditions under which a text was produced and limit interpretation by one's knowledge of those conditions.[13] Yet there is no doubt that response for me represents a kind of presence, one that connects the reader to the work (and sometimes its author), and is an arbitrarily chosen grounding that will allow me to avoid that infinite regress.

On the basis of that admittedly unprovable grounding I propose a tentative model of interpretation and its motives. The meanings open to a seeming discovery in the process of interpretation are those we feel to be hidden or elusive, those that when we formulate them will at least temporarily resolve our puzzlement and still our anxieties about a text. These include those aspects of meaning we conceptualize as the author's or the text's as well as those which we realize are in some sense our own. That is, there are those meanings we believe we are teasing out of a resistant text, and those we think we can identify as dependent on our own process of reading; the latter we may objectify and analyze, but they (and other personal meanings perhaps unidentified as such) affect how we conceptualize the author or text and attribute meaning to them. Whether we can really reconstruct, construe, or only construct the author's or the text's meaning has come to seem an idle question, for we can never know with certainty whether what we seem to have found is objectively true, except perhaps at the most obvious lexicographical level. But this is a part of the human condition, in which all knowledge is mediated by our organs of perception and cognition, our need to think in language, and our cultural and individual histories.

We may regard literary meanings as seeming "hidden" through the modes of indirection and duplicity that characterize imaginative writing, by the latency of an author's ideology and the deepest parts of his psychology, and by the blocks in our psychological and cultural make-up, which occlude parts of what is "outside over there," as well as what is "inside in here." All of these modes of the hidden can motivate interpretation. What I might denominate the dual nature of the need to interpret—to understand what we experience as the author's or text's meaning, and as our own—is perhaps parallel to what one might call the dual form of literary apprehension: the perception of literary works as both utterance and representation. For the sense of a text as utterance is a sense of the other (perhaps an other speaking directly to us), while the experience of the text as representation involves us in the imaginative world and the voices and characters populating it; that is, we experience them not only as others, but also the world as ours and the characters' experiences as happening to us. In this model the experience of literature moves along two affective and cognitive continuums: between other and self, and between utterance and representation. And thus meaning is elaborated and disguised by the author through his particular modes of utterance and representation and is in part hidden from the reader by himself, according to his or her defenses and anxieties, and in part constructed along those two related continuums.

David Bleich makes a distinction between the use of biographical knowledge in the process of reading as a subjective experience, and the purportedly objective products of biographical research (*Subjective Criticism*, 259), but he qualifies this by stressing that "the value of a biographical study lies in the kind of subjective interest the biographer has applied to his task" (263). In other words, every biographer is, like every reader, motivated, and no biographer fully "knows" his subject as other. So a crucial part of the work of biographical research and its products is related to the process of an individual's reading. On the other hand, even if everything an interpreter does ultimately comes down to response, we still must, in order to talk about it, divide response into how we perceive the other and how we perceive our response to it.

There is an interesting parallel between Bleich's saying that "biographical documentation is sought in order to validate one's conception of the author" (*Subjective,* 259), and Morse Peckham's comment that " 'to infer an intention' means to make a linguistic construct of an historical situation so that by responding to the semiotic constellation of that constructed situation we may gain additional instructions for deciding the appropriate verbal response to an utterance to which our initial response was decisional uncertainty" (155). In other words, readers look for biographical information to decide what response they should have (Peckham), or to confirm the response they have already had (Bleich). Peckham assumes that reading behavior involves an imperative wish to have a "correct" response, and that response is cognitive rather than affective, but he does assume that supposed knowledge of intention is always a psychologically motivated construct.

I offer now a further brief demonstration of how meaning-for-a-reader relates to both personal response and a concern with "the author." I shall argue that psychoanalysis on the one hand should not be considered a privileged basis for an approach to response; for when psychoanalytic concepts as applied to literature are taken beyond the basic model of interpretation as the discovery of ambiguity and of latent meanings, they tend like any systematic methodology to reify disparate details, to get between the reader and his or her experience of the text. But on the other hand, Freud seems to be lurking in the background whenever we (or at least I) talk about ambiguity and affect, hidden meaning and response.

In reading *Treasure Island* in my mid-forties for the first time since childhood, I found myself even before finishing the book laying out in my mind a neat pattern of "Oedipal" meanings: Oedipal, that is, with the incest phantasy repressed and the son's phantasy of defeating or killing his father dominant. Jim Hawkins loses his actual father early in the story, encounters a series of substitute fathers on both sides of the law, and ends in triumph over them all, defeating the pirates and exonerating himself in the eyes of the doubting "good" fathers. Yet at the novel's center there remains Long John Silver, towards whom Jim's feelings fluctuate among affection and admiration, jealousy, and fear and hatred, and who by the novel's conclusion has embodied both paternal love and paternal threat.

The pattern seemed neat, but also felt trivial because it seemed to have little direct relation to my feelings while reading. My motive for immediately laying out that kind of schematic Freudian interpretation seemed to stem from a habitual need to come up with coherent and plausible interpretations for the purposes of teaching and "doing criticism." But at the same time I had a deeper motivation for wanting to understand *Treasure Island,* for to my surprise this boys' adventure story (which I had not liked as a child) moved and disturbed me in ways that the Oedipal reading did not explain, or explained only intellectually. So I turned from approaching the text as objectively meaningful and sought for associations between my feelings about the text and my life. And, despite my fear by this point that Freudian abstractions might have blocked any understanding of my response, I did find one dominant personal, affective association. As Bill Bones, Doctor Livesey, Squire Trelawny, Captain Smollett, and Long John Silver provide Jim with important but ambiguous surrogate-father relationships, so I in childhood and adolescence had valued my five uncles as alternatives to my father. But as Trelawny, Livesey, and Smollett appear to give up on Jim after he leaves the Block House, and as Silver is alternately fatherly (or avuncular) and dangerous, so my relationships to those uncles alternated between close and distant, affectionate and antagonistic, and sometimes provoked jealousy and conflict between my parents and myself. I could not help but consider this personal background to be responsible for a good deal of the strength of my response to what might otherwise have seemed merely an adolescent power phantasy, specifically in Jim's defeat of the pirates and his vindication at the novel's close.

The difference between these two ways of reading the text was that between a detached, seemingly objective interpretation along consciously Freudian lines, and one that brought out the nature of my individual way of relating to the text. One obvious catch, however, a part of the inherent nature of reading in a post-Freudian age, is that I probably could not have conceptualized my "response" at all without having gone through the Freudian schemata, or at least without already having the Freudian concepts (including that of the Oedipus complex) as a part of my mental baggage. And indeed the personal associations I describe are somewhat analogous to a description of Oedipal conflicts. Yet experientially the processes of intellectualized psychoanalytic interpretation and the analysis of an affective, associative response, were qualitatively different—the first seeming to take me little distance toward real understanding, the second enabling me to understand what I have above referred to as the initially surprising strength of my response to *Treasure Island*.

Although I did not at the time define authorial intention in Peckham's terms, I did feel a need to discover a connection between my response and what I must call, problematically, Stevenson's meaning. In considering the extrinsic context, the most relevant fact seemed to be that Stevenson wrote the novel in the company of, and to some degree for the benefit of, his stepson Lloyd Osbourne, who was fourteen at the time (Pope-Hennessy, 155). A story involving the death of a father, a series of father-surrogates, and ultimate triumph for the boy-protagonist might well be an appropriate fantasy for a stepfather to write for his recently acquired stepson. In particular Jim's feelings of love, jealousy, fear, and hatred toward Long John Silver suggest ambivalences on both sides in the difficult situation in which Stevenson and Lloyd had found themselves during the previous six years in regard to the boy's vivacious but emotionally high-strung mother, and his handsome, dashing, but philandering and irresponsible father.[14]

The still unsettled family context in which the book was written suggests that both the "objective" (Freudian) and associative readings have a bearing on the emotional and symbolic meanings of the text for its author and its first reader. It seems especially relevant that Stevenson reported, "It was to be a story for boys, no need of psychology or fine writing; and I had a boy at hand to be a touchstone. Women were excluded" (Pope-Hennessy 156). I originally called this statement a "denial" or "disclaimer," on the grounds that the novel actually contained plenty of "psychology" in its insights into childhood and adolescent emotional conflicts, and that women were not *quite* excluded, since Jim's mother is there in the earlier chapters, and Silver's mulatto wife is referred to several times. But I now also read Stevenson's last sentence in a slightly different way: as an assertion that we men (himself and Lloyd), in conspiring to create a story without women, are setting ourselves apart from them—they who are somehow the main source of trouble. Or to put it another way, we exclude Fanny Osbourne, thus denying that she is of importance to us; men (as in *Treasure Island*) can do it all by themselves, in effect making the mother disappear, as she does in the text without any comment from the first-person narrator, Jim.

These are of course only my inferences about Stevenson's "intention"—in the sense of what importance the book had for him—even if they seem to be based on fact. And they serve the purpose of validating my response to the novel as something more than idiosyncratic or solipsistic because they deal with matters of family conflict and the problems of a child with a substitute father, as well as with male companionship—both very much a part of my conflicted relationships with my uncles and matters that are hardly unique to me. The motive for creating such connections is a desire to define and stabilize my response to the text by positing a link between the author's subjectivity and mine, which undoubtedly stems from a need to establish some kind of authority for my interpretations even while acknowledging them as constructs. As such, this sense of authority functions to fulfill my needs as reader, teacher, and critic rather than to establish a verifiable meaning; but if another reader should find that the biographical link and the associations create a feeling of greater understanding of the novel, then that authority has been established for him or her, as well as for me. A biographical construct is involved even in the simple attribution of some aspect of a work to an author; "Shakespeare shows," "Dickens says," or "Joyce alludes to" are rudimentary but widely used forms of constructing a phantasy-author, just as Foucault insists, rather than statements about the "real" author. The author we refer to is indeed a function of the process of interpreting, but Foucault's rejection of the "author-function" as no longer necessary and restrictive to the full play of discourse is not self-evidently true. What may be restrictive for one reader may be liberating for another.

I suggested earlier that abstract statements of themes or messages, which still despite reader response and deconstruction often tend to be the end-product of interpretation, are inadequate to communicate the richness of the experience of reading imaginative literature. But our only alternative to making statements is to be silent. And if our statements are to embody both the personal experience of reading as well as a sense of the work and sometimes the author as distinct others, we cannot give up our sense of presence, of something real, to become what Hirsch calls "cognitive atheists," even as we recognize that anything approaching conclusive knowledge of textual meaning can be attained only at a relatively trivial level.

In the chapters to follow I am concerned with demonstrating a variety of problems in and approaches to the discovery (recognizing the problematic status of that word) of "hidden" meanings rather than with tracing a pattern of historical development within a genre. Most of the narratives discussed here are connected (in my mind) not only by problems of interpretation but also by certain preoccupations within these works, as well as the seeming *lack* of certain kinds of overt content. Although it still seems a widely accepted belief that the Victorian novelists and their immediate predecessors and successors could not talk or write about certain subjects, so that when certain meanings appear to twentieth-century readers they are granted only as a part of the author's "unconscious intention," I should prefer to dispense with the latter concept as a contradiction in terms, and one unnecessary to the discussion of hidden meanings.

I return briefly to Housman's "1887" to help clarify the problem of unconscious intention. If we are to take Housman's disavowal of irony as sincere, then we must accept that he intended to write an unambiguous paean to the queen on her Golden Jubilee. But many readers, including myself, do not feel that he wrote one. Thus his *original* intention was different from the mental object, the particular language-structure, that he seems to such readers to have created. The irony of the concluding lines of the poem is "unintentional" only in the crudest sense—since Freud, we can certainly not consider it accidental. And if we do perceive that irony, we may conceptualize the process of Housman's writing the poem as one of discovery, a process that has become public whatever denials the poet may have made. Throughout the chapters to follow I shall be "discovering" meanings of the sort that have customarily been called unconscious by psychoanalytically oriented critics (and surely most of us are Freudians whether or not we acknowledge it): sexual puns, Oedipal patterns of desire, aggression and guilt-feelings, and contradictions between the apparent didactic meaning and the dramatically realized meaning. In many instances these meanings are likely to have been absent from the author's conceptualized, originating intention; but we cannot limit meaning—or even "conscious" meaning—to what is fully conceptualized.

In calling the process of my reading "discovery," however, I reveal the inevitably circular nature of any approach to interpretation. For there is no way past the reader's conceptualization of the author to the "real" author or his "real" meaning. What then is the value of inferred intention, or of constructed author-figures? Their value in this context has to be that as a part of reading they are aids to establishing a locus of meaning. This does not necessitate, as Foucault suggests, the stabilization or restriction of meanings. Although it does serve the reader by creating a temporary feeling of such stabilization, this need not be equivalent to "closing" a text.

Although the bulk of this book consists of readings of particular texts, one of its aims is to explore what kinds of pointers we use to arrive at our construction of what seems to be a text's meaning, an author's meaning, and our own. In the present inquiry the only truth can be a social, intersubjective one: when readings by critics, by me, or by my students make sense and give new insights to another reader. The creation of such an interpretive community may depend in part on shared assumptions about interpretation, shared values, and similarities of experience in both life and reading; but as I indicated in chapter 1, one of the main points of this study is that the communication of reading experiences is something more than merely the act of talking to someone who already agrees with you, a member of your own pre-existing interpretive community.

II · SELF-DISCOVERY AND LITERARY UNDERSTANDING

3 · Stories of Reading: *Wuthering Heights*

This chapter and the next are devoted in large part to my students' reading experiences and to the ways in which a reader may find her or his "self" in a novel, a process that leads not to solipsism but to the deepening of other readers' understanding when responses are shared in a social context. This chapter contains the largest number of quotations from students' papers and the longest ones, essential for my argument that associative response papers are not just relevant as evidence of the nature of the process of reading, or of the reader's personality, but can actually become new interpretations—or "readings"—not attainable through other approaches.

Wuthering Heights may be an accepted part of the canon of masterpieces among Victorian novels, but upon dispensing in my teaching with preconceptions about the unquestionable greatness of any work, I found that this novel began to be greeted by many students with intense bewilderment or actual hostility, now that they found themselves free to make their own judgments rather than obliged to invent ones they thought might please the teacher. Many of these students have had great difficulty, at least initially, accepting *Wuthering Heights* as anything but perplexing, disturbing, and unreal, or seeing Catherine Earnshaw and Heathcliff as anything but too self-centered and cruel to arouse feelings of empathy. But Emily Brontë's novel does evoke detailed responses, and for some students a strong motivation to try to understand those responses and to pin down the elusive nature of this particular experience of reading. The author, though she is of concern to two of the readers whom I discuss below, will disappear fairly soon, as I imagine Emily disappearing behind her several narrators. The extent of their other problems with reading

Wuthering Heights has kept most students from thinking much about the author, concerned as they are to find some way "into" the text, by exploring and explaining their responses. Some have found crucial aspects of themselves in Brontë's novel, but in the classroom context we also have seemed to uncover important aspects of the novel in their responses.

I preface the account of my experiences of teaching *Wuthering Heights* with a brief treatment of one of the earliest and most interesting modern attempts by a critic to arrive at a coherent reading of Brontë's novel. It is a reading that, if one accepts it as correct, pretty well closes the novel to further interpretation and thus serves here as a convenient straw man. Mark Schorer, in what was originally the introduction to the Rinehart edition, seems determined above all to debunk the idea that *Wuthering Heights* celebrates "the moral magnificence of immoral passion" (186). He shows how Emily Brontë exalts "the power of human feeling" through her metaphors (187) and yet insists that the attempt to present Heathcliff's and Catherine's passion as transcending the ordinary with "spectacular magnificence" results not in "moral magnificence" but in "a devastating spectacle of human waste" (186); "in the end the triumph is on the side of the cloddish world, which survives" (187). And yet, "the triumph is not all on the side of convention and the cloddish world":

> In *Wuthering Heights,* one world explodes within another—the world of unconscious yearning and of those primary passions from which we construct our myths, within the world of conscious propriety, literary no less than social, and those secondary sentiments on which we base our manners. The fires of this eruption must be put down—that is the habit of civilization; but the outer world has been enriched and cleansed as well as seared by them, and that is the function of art. [188]

Is Schorer trying to have things both ways, or is he suggesting that Emily as novelist is doing so? Notice how neatly balanced is the syntax of the last sentence quoted, and that nonetheless "the habit of civilization" and "the function of art" are not logically parallel in regard to what they would seem to correspond to, namely, the ordinary world of manners and the "primary passions." The function of art is suddenly introduced as if to move from a description of genuine conflict to a reassurance that it is, after all, only in art that such an explosion can be effected, not by conflicts within a represented world that has analogues in the real one. On the basis of my still (perhaps permanently) evolving understanding of *Wuthering Heights,* and the varied but always troubled responses of my students, I cannot accept such a reassurance.

In teaching, I will sometimes write and distribute my own response paper during initial class discussion of a text, and when I do so there is no doubt that it influences the form and subject matter of some students' subsequent contributions. It has been suggested to me by a former student who himself values reader response as a pedagogical approach that I may be setting up an ambiguous power-relationship. To some extent this is of course true: in any classroom, many students are going to try to please the teacher, and my emphasis-by-example on the value of personal associations to account for individual responses does encourage many to try it. I should like to think, however, that the most important result of their reading my paper before they write their own is to open up possibilities for them, to relax inhibitions about revealing personal feelings and experiences. Although I do not limit what they are permitted to write, it would be disingenuous of me not to acknowledge that there is a range of topics and approaches that I am more likely to praise—something they perhaps catch on to very quickly. My experiences of teaching suggest to me, however, that students value the opportunity to attempt a kind of thinking and writing about literature that they can do in few other courses, whether or not they do eventually write personal-response papers; for a number who find writing associative papers very difficult and who do not receive particularly high grades have chosen to take a second or even a third course with me. But I can best tackle this question by commenting on the relation of my own paper to the student papers that I quote or summarize here. I present first a somewhat condensed version of a paper on *Wuthering Heights,* which I distributed and which formed part of the immediate context in which most of the student papers referred to here were written:

1. The last time I tried to come to terms with my experience of reading *Wuthering Heights* I produced a paper for my class which was almost entirely associative, and which avoided certain problems with my response. Yet those particular associations are the source of some of my strongest feelings about that novel, and I can't dismiss them. The primary life-experience which makes the story of Catherine and Heathcliff at all comprehensible to me emotionally is having grown up from very early childhood in the company of a girl a couple of years older, who came to call me her "little brother," and whose first name still arouses a special feeling. Most memories of J as a child are set in the summer place my parents owned in Connecticut and sold for a song in 1945. J and I roamed over the twenty-seven acres of lawns and

woods, pretending to be spy-hunters (this was during World War II), or imagining that the undersides of leaves bobbing in the wind were mysterious and comfortably threatening things called "White Bobbers." And we loved walking in the woods, especially to a certain place by the brook called by us "Joe's Island," where my grandfather had a hammock and frequently went to escape my grandmother's nagging. Like Catherine and Heathcliff we could stay in such a specially loved place most of the day, looking at the water running in the brook, at butterflies and caterpillars.

2. There are still extant some marvelous photographs of J and me swimming naked in a shallow swimming hole which had been dug out by my father and uncles; and we had our own names for things: for example, we called a big rock at the brook-side "Seal Rock," and pretended to be seals sleeping on it, or sliding off into the water. Another favorite activity was to climb up on the roof of a building called the "shed," to pick the trumpet-vine blossoms and suck out their sweet nectar. If we were not such wild things as Catherine and Heathcliff, we certainly did have a lot of freedom, and yet also felt in league against the grownups, of whom there were normally seven to nine on the property (in two separate houses), each with his or her own word to give us—too many adults for just two young children—and J taught me lots of snotty behavior, such as the retort, when asked to do something, "I re*fuse*!"

3. If I didn't imitate Heathcliff in considering J superior to everyone else in the word, I not only loved her, but thought of her as tremendously brave and daring. Probably the one adventure that most resembles anything Catherine and Heathcliff do as children was our walk into Sherman, the small village about two and-a-half miles away. It was J's idea completely, and I had some hesitation about it, being sure my parents wouldn't approve; that was easily dealt with: we didn't tell them. Two and-a-half miles may not sound like a great distance, but it involved a considerable number of what seemed steep upgrades, and on a hot summer day was pretty tough for two children with short legs. (I'm not quite sure about our ages, but they were probably five and-a-half and eight, which would make it the summer of 1941.) And J developed a painful blister on her foot long before we got to the village (cf. Catherine's bravery about the Linton dog's bite). With our small change we decided to buy some chewing gum in the only store in the village, but because the salesperson kept ignoring us, we left, though not before J simply lifted a pack of gum—something she only told me about afterwards, and which I, as a good little boy, was shocked at, but at the same time admired. By the time we turned back for home we were both tired, thirsty, and hot, and J's foot hurt badly. To make things worse, J decided that we should take a different route, which probably seemed shorter because it was different from the way we had come, although we knew that it was always referred to as "the long way." Luckily my father had set out in the car to look for us, and had tried "the long way." What a relief to see his 1938 Plymouth coming towards us! This great adventure was often spoken

of subsequently by my mother with amusement, but also some annoyance at J, whom she blamed for the whole thing as she had blamed her for the defiant attitude I was developing and the rude language I had learned to use.

4. By the summer of 1943 or 1944, however, a change was taking place. J was reaching early puberty and was less interested in me; as my mother explained it, when girls start to grow up they get interested in other things than their "little brothers." I don't recall any specific event, but rather a general feeling of having been abandoned by my childhood playmate, perhaps the person of all in the world to whom I felt closest. Of course by the time I reached puberty myself I had my own friends and girls of my own age to be interested in; but J remained special. When I was as old as sixteen, possibly even seventeen, the suggestion by an older male friend that I should take advantage sexually of my special relationship to her shocked me—both because it would have seemed like incest, and because I had for several years refused any awareness that she might be involved in sexual relationships.

5. It is time to return to *Wuthering Heights,* though I don't really feel I have left it. I am not Heathcliff, and never banged my head against a tree until it bled, out of sorrow at "losing" J. But it always turns out in a reading of the novel that I can only come to terms with the most disturbing elements, such as Heathcliff's and Catherine's cruelty to one another, Heathcliff's seemingly inhuman desire for revenge, and the absurd violence that is described, by seeing the novel as a series of childhood phantasies carried into adulthood. Catherine's belief that she can marry Edgar and still have Heathcliff as a "friend" recalls my own denial of J's sexuality, but it also suggests that she is a girl playing at being a woman. And to feel that someone else is your *self,* your *soul,* is to deny difference and (as one Victorian reviewer pointed out) your body's urges. The violence in *Wuthering Heights* doesn't really seem physical, but reads more like the imaginings of children who want to avenge themselves on the world for denying their needs. One of the most remarkable passages in the novel for me is that in which Catherine, by infecting Linton's parents with the illness she herself survives, dispatches them in one sentence: "But the poor dame had reason to repent of her kindness; she and her husband both took the fever, and died within a few days of each other" (88). Granted that this is Nelly speaking, and her style is frequently terse, I nonetheless feel it as a kind of symbolized infantile megalomania—the belief that one's wishes determine what happens in the world—together with the child's inability to understand what violence or death (or, for that matter, sex) really are.

6. None of this does adequate justice to Emily as a writer, but one reason I admire the novel so much is because of her ability to present primordial and disturbing human feelings in a dispassionate way through the use of multiple narrators, one of whom (Lockwood) is unconsciously comical, and another of whom (Nelly) repeatedly condemns herself by her own statements. I have stopped feeling, as I used to in my younger, more cynical days, that the conclusion (Cathy and Hareton's marriage) is a sentimental denial of the

Romantic passions in the rest of the book (but see Heathcliff's scornful statements about Romantic love [150]); the resolution is necessary for me, because I need to believe that there are "normal" adults who don't devour each other in their love, and that the world will go on after a love has been refused. And yet that love and that violence are tremendously moving because they speak to matters that are a part of me. So perhaps I am, after all, Heathcliff, in the disappointment of my childhood love, in the violence of some of my phantasies, and in the hairspring temper which I have far from altogether conquered.

7. But why should Emily's "dispassionate" presentation of horrible things please me? Here I seem to be constructing an author, and admiring her for eluding me: which means that ultimately I think Emily really must be expressing her own emotions and phantasies, and yet I would be less comfortable with the book if I could detect that expression *directly*. Some of this may be the result of re-reading *Wuthering Heights* right after *Jane Eyre* and *Vanity Fair,* in each of which the narrator rather buttonholes the reader, in Thackeray's pronouncements and in Charlotte Brontë's way of letting us in on Jane's deepest feelings and her narrator's way of addressing us as "reader." And given what I know of Emily's reserved but tough personality, maybe I would just as soon *not* be able to attribute any phantasies to her which take the scary forms they do in her novel.

Most of my students do not find it a priority to come to terms with the novel by searching for that author whom I find so elusive, and one of them, Carol, has on the contrary described her continuous *awareness* of the author (her response is discussed below). Experiences of empathy and identification are generally distinct from a response to authorial elusiveness, yet in the first student response paper I discuss the two are definitely connected. My own sense of elusiveness in Emily Brontë stems not only from her use of multiple narrators, but also from an uncertainty about the origin and identity of the demonic character, Heathcliff, and an ambiguity between dream and reality, especially in regard to the supernatural (Lockwood's "dream" about Catherine's ghost, the report about Heathcliff's and Catherine's ghosts at the novel's end). But I would further describe the way I conceptualize Emily as an elusive author as my construction of one who, though she may make every effort to efface her presence from the narrative, somehow also inspires the belief that she is expressing her fullest being in *Wuthering Heights*. Yet if we acknowledge the brilliance of her achievement, which for many readers can stand on its own, why should anyone feel a need to locate, to define, the author of *Wuthering Heights*? It would seem to be the combination of strong but ambiguous emotional power, factual uncertainty, and the lack of an omniscient or first-person narrator that leads some readers to search for Emily in the novel. And such a reader may be trying to construct the author and her intentions so as to know how to respond and to overcome feelings of anxiety and vertigo.

Margaret, who like others reports feeling "an ever increasing sense of discomfort" as she reads, describes her distress in this way:[1]

> Both the imagery and the behavior of the characters is disturbing, even frightening. I can't remember reading a novel that seemed quite so foreign or alien to me in this respect. The world of the novel is one of isolation, coldness, darkness, where houses are more like prisons or fortresses than homes, and where whole lives are indiscriminately consumed by either a killing passion or a killing disease.

In the context of such feelings Margaret also finds the problem of the author's ineffability significant and devotes most of her paper—titled, "*Wuthering Heights:* 'Where are you Emily and why do I need you?'"—to that question. I quote her paper from its third paragraph to the conclusion:

3. The second source of discomfort is the direct result of being thwarted in my attempt to identify Emily Brontë. When I look back over my papers for this semester, I could describe each of them in part as a search for the author: for Jane Austen through Elizabeth, for Charlotte Brontë through Jane, and for Thackeray through his handling of the puppets and their handling of him. But as I read *Wuthering Heights,* I found that I was frequently having to remind myself that the novel was written by Emily Brontë, a woman. Was it more upsetting for me to think Emily Brontë wrote from an appreciation of this kind of experience or the possibility that she was capable of imagining such things? I still can't answer this question. But, it seems unfair if I say yes to either possibility. Why shouldn't she write about such things? Why should it be paramount that I make my peace with the author before pronouncing judgement?

4. In partial answer to this question, I know that one of the major impediments in my search for the author is as I've suggested before, the lack of a suitable heroine. Unlike Elizabeth *(Pride and Prejudice)* or Jane *(Jane Eyre),* Catherine is inconsistent, naive, cruel, self-centered, and child-like. There is little that I can find in her behavior that is heroic save for her persistence in maintaining Heathcliff as her only possible lover. Yet as I write this, I feel that I'm being unfair to her. After all, Catherine is barely an adult when she dies. But another source of discontent with her behavior outweighs any feelings of magnanimity I might have for Catherine. It stems from an experience I had with a group of "feminists" who often "quoted" Catherine as a heroic figure in their cause of "sexual liberation." What this cause amounted to was a rather dim reversion to child-like behavior. They tended to dismiss any of their sexual partners who had difficulty in coping with their particular

practice as the "manifest contradictions of living in a capitalist society"; a convenient way of avoiding taking responsibility for the feelings of others as they sexually steamrollered their way through the community (setting sexual liberation back at least 10 years, if indeed it should ever be considered seriously again). This association is a very strong one and possibly distorts my reading of the text, but nevertheless I am uncomfortable with what I feel is the valorization of this kind of behavior.

5. It's interesting on the other hand (and maybe this is an attempt at salvaging) that I can accept Catherine in parts rather than as a whole character. Of course, I can identify with Catherine's position as a young woman. Her major source of positive attention, comradery, friendship, and love until she meets the Lintons was Heathcliff. As Mike pointed out, Catherine suddenly becomes aware of a different kind of power she has over people. She is admired for quite different reasons than those for which Heathcliff admired her and begins to see the advantages of altering her behavior. Perhaps Catherine merely exchanges one image of herself for another—from a wild and free spirit to a princess. Unfortunately for her, there is no opportunity to understand what claims this new image will make upon her. In this regard, it is easy to empathize with the Catherine who suffers the tyranny of adulthood with its demands that she must deny the person she is. That point at which I feel most empathy for Catherine is when she exclaims to Nelly: "Oh, I'm burning! I wish I were out of doors—I wish I were a girl again, half savage and hardy, and free . . . and laughing at injuries, not maddening under them!" (126).

6. The other significant impediment in my search for the author has to do with my surprise at Catherine's death so early in the novel. Did she tire of Catherine as I did and want to get on with writing about Heathcliff? Was he the true object of her fascination; the personification of the savage and the powerful, a happy antithesis to the other much less noble male creatures in the novel (with the exception of Hareton whom she shows some favour for)?

7. I think that what is most troubling to me is that Catherine never quite reaches this level of power independently of Heathcliff. In fact, Catherine as a character seems to lose power as she is separated from her mate. Her greatest strength reaches its apex when she and Heathcliff are still children. In fact, both characters are most fascinating, most heroic when children. This is the only way that I appear to be able to share Catherine with Heathcliff, a kind of consolation prize in light of the fact that Catherine does not emerge as another "Elizabeth" or "Jane." Something tells me that Emily would despise the idea of Catherine becoming a woman like either of them. Something tells me she preferred Catherine's going out in a blaze of glory. There I go again: "Where are you Emily?"

It seems likely that both Margaret's search for the author and her ambivalence about Catherine Earnshaw represent a need for her to stabilize her response by, first of all, figuring out what the author is doing in a way that she can relate to her own current values and conflicts; and second, by finding some point of identification with Catherine. The fulfillment of either of these needs eludes her, and it is difficult to say in what proportion this is the result of the author's seeming elusiveness or of what, as an individual, Margaret brings to the novel. Certainly her sense of herself as a feminist, together with the disturbing experience she describes with a group of women who considered themselves feminists, has an effect on the way she reads *Wuthering Heights.* I might have felt that in this paper Margaret somewhat avoided confronting her anxieties about the novel by bringing in that particular experience, had I not some years before myself had an experience parallel to this one, which in my mind gave credibility and authority to the report of her difficulties in reading the novel for the first time *after* having heard her acquaintances' lauding of Catherine. Supervising a special undergraduate project consisting of a lengthy reading of *Wuthering Heights* by a woman who considered herself a feminist, I read in her paper that Heathcliff is Catherine's "whip,"[2] and in the course of thirty-five pages found this student erecting Catherine into a feminist super-hero, a woman with true power over men, using not only Heathcliff as a weapon against both Hindley and Edgar, but also her own illness and death to punish Edgar and Heathcliff. While not claiming that Catherine embodies an ideal of "sexual liberation," this student seemed to believe that the liberation of women necessarily involves their exercising power over men and the withdrawal of their concern for men as individuals with feelings. I had been as horrified by this student's glorification of Catherine as an embodiment of female "power" as Margaret was by her "feminist" acquaintances calling Catherine a symbol of sexual liberation.

Although Margaret cites me on one point, she by now (having already written on three novels earlier in the course, and having taken a course with me the semester before) had plenty of experience with response papers and was fascinated with the whole process as an adjunct and contrast to the work she was doing in film with a teacher who was both a feminist and Lacanian. The wish to please me as her teacher seems to have been less important; she very much took her own path.

While Margaret, at thirty, was seeking self-definition, some younger students found disturbing fragments of themselves in *Wuthering Heights,* which were difficult for them to acknowledge as such. Much of the interest of these discoveries lies in the ways in which that process varied. Carol, in her early twenties, was the only student besides Margaret who seemed to concern herself directly with the author of *Wuthering Heights;* but although her overall response of fear and distress resembled Margaret's, in direct contrast to Margaret's troubled sense of the author's absence Carol claimed that she felt the author's presence more strongly in *Wuthering Heights* than in any other novel she had read. She wondered what could possibly have motivated the author to depict the bitterness and rage that she, Carol, found in the book. Above all, it seems to have been the consistency of this response throughout her reading of the novel, a sense that the novel was all of one tone and thus had been created by a definite person who may have shared some of those disturbing emotions of anger and bitterness, that caused Carol to say that she felt the author as a brooding presence everywhere. It is not in my experience a frequent occurrence for a student to describe a dream that he or she believes to stem from reading (although I do give an extended example in chap. 6), but Carol's paper in fact centered on the nightmares that she felt were caused by reading *Wuthering Heights.* These dreams involved her limbs being ripped off, or her being mutilated or murdered by unknown persons with incomprehensible motivations. She also dreamed of the panic of finding her arm going through a solid wall and getting stuck there, much as happens to Lockwood in his (presumed) dream about "a little, ice-cold hand" pulling his arm through the window.

Carol described a feeling of confusion in those dreams: a feeling that acquaintances' and family members' roles were shifting, so that she could not tell who was a relative, who a friend, who a stranger, or who an enemy. She attributed this to her confusion, in reading, about the nature of the relationship between Heathcliff and Catherine—whether they were brother and sister, or lovers, and another confusion as to whether Nelly Dean was a good or evil influence in their lives. Above all, she was depressed by what seemed to her Emily Brontë's tormenting of her characters—as when the younger Cathy is imprisoned at the Heights by Heathcliff and forced by him to marry young Linton; such episodes disturbed Carol by giving her both the sense of an unremitting, irresolvable tension, and a feeling of ultimate hopelessness. Finally, taking up the question of whether *Wuthering Heights* is a love story, Carol denied categorically that it is, because of what she considered the obsessiveness of the characters' needs for one another. Even the uniting of young Cathy and Hareton seemed to her to be motivated primarily by their own need to avoid the misery and early deaths of so many of the other characters, rather than by love.

Carol's paper was one of the most extreme reactions of horror at

Brontë's novel that I had ever received and did not at all resemble her other work for me. As she attempted no associative analysis of her response, it would have been an especially puzzling reaction had I not known that she had had some recent, very trying experiences that were too painful to write or talk about. Her response might have been substantially different had her own immediate circumstances been different, though I can't be certain of this. But it seems more than likely that the experience of reading *Wuthering Heights* brought back recent events in a symbolic but all too vivid form. Her apartment had a month before been completely gutted by fire, destroying all her (uninsured) possessions, and while standing outside in the rain she had had to endure the taunts of the arsonist himself, whose identity she learned only a day or two later—all of which suggests a considerable overdetermination of the nightmares in which unknown persons were mutilating her for incomprehensible reasons. On top of this, she had told me about a week previous to handing in the paper that her mother had a serious medical condition about which she was very worried. I would call Carol's response as a whole an instance of not fully conceptualized but very close identification, as distinct from empathy, in the sense that she experienced *Wuthering Heights* as if it were happening directly to her, as if Heathcliff were one of the unknown persons motivated by an incomprehensible anger, and she the object of that anger. In addition, her feeling of hopelessness was related to both the arson and her fear that her mother might die. My guess is that these new feelings of there being an irrational, evil force in the world were so strong that they dominated her emotional life at that time, and thus also dominated her reading of a novel with more than its share of violence and irrationality. (When we discussed Carol's paper in class I made the foolish error of suggesting that her reactions in dream and waking might be due to recent events that had created confusion and anxiety in her life. I did not specify what I was referring to, thinking that she might be able to acknowledge calmly that I was probably right, but I should have known better than to allude to these matters, for she burst out crying and had to leave the room. I mention this as an example of how careful one has to be when teaching in a way that requires personal responses and a discussion of them.)

Margaret's and Carol's response papers on *Wuthering Heights* are atypical and yet at the same time exemplary, in the sense that they both demonstrate how very specific personal associations can affect the experience of reading. Among my students there have been only a few who spontaneously connected *Wuthering Heights* with feminist issues; much more common (among both men and women) is either a revulsion, which sometimes is not overcome, an acceptance (though usually carefully qualified) of the power of a destructive but transcendent love between "soul-mates," or a retrospective and sometimes painful set of associations with one's childhood or adolescence. Vicki, a student in a class a few years earlier, reading the novel for the first time, reported a strong initial revulsion from Heathcliff's violence, but as she thought about her responses this changed into a recognition of herself in the character. For, having described Heathcliff as cruel, selfish, and constantly seeking vengeance against those who have oppressed him, she was suddenly struck by the similarity of this description to her memories of herself as a child constantly in rebellion—in feeling and sometimes in deed—against the constraints placed upon her by her strict, religious family, constraints especially strong because she was a girl. Feelings of anger against the world had persisted well into her early adult life, feelings that sometimes spurred her to wild and irrational behavior. Her distrust of others, men in particular (who in her experience tended to be betrayers), and doubts about herself had to some extent dominated her life until fairly recently, when she had entered the university and also established a successful domestic relationship. This recognition of herself in Heathcliff (or of the Heathcliff in her) changed her reaction to *Wuthering Heights* from one of revulsion to one of acceptance, in the very process of reading the novel. Such a complete turnaround based on a sudden discovery of oneself has not been reported in quite such a succinct and dramatic way by very many students, and it seems likely that one factor in Vicki's ability to accept the novel in the way she did was her relative maturity (she was twenty-eight at the time) and the strong sense of self she had already acquired. Margaret, equally mature and having gone through an equally intense process of self-searching, was still more actively involved in trying to solve for herself the problem of being a woman in a male-dominated society; this led both to her ability to accept the novel to a degree, but also to her feeling of a frustrated need to "place" Emily as author and woman.

The retrospective papers (among which I include Margaret's and Vicki's) have seemed the most significant for the question of how reader response may relate to literary understanding. This is in part a matter of personal bias, because my two classroom response papers on *Wuthering Heights* themselves were based on memories of childhood. But although those papers of mine set a context and perhaps a model for some of the students, the kinds of childhood memories that turned up were quite varied, some affording more striking instances than others for understanding the novel by concretizing and clarifying its (or its readers') emotional confusions. One woman, Beth, identified most fully with Heathcliff as the rejected child in a family; her strongest association was with her own rejection by her stepfather, and her resulting feelings of inadequacy. And she remarked that her mother's favoritism, although it made her stepfather more antagonistic just as Earnshaw's favoritism for Heathcliff drove Hindley into violent acts, was the saving factor of her childhood, without which she might well have become "as cold and brutal" as Heathcliff when he had lost, first, Mr. Earnshaw, and later, Catherine. As in Vicki's response, this paper describes an initially resisted identification with Heathcliff, but here it is with his position of alienation within the family rather than his "evil" qualities. While Vicki suddenly recognized her resemblance to Heathcliff as both victim of injustice and hater of the society that had made him a victim, Beth empathized with him more specifically through the feelings evoked in her by Heathcliff's rejection by his adoptive family. Beth also related her sense as a child that all the troubles were her own fault to what she assumed to be Emily Brontë's detestation of Linton Heathcliff (which, is, in the text, actually Heathcliff's attitude, though it could be Brontë's as well).

In contrast, Pat's response paper concentrated on her retrospective association with Cathy's deathbed nostalgia for her and Heathcliff's freedom on the moors in childhood. In the midst of holding down a full-time job, attending university, living in a "messy apartment," and being sick with the flu, she longed for the "huge, slimy" drainage ditch she had known as the one touch of nature in the barren southern California landscape in which she had lived. This ditch had given her and her brother some contact with nature, even if it was in the form of tadpoles and stagnant water, that caused them to return home "filthy and reeking." Though in her present life the idea of the ditch seemed repugnant and disgusting to her, she nonetheless sometimes longed to experience once again feelings of self-abandon of the kind that Catherine so longs for in the novel. Elsewhere in the paper, Pat refers explicitly to the influence of my paper on hers, yet her concerns are quite different from mine, focused as they are on the longing for lost freedom by a young adult struggling in an intractable world (which could describe either Catherine or Pat herself), rather than memories of a loss *in* childhood.

Marian's remarkable paper differs from the other instances of response to and retrospective association with *Wuthering Heights,* including my own paper, in that it deals with adolescence rather than childhood and connects readings of the novel at two different ages to a specific relationship presented in detail. It is special also in that it uses a comparison of her two very different understandings of the novel as a means of self-analysis.[3] Although unusually long for a response paper, it requires quoting in its entirety:

1. I wasn't sure I really wanted to read *Wuthering Heights* again. I had read it five years ago and it left me feeling terribly upset and depressed. I recall crying bitterly over it (although at which point in the novel I have no idea), and feeling down for days. The reason for this was, and is, no mystery. I saw in *Wuthering Heights* reflections of my own relationship with a very special childhood friend—Ted.

2. In that first reading, the characters that stood out in my mind were Cathy and Heathcliff/Ted and myself. I was entirely engrossed in their/our relationship. All the other characters were forgotten, so much so that in rereading the novel this time, they (Ellen, Lockwood, Edgar, Isabella, Joseph, young Cathy, Linton, Hareton and so on) were not in the slightest bit familiar. Whenever I did think of *Wuthering Heights* after that first reading, I recalled only Heathcliff's/Ted's haunting expressions and all the pain associated with the loss of my friendship with Ted.

3. When it came time to reread the novel, I found myself feeling agitated, apprehensive and depressed. I hadn't given old Ted much thought over the past couple of years, having finally managed to bury him in the past where he belongs. I was afraid in a way of retracing those old memories, knowing I would have to face again the feelings of rejection. What could I do other than assure myself that it was far enough behind me and not likely to really affect me. All the same, recalling how strongly I had reacted the first time I read the novel, I decided to jot down before rereading as much as I could recall about that reaction so as to make a more comprehensive comparison should I experience a change in response. Incidentally, underneath my rational exterior, I was quite convinced I would react in exactly the same way.

4. One of the first things I jotted down was that it was a love story. I did not mean love in the traditional, romantic sense. Rather, I recalled the intensity of the emotion between Catherine and Heathcliff, recalling it as a love quite apart from physical, sexual or natural love. I know there has been some argument in class as to whether such an unnatural relationship *is* love. To some I suppose it is inconceivable and unacceptable and yet, while I admit it *is* unnatural, I think it is possible. In that first reading, I very clearly paralleled my love for Ted with that love experienced by Cathy and Heathcliff, not seeing it at that point as in any way unnatural.

5. I began the novel the second time, expecting to find those striking parallels between Heathcliff and Ted, myself and Cathy. Immediately I was confused. Things seemed unfamiliar. I was seeing an entirely new Heathcliff and Cathy and an entirely new relationship. And yet, Ted and I were there, only this time not so much literally as perhaps symbolically. Our roles in the

drama were less defined now than they had been in the first reading where Ted *was* Heathcliff, and I Cathy. This time I was more an observer, identifying with rather than interacting with Cathy and Heathcliff's experience. In this reading, I was not restricted to Cathy, but identified also with Heathcliff. And, oddly enough in this reading, I did not become emotional but was left feeling strangely numb.

6. Underneath the numbness was an uneasiness, an uneasiness which increased as I tried to understand, looking over the notes I had made, why, when I could draw so few direct parallels between the novel and my life, certain things seemed so very very familiar. Not able to distinguish between memory and reality after so many years, I decided that I should read through my diaries—diaries I kept religiously for the three years I knew Ted—hoping to find some explanation for my unrest. It was the first time I had ever had the courage to wade through the seven volumes and what I found, to my alarm, were passages remarkably similar to some which appear in the novel. But first, let me explain the nature of my relationship to Ted.

7. We met in eighth grade on a warm windy September afternoon on the back steps of the high school where a group of us had gathered to chat. Our eyes met and very quickly we became best friends. For a year, we spent all our free time together and talked on the phone every night for an hour—or until one of our mothers caught us and made us hang up. We were never boyfriend and girlfriend, and actually had other boyfriends and girlfriends. There was no jealousy. In fact, often we recruited our respective friends as boyfriends/girlfriends for one another. This went on until ninth grade, when one day I "excused" one of the boyfriends Ted had set up for me. Ted was enraged and refused to speak to me for a full year after that, going out of his way to abuse me. Not understanding what I had done wrong, I grew defensive and as a consequence, we developed quite a hatred towards one another.

8. Then, one day in the tenth grade, our eyes met and somehow the war was over. Even so, we were never really close again and within four months of our "reunion" Ted moved away. On the day he left, quite out of the blue, we swore we would be friends forever, and Ted hopped onto his bus, brushing away tears with the sleeve of his grubby jean jacket. This may not sound like a terribly remarkable parting, but you must know that by this stage, Ted had grown into a tall, bushy-haired, loud-mouthed troublemaker—into drugs, alcohol, theft and "sleazy" girls. Tears in the eyes for one such as Ted were simply *not* cool.

9. Friends from our respective/separate groups only shook their heads at us wondering what on earth we could see in one another. Indeed, in many ways we were entirely different. Even so, I always maintained that Ted and I had a very special kind of love between us—that we were somehow "soul mates" (to use Janet's term). As I read through my diary, this became quite evident:

> Ted is one of my best friends. He's just like a brother. We seem alike in so many ways. We think the same way. Ted is my pal. We tell each other

everything, secrets and all. I feel at home with him, like someone I've known forever. He reminds me of someone. Sometimes it flashes through my mind when we look at each other, that I'm seeing myself. It's weird. We're not like the others.

Ted's the only one who really knows me, so if I ever die, I want him to have this diary. Ted, if I ever die, remember to keep talking to me because I'll always be listening.   (written at age 13)

I think you will see the parallels between what I said about Ted and what Cathy says about Heathcliff.

10. I equated myself with Cathy in both the first and second reading, but in the second reading, that identification wasn't as fixed. I found I did not like her at all in the second reading. It was only after reading my journals that I began to understand what it was about her I found disagreeable. It has been suggested in class, and I must now agree, that Cathy betrayed not only Heathcliff, but also herself. She denied him his natural/sexual feelings, and possibly even her own.

11. For years I believed that Ted and I had drifted apart because *he* had lost interest in *me*—outgrown me—rejected me. Before I read my journals, I wondered why I was identifying with Cathy so strongly when really, I had been rejected like Heathcliff. However, as I went over the diaries, I was shocked to discover that it was I who was fault—I who had betrayed and rejected Ted. All through grade eight our friends had made jokes about us, always trying to force us together at parties and dances and writing our initials together in hearts on the blackboard. I used to become enraged and deny their innuendoes and Ted would turn red, avoid my pleas for support, and pretend he hadn't heard. Like Cathy, I believed that Ted was like a brother and that nothing could separate us. There was a certain physical element to our relationship, but in my mind it was all in the name of friendship. We would wrestle and chase one another about, but if anyone suggested we participate in a game of spin the bottle . . . one of us always sat out.

12. Once Ted offered me his hand at a skating party but I refused, afraid people would laugh at us. I didn't receive my routine phone call the next evening. This was a sign of things to come. The clincher was my dismissal of one of the boyfriends Ted had set me up with. I think he must have seen it as a final rejection. I had humiliated him—after all, here was this friend of his who was incapable of holding down a boyfriend. Ironically, I had broken up with the boyfriend so I could spend more time with Ted. I have only just now realized the nature of Ted's bitterness towards me following the termination of our friendship. His insults, carefully recorded in my diary, were very directly aimed at my sexuality, or what I now think he must have perceived as a lack of it. So, just as Cathy signed the death warrant for her and Heathcliff's relationship by believing they could always be lovers "in the head," perhaps it was I who was to blame for the destruction of Ted's and my relationship.

13. And yet, even if it was I who cast Ted off as Cathy did Heathcliff, it was I, not Ted, who was to suffer most and who was to be haunted, like Heathcliff, for years afterwards. I was the one who felt betrayed, thinking I had been traded in for a packet of Export A and a big-busted bottle-blond. I agonized over Ted's endless stream of girlfriends, and like Heathcliff, I wanted revenge. My revenge was flirting with other members of his "tough" group, while ignoring him. It never dawned on me that I really could hurt his feelings and I never noticed that his behavior towards me intensified from ignoring me to purposely abusing me—kicking me, punching me, spitting at me and so on. For instance one day while a group of us were standing talking and I was engaged in a conversation with another male friend, Ted, who had been chatting with someone else, interrupted his own conversation, looked directly at me and hollered "Why can't you shut up." He said it with such bitterness that there was a shocked silence and I, bewildered and humiliated, literally ran away. Later that day I wrote:

> What is he trying to do? Hasn't he hurt me enough? Why does he always make sure I'm looking at him when he yells at me—and I can't look away. I think it gives him a feeling of satisfaction because he knows it crushes me. But what have I done to him? He's the one who started all this, not me.
>
> (written at age 14)

So, perhaps too, Ted was haunted to a certain extent, only I never realized it.

14. But still I am confused. If Ted does play a Heathcliff role and I a Cathy role, why is it that I sympathize with Heathcliff? Perhaps our tales are closer than, even now, I care to admit. After all, if they are truly similar then is it not I, like Cathy, who is to blame? Am I not then Ted's as well as my own destroyer? Why should I wish to shoulder the responsibility for all the hate and hurt both Ted and I endured?

15. As I mentioned earlier, Ted and I parted on speaking terms but by that time it was too late. The scars ran deep and we had grown our separate ways. We belonged to different groups and except for the occasional meeting, our paths seldom crossed. Then, he moved. It's been six years since I saw Ted and we only hear about one another every few years, through a mutual acquaintance. Always there is that promise to call one another but neither of us I think are willing to risk it, for now, more than ever, our lives are different. Whether or not Ted is haunted by the memory of our friendship on occasion as I am, who can say? In any case, it is unlikely that either of us will rush to the grave in anticipation of some final reunion on the other side!

16. Where, you may ask, is the response? It is hard to say because from that first half of the novel, I can not separate my own "love story" from that of Catherine and Heathcliff. The association is still too strong. Do I like *Wuthering Heights*? Yes, and no. Yes because along with all the painful memories come fond ones of someone who was, and is at least in memory,

very special to me. No, because I had to relive much of the pain I had tried for years to bury—pain which arose not only from reading the novel, but from reading my journals.

17. If there is any value in this rather heavily autobiographical response-paper, it is perhaps to see that fiction, for some of us anyway, can be used as an instrument on which we play out our own experiences, for it allows us to move in close to our emotions through association while at the same time remaining far enough removed so we are able to look at them more objectively.

Marian's closing comment about the paper she had written suggests an embarrassment at having concentrated so much on her personal experiences. Her embarrassment is not over having let out too much that was personal and private, but rather arises from her doubt whether communicating such an account to twenty classmates is appropriate or too self-centered to be of value to a group of people who have come together because of their love of literature and desire to know more "about" it. Receiving this paper, however, and one or two others during the same year of teaching, was something of a milestone in my attempt to develop a way of describing how individuals' "stories of reading" can be uniquely apt vehicles for the communication of certain kinds of literary understanding. The fascination Marian's paper held for those of us in the class was that it did *not* just demonstrate the use of a literary work for playing out one's own experiences and emotions, but also communicated a way of understanding some of the most puzzling aspects of Emily Brontë's dark novel. In short, in addition to clarifying for Marian herself at twenty-two things she could not understand about her and her friend Ted's emotional lives when they were thirteen or fourteen, or when she first read the novel at seventeen, the paper allowed us to see how the intense and tangled feelings of Heathcliff and Catherine could have some connection to the world of real persons and relationships as we perceived that world.

One of the things that came out in the subsequent discussion of Marian's paper was a clearer sense of something already implicit: that her sense of Ted's and her affinity, their unique ability to understand one another, was experienced across a gulf of difference—a gulf defined by "his group" and "my group," that is, by what for North American teenagers seems to be the equivalent of social class in the England of Emily Brontë's time. But at the same time, as Marian clearly recognizes in her twelfth and thirteenth paragraphs, the gulf was also for her and Ted defined by their different, though both clearly inadequate, understandings of love and its relationship to sexuality.[4] In *Wuthering Heights* the difference between Heathcliff and Cathy in this regard perhaps has something to do with the Victorian belief in the differences of levels and kinds of desire in men and women; in the case of Ted and Marian, it has to do with the inevitable confusions that arise in the early teen-years in a culture in which children are still often left ignorant of sexuality, and adolescents more often than not have to work out the meaning and gratification of new desires completely on their own. I am confident that Marian's descriptions of Ted are accurate, stereotyped though her language very occasionally sounds—accurate, that is, as accounts of memories of the way she was able to see him between the ages of thirteen and sixteen. What is also noticeable is how little then or at seventeen, and how much more fully now, she can understand the significance of his hostility toward her. For her as a young adolescent the physical element between them was one of "play"; clearly she knows now that for Ted, and perhaps for herself unconsciously, there was more to it than that. The interest of Marian's account for an understanding of *Wuthering Heights* is that it is virtually a retelling of Cathy's ignorance or repressed understanding of Heathcliff's feelings, and of her own. And it is a retelling based on Marian's contemporary records of her teen-age confusion, seen through a more mature understanding. As a result, the details of the novel at first seemed wrong to her, yet strangely familiar; reflection then led her to recognize how much more complex the analogies between the roles of Catherine/Heathcliff and Marian/Ted were than she had originally thought.

Especially relevant to this question of childhood and adolescent self-understanding is one of the most interesting of Victorian reviews of *Wuthering Heights,* by G. W. Peck, which appeared in *The American Review* in 1848:

> The physical condition of our bodies, the changes which take place on arriving at an age proper for marriage, do not allow of the ignorance which our author requires us to suppose in his heroine . . . especially after Heathcliff's absence and return, when she is the wife of Linton and about to become a mother. . . . Could Mrs. Linton, after Heathcliff's return, desire his presence without being conscious that her feelings towards him were such as his presence would only render more intolerable, unless, as the author leaves us no room to suppose, she meant to be untrue to her husband? We think that when any one considers the matter, he will find in what we have said above, a very plain explanation of what has been talked of as a puzzling character. . . . There is in these characters an absence of all that natural desire which should accompany love. They are abstract and bodiless. . . .

The children know too much about their minds and too little about their bodies; they understand at a very early age all the intellectual and sentimental part of love, but the "bloom of young desire" does not warm their cheeks. The grown-up characters are mere tools of fixed passion. [Allott, 239-40]

This seems remarkable because of its emphasis, without gender distinctions, upon physical desire and its apparent absence in *Wuthering Heights,* as well as, implicitly, Catherine and Heathcliff's fixation upon their childhood relationship. Although it may be limited in psychological insight by the lack, in 1848, of any concept of repression, the idea of persons whose feelings have remained fixed in childhood seems strikingly modern—even granted that it is not a point of praise for this critic. Peck's has always seemed to me a plausible reading of the confusions in *Wuthering Heights*: that Cathy and Heathcliff are really like children acting out the passions of adults (or is it adults trying to act out the phantasies of children?). And why, after all, should these barely adult characters (by some definitions still adolescent at the time of Cathy's death), or Emily Brontë, whose strongest heterosexual feelings seem to have been for her dissolute brother Branwell, have any more ability to understand their own feelings than did Marian and Ted at age thirteen or fourteen?

Marian's exploration of the meaning of *Wuthering Heights* for herself at two different stages in her life through the medium of the response paper communicates those meanings to other readers in ways that potentially open up a new understanding of the text—if we define the text specifically as a symbolic structure accessible only in readers' "resymbolizations" (David Bleich's term) of their response to it. For Marian the process of objectifying and analyzing her earlier and current involvement with that text was an act of discovery, of increased self-knowledge, but also, in what she ultimately recognized about Ted and herself, provided new knowledge of the "other" of the text. And the process of reading and discussing Marian's paper was less a coming to know *her* than it was a matter of coming to know a new text that, by being placed against Brontë's, afforded a resymbolization different from my and others' readings of *Wuthering Heights.* Her paper strongly supplemented our understanding of the mysterious relationship of the two main characters in a way only touched upon in my own set of associations with the loss of a loved person in childhood.

It may be thought that Marian's account of her failed early adolescent love is nothing all that remarkable—after all, misunderstandings occur between adolescent boys and girls all the time, and sometimes they take on a class and gender-specific configuration quite like the story of Marian and Ted. But it was not so much the account of the relationship as it was that of the process of coming to understand it as it seemed to be reflected in *Wuthering Heights*, first to an adolescent girl and then in a quite different way to the same person as a young woman, which seemed to provide a new concreteness and solidity to Emily Brontë's alien and isolated characters. In the fullness of its account of the relation between two readings and their developing associations, and its analysis of a personal quandary very much as though it were a crux in a narrative text, Marian's paper is special, though not unique. For in that same course Margaret produced a shorter but equally striking paper on the puzzling relationship between Jane Eyre and St.-John Rivers, as she associated it with her own disturbing friendship at sixteen with a young man who, though she didn't really even like him, threatened her sense of self with the same kind of "Christian" assuredness and simultaneously ascetic and sexual domination that Rivers seems to exercise over Jane. Charlotte Brontë presents one of the stranger male-female relationships in Victorian fiction, and Margaret's paper made us feel that it had become more tangible and comprehensible. Like Marian, Margaret also expressed doubts about the value of her personal associations except as self-therapy, but the other members of the class had no doubts that she had thrown more light for us on *Jane Eyre* than on her own personality and emotional history.[5]

These two papers, together with several others, such as Beth's account of her feeling herself the "outcast" in her family as a child and Pat's story of her longing for the pleasures of the California drainage ditch, convinced me that personal analysis of the associative aspect of a response can increase literary understanding by communicating to other readers experiences that are special to certain individuals and that normally do not get written about except in autobiographies. The communication of such self-understanding, even when the writer expresses doubts about its relevance, in a mutually trusting social context effects an understanding for others, in a special way, of the text. It is not, however, a matter of claiming that certain canonical texts have "universal" appeal that can be discovered through the approach I am describing. Rather, the kinds of communal insight generated by coming into contact with others' ways of reading are most usually experienced as new discoveries, and they may not be permanent judgments about a text for any given individual. A group such as a literature class may by and large come to a consensus about the value of a given response paper for reading a given work, but because such a group is made up of individuals, their individual views will not be identical and are likely as not to change with time.[6]

When planning this chapter I had at first thought to emphasize the "discovery of self" in readings of *Wuthering Heights* by centering on Vicki's sudden switch from recoil to recognition of her own worst traits in Heathcliff. Subsequently I taught the class whose response papers now form the core of my discussion here, and the topic is still "the discovery of self." But that expression should not be misunderstood: it is based neither on the observation that readers impose their personal experiences on a text, nor on the belief (as in Norman Holland's theory of "identity themes") that the reader always experiences reading in terms of a fixed pattern of dealing with the world. Marian's paper is probably the best example I have seen of how the self is not just eternally rediscovered as what it has always been, but may be revealed as something that has changed—just as the rereading of the text amounts to a change in that text.[7]

Nor is the self-reflective process of considering one's responses and the associations that are their basis solipsistic, as long as the subject does not assume that he or she is talking about *the* correct meaning of the text and does communicate the process to other readers. Personal response and association are not always interesting, nor do they always result in new understandings; but I have had a pretty high percentage of student papers that concretize through association and analogy difficult aspects of a text. In the case of *Wuthering Heights,* elements that had previously remained hazy, disturbing, or puzzling, such as the personalities of Catherine and Heathcliff, the way they interact, and the nature of their "love," took on a new clarity, concreteness, and a clearer connection with adolescence in both Brontë's society and our own, thanks especially to Marian's story of her readings. Conversely I, at least, have also been made much more aware of just how problematical this novel can be as a reading experience and an object of interpretation.

4 · Reading Esther Summerson: Reception, Response, Gender

Reception

Marian's particular experiences of reading *Wuthering Heights* and the paper she wrote as an account of them, if they are not unique, represent a deeper level and a broader scope of response and association than I usually expect from students. But there have been other, seemingly more fragmentary occurrences of what I have called the "discovery of the self" in literary texts which provide insight into problems of interpretation—problems I am here defining as ones of response as well. Because this chapter deals with the public history of reactions to a certain vexing element in a novel, as well as my students' and my individual responses, I have appropriated the term *reception* from German theorists in order to make a crucial distinction. I take *response* to refer to individual reactions considered separately or comparatively and *reception* to be a theoretical construct used in attempts to chart and account for the reactions of readers in a text's original historical context, as well as changes in the responses of readers from one historical period to another.[1] And it would seem obvious that without individual responses there is no reception.

Vividly presented fictional characters are perhaps what remain most enduringly in our memories of reading, although there are no rules for predicting which characters will endure for a given reader. Some have claimed that Mr. Micawber is the most memorable character in Dickens, and yet for me and some other readers he is a windy old bore and, as the late Leonard Manheim suggested years ago, something very like a psychopath.[2] Although he is given no more inner and less past life than Micawber, I find Quilp, the goblinlike villain of *The Old Curiosity Shop,* far more memorable, perhaps because in his carefree aggressiveness he acts out repressed wishes of my own. But I also find Myshkin more interesting than Raskolnikov, and Fanny Price more so than Emma. I could probably account for each one of these preferences through introspection and association, but offer these examples of what may seem to other readers of classic novels to be perverse reactions only in order to stress the problem of the variability of response to and understanding of fictional character.

One of the most striking instances where there is a substantial history of the reception of a character by reviewers and critics and a significant shift in that reception is the case of Esther Summerson, heroine and one of the two narrators of *Bleak House*. In my teaching *Bleak House* to undergraduates this character has been one of the greatest obstacles to students' reading the novel sympathetically. My students of the late 1960s were less outspoken than those in the late 1980s about their revulsion at Esther's habit of continual self-effacement by attributing other's praise of her to their goodness, but it was clear that those students of two decades ago did not see her as having any connection with their own lives. A common explanation for this was that "after all, Dickens was writing about the Victorian ideal of a woman, and that is not the way we think in the twentieth century." As a result of this reaction, I made it a regular practice when teaching *Bleak House* to read to students from contemporary reviews in order to demonstrate that not all Victorian readers were pleased with Dickens's handling of the character, and that they certainly did not all consider her the ideal type of Victorian woman. This was done in the process of my trying to persuade students that Dickens actually had created a detailed and convincing portrait of a person who, damaged by her treatment as a child, carried the signs of that damage into adulthood and never totally lost them. In a sense, this attempt was contradicted by demonstrating that *even* the Victorians (and thus, implicitly, not only we moderns) were unhappy with Dickens's portrayal of Esther. The oddness of that self-contradiction is one motivation for my writing about the reception of and response to Esther.

From the first publication of *Bleak House* until very recently, Esther Summerson has not very often been recognized as a successful instance of literary portraiture. George Brimley, reviewing Dickens's novel in the *Spectator* (24 September 1853), remarked that

the love of strong effect, and the habit of seizing peculiarities and presenting them instead as characters, pervade Mr. Dickens's gravest and most amiable portraits, as well as those expressly intended to be ridiculous and grotesque. His heroine in *Bleak House* is a model of unconscious goodness; sowing love and reaping it wherever she goes, diffusing round her an atmosphere of

ers quoted here, but it is clear that he was disturbed in the same way as Brimley at Esther's tendency as narrator repeatedly to advertise her superior qualities while purporting to deny them. Forster apparently believes that it is part of Dickens's intention to make Esther an ideal woman or at least to praise her self-effacing nature, and it is this to which he is referring when he speaks of the improbability of such self-conscious behavior in "a person of the character depicted."

Such doubts about Esther as a successful characterization prevailed among critics until A. E. Dyson argued in 1970 (the Dickens centenary year) for her as "that rare thing in a novel, a convincing depiction of moral goodness." Dyson is quite aware of modern readers' doubts about Esther, but attributes them to the "changes in attitude towards humility and gratitude [which] have followed the rise of welfare services and the emancipation of women" (173); he is evidently not aware of the very "modern"-seeming negative responses of some of Dickens's contemporaries. A more radical shift from the general view of Esther is to be found in two articles that appeared in the early 1970s, Alex Zwerdling's "Esther Summerson Rehabilitated," and Crawford Kilian's "In Defence of Esther Summerson," both of which present Esther as a psychologically consistent case history.[4] The previous negative reception of Esther (in both the nineteenth and twentieth centuries) depends on an assumption that Dickens intended to present her as an ideal heroine—whom the critics then judge wanting. Zwerdling's and Kilian's being historically post-Freudian, if not actually Freudian in their approaches, and their awareness of the modern psychological novel from James onwards, are the historical conditions that make it possible for them to stress the fullness and accuracy of Dickens's portrait of an emotionally damaged child, whose sense of guilt and lack of confidence in her self-worth have been imposed early in life by her "god-mother," Miss Barbary. Zwerdling in particular argues that Dickens's interest in Esther is "essentially clinical," and her portrait that of someone "who remains trapped between childhood and real maturity" (429), while Kilian claims that Dickens intentionally portrays Esther as one who must continually present and think of her identity in terms of a "false self," the "Little Old Woman" image, because she is too frightened of her "real self," the one that could risk love and thus rejection.[5] To again adopt (and adapt) a term from reception theory, the possible "horizon of expectations" for critics has thus changed, although those necessary historical conditions do not explain why it changed so late, or why for these particular critics.[6]

Zwerdling and Kilian find value in what they see as a mimetic presentation of a character's complex personality. In reaction to an overtly Freudian essay by Gordon Hirsch which appeared in 1975, but also, I think, partly to Zwerdling's privileging of the psychologically mimetic, Albert D. Hutter attempts to present a new way of approaching the problem of the reader's response to *Bleak House*. Hutter (himself a nonmedical psychoanalyst) rejects the orthodox Freudian emphasis on very early childhood as the primary basis for explaining the psychology of adults or adult fictional characters. He further argues that the really significant aspect of the reader's response is to the symbolic implications of the *form* rather than to the overt content of Dickens's novel, in particular to the way in which Inspector Bucket assumes an omniscient role, and in so doing connects the first-person narrative with the omniscient one. The transformation of Bucket from sinister minion of Tulkinghorn and the Law to all-knowing and humane father-figure (in the search, with Esther, for her mother) seems contrived, Hutter says,

only when we expect Bucket's character to develop realistically and when we ignore the thematic significance of his behavior and its impact on the reader. From the "high tower of his mind" Bucket identifies imaginatively with Lady Dedlock. His action and the language in which it is described enlarge the reader's empathic understanding.

Bucket's progress guides our progress until Bucket eventually bridges the narrative gulf of the novel. Linked from the beginning to the omniscient perspective, knowing, observant, cool to the point of apparent heartlessness, Bucket's alliance with Esther in the final chase symbolically connects him with the emotional subjectivity of the first person narration, and the plot now ties the various strands of the novel together. [307–8]

Bucket's transformation from a sinister to a humane character is also taken by Hutter as analogous to the general theme of transformation of character, of which Esther is the central instance.[7] It is difficult to do justice to Hutter's complex argument through paraphrase or limited quotation, but my main problem with his admittedly brilliant article is that it seems to be based on an assumption that there is a universal, or at least a *best,* way to respond to a text. That the idea of a universal response has been discredited as an epistemological or interpretive principle by such as Stanley Fish, Norman Holland, and David Bleich in their major theoretical works is of less significance to me than the fact that, after reading and rereading both his article and *Bleak House,* I cannot respond as Hutter says "the reader" does.

One question that bears on both reception and interpretation is whether all those critics are "wrong" who from 1853 until at least the 1970s have regarded Esther Summerson as a repugnantly self-conscious, simpering goody-goody who always lets us know how wonderfully humble she is. I suggest tentatively that those of us who have taught or written about Esther Summerson as Dickens's intentional portrait of a neurotic who continually reveals just how damaged she is by her denial of her own evident goodness are motivated by something in addition to what is "in" the text. I know that I have been motivated consciously by an unwillingness to believe that such a substantial portion of what I think a great novel is flawed, and I shall discuss other less conscious and probably stronger motivations later in this chapter.

Although the idea of Esther as an emotionally damaged child who carries the effect of that damage into her adult behavior occurred to me in the 1960s, Zwerdling's "rehabilitation" of her greatly strengthened my conviction that this was *the* way to see Esther and to teach *Bleak House*.[8] But holding such a conviction would seem to require that one be convinced that Dickens deliberately caused Esther to reveal her "clinical" symptoms through her role as narrator of her own story, contrary to the apparent assumption of her earliest reviewers and most later critics—and as Zwerdling and Kilian both claim. There is virtually no direct textual or external evidence as to how Dickens regarded Esther. About the closest we come to this is in Dickens's memorandum to himself for Number 10 of *Bleak House* (chaps. 30-32), in which he writes, "Esther's love must be kept in view, to make the coming trial the greater and the victory the more meritorious" (786). This must refer to Esther's love for Allan Woodcourt, which Dickens frequently reminded himself to "carry through," and it is "kept in view" in Number 10 by the introduction in chapter 30 of Allan's mother, who knows of her son's feelings about Esther and takes pains to stress to her in conversation that he pays attentions to young ladies without being at all serious about them. Esther makes it clear she understands the motive behind this: "Why was it so worrying to me to have her in our house, and confidential to me every night, when I yet felt that it was better and safer, somehow that she should be there than anywhere else? These were perplexities and contradictions that I could not account for. At least, if I could—but I shall come to all that by and by, and it is mere idleness to go on about it now" (368).

In the novel's immediate context "the coming trial" is Esther's smallpox. But Dickens in his memorandum may be thinking ahead to Esther's belief that the disease has destroyed whatever beauty she may have had, and still further ahead to her belief that Allan

Woodcourt upon his return to England is only sorry for her, with her scarred face; and if he *is* thinking that far ahead, then it seems likely that "the coming trial" also refers to her acceptance of John Jarndyce's proposal of marriage and the fact that it prevents her from accepting Allan's subsequent declaration of love (chap. 61). What I find most interesting here is Dickens's emphasis to himself (in a sense writing of his own intentions—or as an interpreter of his own novel as he is writing it) on the need to make the trial harder, and the "victory the more meritorious." Here, the novelist indeed sounds as if he is thinking of Esther as an ideal woman, who merits a victory in the form of an ultimate marriage to Woodcourt, especially because she has been through much suffering, including the belief that she has lost him forever.

Of course, Dickens could be simultaneously idealizing and clinically analyzing Esther, and so why should I be grasping at straws of "objective" evidence as to how Dickens himself regarded his character? Why is the text not enough from which to infer Dickens's intentions, especially now that Zwerdling and Kilian among others have elucidated the defense-mechanisms Esther brings into play, or the "false self" with which she identifies herself? As indicated earlier, I often feel a need to conceptualize an author and his intentions as a way of stabilizing my subjective understanding of the text; but because several students' strongly expressed feelings in their response papers on *Bleak House* have shaken my certainty about the superiority of the psychological-mimetic way of reading Esther, I now feel that to accept the "clinical" reading is to disregard a crucial aspect of the novel and of readers' responses to it. For why was the negative critical view so prevalent for more than a century, until some critics discovered that the others had been wrong all along? Is the newer, favorable, psychological view of Dickens's treatment of Esther really so totally different from the old condemnations?

Response

I always expect some negative reactions to Esther Summerson from students, but since I began to require papers that describe and attempt to explain the reader's strongest response to some aspect of *Bleak House,* the probability and strength of negative responses have increased.[9] In a class taught at the beginning of 1987, the intensity of revulsion at the character of Esther went beyond anything I had encountered previously, and my usual attempt to explain what Dickens was "really" doing with her fell quite flat, for it in no way assuaged the visible anger of some of the students. To convey these reactions adequately, it is necessary to quote from a few of their papers. But first, in order to make clear part of the context in which these were written, I present an abridged version of the paper I wrote and distributed to the class. If it had little effect on the students' most visceral responses to Esther, it seems to have had some on what issues they took up, and I shall suggest later what relevance it has for the whole question of "reading Esther." Its title is *"Bleak House*: My Favorite Dickens, but a Vale of Tears: An Experiment in Psychosomatic Response Criticism."

1. After reading Alison's description of her somatic response to *David Copperfield,* I felt obliged to deal with my own similar responses to *Bleak House*—uncontrollable tears at certain points, if not uncontrolled weeping. (I once mentioned this to a class, and some of them said they had wept, but only at the difficulty of getting through this massive novel!)

2. Reading the novel this time, with careful attention to the language, tone, satirical meaning, etc., I still find my eyes filling with tears at the same old points. I have felt in the past that I must have some residue of sentimentality in my soul, and have been annoyed that Dickens manipulates me into that reaction, but that is probably unfair. Most of my tears come in response to crucial passages involving Esther: when she is told she is to go to school under the patronage of Jarndyce, and is so grateful; when she realizes that she has a "guardian," and again, is so very grateful for his love.

3. There are other passages, but these may stand as typical. What is there that affects me in a way that *David Copperfield* rarely does, and what are the sources of that response in myself? Certain aspects of Esther should militate against my identifying with her: I find her terribly coy as narrator in her repeated denials of how good she is (which really seem to be there to inform the reader of just how good she *is*); and such denials also apply to her own attractiveness, carrying through to the very last sentence of the novel. And although I have learned to see Esther's self-deprecation as a system of defenses for a woman who has been denied love and made to feel guilty as a child, I still feel irritated by those statements of hers. And yet at the same time I must be identifying with her strongly, on the evidence of the way my tears so easily flow. To get at the reasons for this will require some digging into my past.

4. As I think about my life, it occurs to me that it has been a typical pattern that I am frequently surprised at discovering either that someone liked or loved me, or that I had received approval for something I had done: that my undergraduate grades (which, at Reed College, we didn't receive until after we had graduated) included a number of A's; that my written work is accepted for publication. I can still feel surprised when my wife tells me that she loves me, or that I'm good-looking; when my kids tell me that I'm a terrific father; or when a student tells me that he/she really enjoyed a course.

Thus it seems to be my own propensity for self-doubt that accounts for my tears whenever Esther feels surprise and gratitude at others' good feelings about her.

5. My childhood was certainly not one of constant rejection, like Esther's, and I should be *used* to success. I always did well in school, I had friends, and "girlfriends," as child, adolescent, and young adult. And I have not been unsuccessful as a teacher and critic. Yet as a child, and to a degree later on, I was hypersensitive to any hint of disparagement or rejection—to the extent of swinging my fists when I sensed or imagined it.

6. The association that may explain this is what I recall of a sense of being made to feel inadequate about some things, while being over-praised for others. The first was the work of my father, the second, that of my mother. My father was first successful for a time as a cartoonist, then as a writer of fiction; he also had been a musician and was trained as a visual artist. Incredibly good with his hands, he taught himself to be a machinist during the war so he would qualify for defense work; later, when his writing stopped selling, he collaborated with a brother in developing a successful business manufacturing paints for commercial artists; when it became evident that there wasn't enough profit for the two of them in that, he taught himself, at 44, to design and make modern jewelry, his main source of income from then until his death at 67.

7. With this kind of competence, my father could not tolerate my attempts to make or fix things with my hands; typically, whatever I was working on with difficulty would be taken away from me and he would finish the job. Even my piano-practice irritated him when I would stop and go over phrases if I made a mistake. I bear no anger against my father now, though I certainly did as a child. In many ways he was warm, loving, and approving. For those things I did well I got praise, and he spent much time with me when I was a young child—taking me to parks, to movies, talking with me in an uncondescending way, virtually as an equal. Being made to feel inadequate by a father whom I loved greatly is probably the emotional source of what I·have called my frequent surprise at love or praise, the basis of my identification with Esther and my tears at all her similar surprises. But an additional factor which probably made that whole complex of traits even more dominant in my personality was my mother's habit of praising me *too* much for what talents I had, a kind of praise which may well increase one's sense of inadequacy. And thus my empathy, to the point of tears, with Esther when she repeatedly is astonished that people really like and praise her, really think she is competent, good, and even beautiful.

At the least, some students picked up my references to Esther's emotional damage as a child as the source of her repeated self-deprecation, but, most significantly for the whole question of my influence on what my students write, my expression of this idea did not lessen the violence of their rejection of the character. I think, rather, that the negative feelings about Esther in my paper allowed them to express their own hostility, without necessarily buying my psychological view of Esther.[10] Wanda's paper deals predominantly with a conflict between the view of Esther as an emotionally damaged person, and her own response to Esther as impossibly coy and hypocritical.

1. My overall reaction to Esther is confused, and seems to encompass a variety of emotions. Much of what Esther does I consider to be game playing. I am disturbed myself when I as well as others resort to this. I also find myself making excuses for Esther's behavior, yet as the novel progresses, I find these excuses wearing thin. I feel as if I should be sympathetic to Esther throughout the novel as I was at the beginning, but instead I find my tolerance for her behavior vanishing. I do not consider her a very interesting character and sometimes wish that she would do something daring. Yet I feel guilty that I am so annoyed with her.

2. I was happy for Esther when she was at Greenleaf, because she seemed to be happy, well liked, and accepted. However, shortly after that point, my impatience started growing. I became royally sick and tired of her constantly letting me know how nice everyone was to her and how well liked she was. She seemed to do this under the guise of trying to make other characters look kind and charitable, but from my own experiences I have found that people describe the kindness of others in at least two ways: 1) "They were *so kind*." 2) "They were so kind to *me*." Those who use the second expression are trying to praise themselves by using someone else's kindness as an excuse to do this. This is where I have a problem with Esther. It seems as if she talks about how kind other people are to her with the ulterior and overriding desire to let me know how wonderful she really is. I am irritated and annoyed with this behavior and consider it to be a kind of game. I don't like to see it in my friends or myself. It is almost an insult to the listener's intelligence.

3. I think that some people try to make themselves look popular and well liked because they really are insecure. I know that Esther's childhood was probably the cause of this insecurity, but I found that excuse wearing thin. I don't want to sound judgmental, and I realize that some emotional scars will always be part of a person and will continue to affect their outlook on life, yet I don't think that it is right to let those scars control a person's life. I feel as if Esther has never really come to terms with her past and as a result is very insecure. I find her way of coping with the past to be nauseating. She is coping, but hasn't dealt with the root of the problem. Frankly, I'm tired of reminding myself that Esther had a rough childhood and therefore I should excuse her behavior. (Please note that I realize that Esther does not really use this as an excuse. It is the excuse I use to explain her behavior.) The irony of this is that after four years I still have trouble overcoming an experience of my own. [After an accident in a car that was hit when going through a yellow light] I still can't drive through a yellow light without my heart beating madly. I freak out when I drive through lights that have been green for a

long time, and I could scream when I am a passenger and the driver deliberately runs a yellow. It annoys me that I have not been able to completely overcome this. I realize that this experience is by no stretch of the imagination as damaging as Esther's was, but I feel the principle is similar. Maybe I am partly frustrated with Esther's behavior because I haven't been able to overcome my own problem or take my own advice; instead, I rely on an excuse.

4. One interesting slip that I made almost to the end of the book was in reading Esther's nickname Dame Durden as Dame Drearden. This basically expresses my feelings about Esther. I find her to be a tiring and dreary character who had some psychological problems. She was dreary as a child and as an adult. She never did anything mischievous or daring. Lately I have wished that I could have been more mischievous during my childhood. My brother tells some great stories about his adventures as a child, but I don't have any really exciting adventure stories. I hated getting in trouble and that pretty well kept me in line. I wish I had been more daring and even suffered the consequences.

5. So why does Esther bother me so much? Perhaps because some of her problems cause me to think of some of the shortcomings and insecurities that many people (including myself) have. I guess I don't like many of the games people play, although in some cases I feel sorry for those who feel the need to play them constantly. Perhaps Esther's shortcomings "bug" me too because they occur in a relatively short period of time, that is the time it takes me to read the novel. In real life, I come across these games, but they seem to be more evenly distributed and not as condensed. I think I may be better able to handle them because their occurrence is usually less frequent.

In addition to the conflict evident in expressed feelings of guilt, what is most interesting about Wanda's paper is what she fails to cover in detail or omits. For while she does mention that Esther's shortcomings are related to her own, especially her lack of adventurousness, and that this is some of the cause of her nausea, only in class discussion did it become clear that she also considers herself an extremely dependent and malleable, as well as quite insecure, person, and that these qualities may be what she most dislikes about Esther. Wanda describes her home-life as loving and secure and is anxious about moving out into the world on her own.[11]

Another student, Gwen, in her paper also complains about Esther's constantly calling attention to others' praise of her as "nauseating," but is somewhat more direct in describing the aspects of herself that she finds in Esther:

As a child I did not feel good about my appearance, intellect, or social position, and the only way for me to experience a feeling of self-worth was to do good things for people. I recall my mother calling it "buying friends."

I remember promising all my playmates a treat if they would play with me. You can imagine my mother's horror when she was met at the door with a group of eager eyes, each wanting their reward. When I played with other children I would always give them the best toy in hope of gaining their acceptance. I so compulsively wanted to appease my parents that at one point when they needed help moving I requested the assistance of our land-lord, who had no idea that they were planning to leave. This left them in quite an embarrassing position. I also bragged about many of my kind acts to allow those who had missed them to at least have the pleasure of hearing about them. As I grew older, I realized that my good deeds had really only been a plea for social acceptance and I began to hate the things I had done in the past, despising my insecurity and questionable motives. It is said that what one hates in himself he also hates in others. Although my actions differ from Esther's, she does continually mention her good deeds and seems to do them compulsively, as I did. Thus, as I performed these kind actions owing to my insecurity, I see Esther doing the same.

In her very next paragraph, however, Gwen seems to try to distance this recognition of her own qualities by telling of a girl into whose friendship she was forced by her parents, and who talked about "how well she could sew, knit, and perform in school, and when [she] was not bragging about her skills, she was telling me about how well liked she was by our peers. As I hear Esther continually mentioning her good points, I see my friend who, through the years, becomes more nauseating."

In class discussion Gwen, like Wanda, admitted to disliking most in herself her insecurity and submissiveness, qualities she also attrib-uted to Esther. In contrast to these papers, Diane's demonstrated an ability not only to describe, but to face directly, her own feelings of insecurity, and unlike many of the other students she considered *Bleak House* her favorite among all the novels we read. While on the basis of her way of speaking and her gestures, Diane seemed to me more insecure in general than Wanda or Gwen, she had, for whatever reason, a strength that allowed her to feel "sympathy for and under-standing of Esther," rather than a need to reject her because she is too close to her own negative qualities.

Why did I respond to Esther? A part of me is very insecure and like Esther I need reassurance. I am constantly questioning my abilities. When I started university my parents were proud of me and they kept reassuring me that just getting through was good, the grades were not important. But I've always felt that just getting through was not enough, although I'm not unrealistic. Whenever I write a paper I am so unsure of myself that I refuse to let my brother [a "straight-A" student] read it because I am afraid he will see me as a fraud. Yet in the back of my mind no matter how much I have convinced myself that a paper is terrible, I expect a decent mark. I must admit that on occasion I have tried to milk compliments from my family because I need that reassurance. When someone does compliment me I usually question that compliment (is it valid?). I also have trouble sometimes expressing my opinion when I am around people I think are bright because I am afraid they will laugh at or tear my ideas apart.

Reception, Response, and Gender

It would seem that all three of these young women have conflicts about what are traditionally supposed to be "feminine" qualities, and Wanda and Diane both express envy of a brother's greater adventurousness or intellectual prowess. Wanda's anxiety about leaving home is connected with her distress that so many of her friends are getting married and thus will no longer be friends to her in the same way. And I suspect that part of her disgust with Esther is that she lives out a phantasy of Wanda's own in an almost crudely symbolic way by getting to marry and keep her home as well, remaining always in a "Bleak House." It is perhaps the difference between Wanda and Gwen on the one hand, and Diane on the other, that the first two have strong, unresolved conflicts about their passivity and insecurity, while Diane is able to look clearly at the insecurity and submissiveness that result from her position as the youngest of three children, and to try to deal with them. All three "find" themselves in Esther, but the resulting responses are quite different—anxiety and "nausea," as opposed to sympathy and understanding.[12]

Wanda's and Gwen's papers fit within the paradigm of the anti-Esther critics from 1853 to the present, while Diane's paper is closer to those, like Zwerdling's and Kilian's, which defend Esther. But there are gender complications that prevent these analogies from being perfect. Most of the published critics, especially the negative ones, who deal with Esther have been men, and on the basis of my reading of Wanda's and Gwen's papers I am tempted to conjecture that the strong revulsion felt by these men (of whom I am intermittently one) has something to do with the threat to a man of identifying with the stereotypically feminine: the submissive, the dutiful, the serving, the "good." It would seem that a difficult emotional leap is necessary in order for a man truly to empathize with the extreme embodiment of what were once considered feminine virtues that Esther represents. And though it seems clear that the psychoanalytic concepts of the unconscious, repression, and neurosis have made possible a different sort of reception of Esther by critics, can it be

that those of us who have decided that Dickens's *Bleak House* heroine
is really a sharply focused and profound clinical portrait are using
such concepts to erect our own kind of defenses—in effect denigrating
Esther as "damaged," or "neurotic," so that we may distance her
from ourselves? This would be the opposite of what Wanda in particular does to achieve the goal of distancing Esther, for she argues that
Esther's emotional disturbances are *no excuse* for Esther's "nauseating" way of talking about herself. Seeing qualities of their own in
Esther, Wanda and Gwen disclaim those qualities in the very process
of admitting to them, by blaming the fictional character for the
"nausea" they feel. Is it possible that the male critics who have found
Esther a realistic psychological portrait are using a more complex,
and thus less detectable, process of denying the discovery of some of
our own qualities in Esther?

It is in regard to this last question that I think my response paper
becomes especially relevant. In it, first of all, I affirm that rereading
Bleak House had brought out in me, as it always seems to do, what
at least used to be considered a feminine (or childish) somatic response: uncontrollable tears. Second, I talk about a seemingly irrational insecurity about my accomplishments, which in reading over
that paper sounds almost as self-deceptive and annoying as Esther
Summerson at her worst, however true it may be as a description of
my feelings. And I suspect that all the negative reactions to Esther,
as well as the clinical readings, are in part responses to the challenge
to be selfless, to work only for others' happiness, and to draw one's
own happiness from the result—challenges that are also felt as threats.
In some respects this is a Christian ideal projected onto an extreme
version of a traditional concept of the feminine as submissive and
self-sacrificing, and therefore received with all the ambivalence that
modern men and women tend to feel about it. Whether or not Esther
Summerson is to be taken as Dickens's ideal, or as a model Christian
heroine, many readers seem to feel that she is *supposed* to be taken
as an ideal and resist what they see as the novel's attempt at persuasion. And the three students, in trying to come to terms with the
discovery of part of themselves in Esther, are taking up a challenge
to relate their own personalities and roles as women to the unquestionably good as well as the exasperating qualities in Esther.

There may be a further gender complication that causes men,
especially in the twentieth century, to feel uncomfortable with Esther.
For while a woman may find, and accept, reject, or deny an image
of herself in Esther, a man is faced with the twofold danger of
identifying with qualities supposedly shameful in men, while also

wondering whether these very qualities, especially submissiveness, are not just what he wants in a love-object, which is also a shameful thought, difficult to face in these days when women are trying to escape from their traditional subordinate roles. This could be another possible motive for distancing Esther, by whatever means.

There seem to have been three main ways for critics to deal with Esther. One may reject her as an artistic failure (a term that may be employed to evade the question of the subjective and the motivational in aesthetic judgments) because of her coyness and eternal self-promotion; one may accept her as an ideal; or one may see her as an incisive and full portrait of an emotionally wounded child carrying her scars into adulthood. But to choose any one of these ways of seeing Esther—or Albert Hutter's approach to "the reader's" response as based on narrative form rather than content—is, implicitly, to reject the others and thereby acknowledge that some aspect of Esther, if looked at directly, is a threat. The clinical view, which I had for years promoted, is not the least evasive, because of the way it distances, by labeling "neurotic" or "false," Esther's personal qualities.

Wanda and Gwen also attempt to distance Esther, but because simultaneously they recognize themselves in the image they reject, that rejection cannot be final. So, if my conjectures about the origins of responses to and interpretations of Esther Summerson have a modicum of accuracy, it would seem that the nature and meaning of this character "in" the novel are inextricably tied up with what we bring to the text when reading and trying to make sense of it. There is thus no "best" way of understanding Esther, but it is possible that the fullest kind of reading of any strongly drawn fictional character occurs when we can first acknowledge the elements of ourselves that we find in her or him, before we distance the character to be analyzed as "other." While it may be objected that my emphasis on individual response represents a misuse of the concept of "reception," I do not see any way of plumbing the complexities of reception, either historically or among modern readers, without resorting to accounts of individual response, and conjectures about the responses of those individuals whom we cannot interview, or who cannot or will not provide us with response papers.

5 · Response and Evasion in Reading
The Wind in the Willows

Introduction

I move now from the question of how a reader may discover himself or herself to an expansion of that same question: how the reader's self is relevant to attempts to understand the meanings of a text, and the author's "presence" in that text. The account in chapter 2 of my reading of *Treasure Island,* given as a brief demonstration of the analysis of response as well as the inferring of intention through associations and biographical material, is to some extent evasive. However arid the initial Oedipal reading may have felt, without having performed it I could not have come up with the personal associations that presumably were the real source of a strong affect. But then any ability to unearth the "hidden" (which includes above all the sources of affect) is made possible in part by what knowledge I have of Freudian theory. And the wish to find the hidden is likely motivated by two other factors: a strong desire to understand the present in relation to my past (the hidden source in myself of affect), and a kind of pleasure involved in believing that I know something others do not—the author's hidden meanings, even though they are ultimately my constructs. The evasive nature of that particular account of the associative sources of a reading is defined by the strict limits I had set for myself in the discussion of my response: as presented, the association of the adult male characters in *Treasure Island* with my uncles does not go very far, for I avoided touching on some of the most painful aspects of my relationships to them. The wish not to re-experience pain is probably what most limited me, though I also wished to avoid overloading an introductory chapter with too many personal details. *Treasure Island* was not an especially important book in my childhood, and my emotional involvement with it as an adult is narrow, if strong; and there is also something tendentious in the way I have sought for associations and used them to make a point about psychoanalytic criticism.

The insistence by those who doubt the value for criticism or theory of personal response that it can never really be spontaneous is well taken (see my remarks on Culler in chap. 1), for writing, even what composition specialists call "freewriting," is a formal act. Moreover, reports of responses and associations always involve some degree of evasion: something is always omitted, both through unconscious repression of the painful and conscious selection of which details to present. Nor can the reader detailing associations connected with a response be sure of their accuracy, because the process involves an attempt to reconstruct the past on the basis of memory, whose reliability must be uncertain.

To illustrate just how evasive a detailed "story of reading" can be is one of the purposes of this chapter. My experiment with *The Wind in the Willows* originally took the form of an essay, the first including personal response and association which I wrote for publication. I present the substance of the original essay interspersed with comments about my evasions and how I came to recognize them. At the end of this chapter I comment on its methodological problems, which include above all the confident-sounding generalizations about the nineteenth-century and early twentieth-century novel. This experiment and that with *Alice in Wonderland* stem from my engagement in teaching and writing about both the novel and children's literature, and my attempt to develop a response approach to interpretation and the role of authorial intention (more broadly, the extrinsic). More immediately, because Grahame's and Carroll's novels had been important in my childhood I was motivated by a need to find out just what those books had meant to me, why my adult responses as I reread them and my childhood ones insofar as I could recall them seemed so perplexing.

At the Back of *The Wind in the Willows*: Response

One does not argue about *The Wind in the Willows*. The young man gives it to the girl with whom he is in love, and if she does not like it, asks her to return his letters. The older man tries it on his nephew, and alters his will accordingly. The book is a test of character. We can't criticize it, because it is criticizing us. As I wrote once: it is a Household Book; a book which everybody in the household loves, and quotes continually; a book which is read aloud to every new guest and is regarded as the touchstone of his worth.

But I must give you one word of warning. When you sit down to it, don't be so ridiculous as to suppose that you are sitting in judgment on my taste, or on the art of Kenneth Grahame. You are merely sitting in judgment on yourself. You may be worthy; I don't know. But it is you who are on trial. [Milne, Introduction, x]

Among Victorian and Edwardian fantasy novels, the one that has perhaps retained the greatest power to affect readers emotionally and to claim the lasting loyalties of those who first take it up in childhood or adolescence is Kenneth Grahame's *The Wind in the Willows* (1908). It is indeed a "household book," and certain connotations of "household" may help explain A. A. Milne's interdict against "sitting in judgment . . . on the art of Kenneth Grahame." Such a warning implies that this work is inviolable, immune to analysis or criticism, because the feelings it arouses are too special and private.[1] And it might be said that nineteenth- and early twentieth-century British novels are by and large household books. Austen, Dickens, Thackeray, the Brontës, Eliot, Gissing, Hardy, and James each in his or her own way both reveals and conceals the intimacy of emotional life within the family, in the individual psyche, and between lovers. While Henry James conducts so painstaking and convoluted an analysis that it often hides as much as it reveals, George Eliot merges domestic realism and moral philosophy so that the latter appears to subsume the former. Thackeray, in *Vanity Fair* at least, manages his evasions and sometimes prurient revelations through the wiles of a protean narrator who slips coyly in and out of the story—and the families therein—so that the independence of the story's dramatic reality remains ambiguous. In Charlotte and Emily Brontë, and in Dickens, there is often what looks like an overt symbolism that may lead away from those secrets at the same time that it embodies them, and in the case of Emily there is in addition a cunningly elusive narrative form behind which there seem to be hidden "facts" about the characters. Hardy's usual forms of indirection are a pretension to historical wisdom and knowledge of the universe and his narrators' frequent self-contradiction, or, as in *The Well-Beloved,* endless nattering around the main subject—sexual and "ideal" love. Gissing combines a purported social realism with phantasies of sex and class that are barely concealed. In the pre-Victorian part of the century the most intense chroniclers of domestic entanglements are Jane Austen, from behind whose (sometimes seemingly contradictory) defenses of irony and moral rectitude the household secrets reveal themselves at crucial points, and James Hogg, whose one great novel (*The Private Memoirs and Confessions of a Justified Sinner* [1824]) is an astonishing instance of the uncanny achieved as much by indeterminate narrative and an elusive author as by the supernatural (see the opening of chap. 7, below).

The modernist novels of Joyce, Woolf, and Kafka may once have seemed, in contrast to those of the nineteenth century, to be under a new and fully conscious kind of control, with meaning obscured only by the novelists' erudition and the breaking up of straightforward sequential narrative. With increasing biographical knowledge, however, we are beginning to understand how much these authors' works (which might previously have caused us to believe that they herald the elimination of what Foucault calls the "author-function") embody the personal ambivalences, conflicts, and phantasies of their creators. What Victorian novel is more one of the household and the family than *To the Lighthouse, Ulysses,* or "The Judgment" and *The Metamorphosis?* Yet there *is* a difference for Joyce, Woolf, and Kafka, because though born in the nineteenth century they knew that age with hindsight and could react against it in a way that was only beginning to be possible for Hardy in *Tess* and *Jude.*

Our own relationship to the Victorians is a complex one, for culturally we are their heirs, and though we may pride ourselves on having transcended their limitations in the domestic sphere, we keep returning to them and the household in their novels to try to understand its meaning for ourselves. As Freud found in consulting Daniel Sanders' and Jakob and Wilhelm Grimm's dictionaries, *heimlich* became long ago almost a synonym for *unheimlich*—usually translated as "uncanny"—which should by the normal rules of language be its antonym. Thus, that which is of the household is familiar, yet private, even secret, and thus paradoxically strange and forbidden. What is "familiar" is "of the family," and therefore much of it is not to be discussed and is repressed, so that it becomes unfamiliar to consciousness. Superficially, the household and the family seem *heimisch* (homey, domestic, truly familiar); but much of what goes on in one's own or someone else's household is private, even mysterious and, in art, likely to be expressed by the author and experienced by the reader in indirect ways. The feeling of the *Unheimliche* involves what seems alien suddenly producing a strange feeling based on the sudden return of the feeling of familiarity with what has become unfamiliar (Freud, "The 'Uncanny' ").

The *Heimliche* and its counterpart the *Unheimliche* have a role especially discernible to us, as post-Freudians, in Victorian and Edwardian fantasy novels ostensibly written for children: from Kingsley through the Alice books, the fairy-tales and novels of George

MacDonald, to Kenneth Grahame and Edith Nesbit. While the comment that Charles Kingsley's *The Water-Babies* is all about masturbation (Duffy, 283–84) may reflect one critic's "wild" psychoanalytic approach to fantasy, the first edition's illustrator, J. Noel Paton, in fact came remarkably close to depicting masturbation literally, as we see in his frontispiece the naked water-babies clustered around the beautiful fairy, listening to the story she tells, thumbs in mouths and a rapt look on their faces—a situation that for a real child of a similar age usually finds the other hand on his or her genitals.[2] Such household realities are not likely part of the originating, conceptualized intentions of the author or the illustrator, but they may nonetheless be perceived as a part of meaning; and indeed, one way of simultaneously expressing and concealing such meanings in Kingsley's time was to write fantasy "for children," which left the adult reader with the choice of how to take it, and whether to take it at all seriously.

For a reader attempting to deal with his or her response to nineteenth-century novels, and who perceives in them strains of the *Heimliche* and *Unheimliche*, there is a potential problem in the relation between authorial intention, response, and meaning. Freud's essay on "The 'Uncanny'" is, perhaps above everything else, an attempt to plumb the psychological sources of a particular kind of response to certain experiences, of which Freud's main examples are taken from literature. We cannot identify that which is *heimlich* or *unheimlich* by applying any set of rules for definition; if we do not somehow already know (at least subconsciously) what that feeling is even before we have read Freud's essay, we may not recognize "it" in a text when it occurs for other readers. But if one believes that he or she understands the feeling of the uncanny (and it is likely that no two readers' senses of that feeling are identical), in interpretation one may also feel the need to infer what feelings in the author have generated that component of the text. However much the novels I have alluded to (including the fantasies) may be dominated by the domestic and its *heimlich* secrets—which by virtue of being secrets (i.e., repressed) may unpredictably evoke a sense of the *Unheimliche*—they always contain a modicum of what seems to be propositional meaning, and thus can to an extent be read as utterances, conscious acts of expression and communication. It is arguably even the case that while overt, discursive meanings may be read as (i.e., may be inferred as) objectively present, the reader constructs the meaning(s) of the literary work considered as an aesthetic object, a structure of representations, as distinct from a set of utterances.

As will already be clear, in my reading of literature I have found that biographical knowledge, including an awareness of the author's other works, becomes part of the story of my reading for a given text, materially altering my understanding of it and thus becoming a constitutive factor in the development of that understanding. One way of considering the relation of response (meaning and affect constructed by the reader) to intention (*author* constructed by the reader) is to posit the text as existing simultaneously in the experience of reading and in its own biographical and historical context. And thus the constructed aesthetic object can be seen as a constellation of meanings projected along several axes, including the author's expression of his ideas, feelings, and phantasies, his values in relation to those predominant in his age, and the reader's response to and associations with what I have called utterance and representation, as it relates to all that he or she may bring to the text.

The following story of reading is presented as much as possible in the original sequence of the attempts to make sense of my reactions to *The Wind in the Willows*. I describe the history of reading insofar as I have been able to reconstruct it, isolate and analyze my responses, and specify the related associations. Details include the circumstances in which I first read the book and my search in Grahame's other writings and his modern biography, undertaken to create a pathway from my subjectivity to Grahame's (or rather, to my construction of it). The actual process of reading and response will always be fuller than any description of it because the possibilities for personal association and ways of constructing the author and meaning are virtually endless.

Naomi Lewis, the reviewer for *Victorian Studies* of Peter Green's centenary biography of Kenneth Grahame, remarked that she found it both "comprehensive" and "disturbing" (173). I cannot know what this particular reader's reasons were for feeling disturbed, but the potential sources of disturbance in the biography for someone who loves *The Wind in the Willows* are clear enough. Green develops the thesis that Grahame's major work is a symbolic transformation of rebellious and hedonistic impulses faintly evident in his earlier works, a process that took place under the combined pressures of a late, unhappy, and unfulfilling marriage, being the father of a half-blind son, and years of tedious work at the Bank of England. Such an analysis might well be disturbing to anyone for whom reading and rereading *The Wind in the Willows* has formed a special, private set of experiences, and who does not want the memory of those experiences to be sullied by knowledge of the miseries and frustrations of Grahame's life.

Yet I found my first adult rereading of Grahame's 1908 novel more perplexing than I found the biography disturbing. On the one hand, my childhood reading of *The Wind in the Willows* was an important event for me, while on the other hand there seemed to be several reasons why I and at least some of its other devotees should dislike the book. For the novel's fantasy world seems to be very narrow as an analogue of the real world: its principal (animal) characters are all male, they are all bachelors, and all independently wealthy—conditions that obtain for few human beings, and still fewer wild animals. It is, seemingly, "clean of the clash of sex," as Grahame wrote for the publisher's blurb. The full blurb runs, "A book of Youth—and so perhaps chiefly *for* Youth, and those who still keep the spirit of youth alive in them: of life, sunshine, running water, woodlands, dusty roads, winter firesides; free of problems, clean of the clash of sex; of life as it might fairly be supposed to be regarded by some of the wise small things 'That glide in grasses and rubble of woody wreck'" (quoted in Chalmers, 145). It might also be described as a pastoral fantasy of upper-middle-class life combined with a conservative satire of aspects of that same life.[3] Furthermore, it contains a good deal of what is on the face of it terribly sentimental writing. We can perhaps imagine why a well-fed Edwardian (male) reader might find the book delightful because of these very attributes; but it is difficult at first thought to understand why it should have a strong appeal to modern readers who have some awareness of the novel's exclusion of females and the class presumptions of the four main characters.

This observation about reasons to dislike Grahame's book applies not only to my adult perspective but even to my first reading of *The Wind in the Willows* when I was ten-and-a-half. When I proposed to teach the book in a children's literature course shared with a colleague, his first reaction was, "I hate that book, with all that awful religious stuff," and I found myself nonplussed, being unable to recall anything religious about it at all, and would have expected that, as a confirmed atheist from early childhood, I would have rejected almost any book with an overtly religious content by the time I was ten. Similarly, at ten I was on the brink of early adolescence and extremely interested in girls; and why a book about bachelors, devoid of any significant female characters, should have appealed to me at that age seemed another mystery.

The context of my first reading turns out to be significant for the purpose of reconstructing my first response. I was in a summer camp in the Adirondacks, my first full summer away from home, and was also in the infirmary with a cold. Feelings of sadness at separation from my parents and the loss of a country-place they had sold were complicated by the fact that my parents were counselors at the camp, which meant that while I was away from home I was only ambiguously away from them—and was something of an object of envy and resentment for other homesick campers. Thus I was probably ready for a book that could take me temporarily out of a world containing too many difficulties for me to cope with, and to a very specific place in my imagination and memory.

Upon rereading the text as an adult my first impression was that three of Mole's experiences had been the most important parts of it for me in childhood, and perhaps still are. The first relevant passage occurs in chapter 1, when Mole comes out of the ground in springtime and sniffs the air:

It all seemed to be too good to be true. Hither and thither through the meadows he rambled busily, along the hedgerows, across the copses, finding everywhere birds building, flowers budding, leaves thrusting. . . .

He thought his happiness was complete when, as he meandered aimlessly along, suddenly he stood by the edge of a full-fed river. Never in his life had he seen a river before—this sleek, sinuous, full-bodied animal, chasing and chuckling, gripping things with a gurgle and leaving them with a laugh to fling itself on fresh playmates that shook themselves free and were caught and held again. All was a-shake and a-shiver—glints and gleams and sparkles, rustle and swirl, chatter and bubble. The Mole was bewitched, entranced, fascinated. By the side of the river he trotted as one trots, when very small, by the side of a man, who holds one spellbound by exciting stories. [2]

The connotations of sexual renewal in the first of these paragraphs, and of sexual pursuit in the anthropomorphic (zoomorphic?) metaphors of the second, are vivid to me as an adult and certainly influenced my feelings during that first reading as a child; indeed, the sensuality of much of Grahame's language may have been the primary attraction that brought me back to *The Wind in the Willows* more than once in early adolescence. But in the particular context of that first reading my response combined delight with a strong sense of melancholy and loss. For the first eight years of my life summer vacations had been spent at my family's house in Connecticut, away from the deadness and heat of a New York summer; this property was sold in 1945, and we summered that year on Long Island. Only now in my first summer in camp did it come home to me (a stock phrase but also a significant metaphor that arose here without calculation) forcefully that "Connecticut" was lost forever. And so Mole's rediscovery of spring and first discovery of the river are inescapably linked for me with each summer's return to the green woods and the wide brook bisecting our property, layering several kinds of regained delight and felt loss in my memory then and in the adult experience of Grahame's text.

Such feelings are increased and deepened in my response to Mole's return to his underground home in chapter 5 ("Dulce Domum"). Having entered the upper world, and then in winter the dangerous Wild Wood where he and friend Rat have been given shelter by Badger, Mole is struck with a nostalgic longing for his home, of which he has suddenly caught the smell. But because Rat won't listen to him and keeps on walking, Mole is finally overcome:

> The Mole subsided forlornly on a tree-stump to control himself, for he felt it surely coming. The sob he had fought with so long refused to be beaten. Up and up, it forced its way to the air, and then another, and another, and others thick and fast; till poor Mole at last gave up the struggle, and cried freely and helplessly and openly, now that he knew it was all over and he had lost what he could hardly be said to have found.

Mole then explains to Rat, amidst further sobs, what his trouble is.

> "It was my own little home - and I was fond of it - and I went away and forgot all about it - and then I smelt it suddenly - on the road, when I called and you wouldn't listen, Rat - and everything came back to me with a rush - and I *wanted* it! - O dear, O dear! - and when you wouldn't turn back, Ratty - and I had to leave it, though I was smelling it all the time - I thought my heart would break. - We might have just gone by - but you wouldn't turn back, Ratty, you wouldn't turn back!"[4] [50]

This is followed by Rat's insisting in a fatherly way that they go at once to Mole End, and by the rhapsody of Mole's rediscovery of his home, beginning with an "electric thrill . . . passing down" his body, which, though described as "faint," is strong enough to be felt by Rat through physical contact with Mole (51). Smell has led Mole to his home, but once Mole End is reached smell is replaced by Mole's childlike but also bourgeois delight in seeing his possessions again, as well as an oral delight in the "provender so magically provided" by fieldmouse children who have come singing Christmas carols (57–58). Again, there are things I might, as an adult, find offensive, in particular the obvious class distinctions (the fieldmice call Rat "Sir," speak with Cockney accents, and function as servants). But this is subordinate to the vividness and specificity of my associations from childhood.

Apart from the feeling of having lost a home, and what was for me well into adulthood a daydream of regaining the Connecticut property, an incident from about age four has the most direct connection with my response to "Dolce Domum." Mole's speech that ends, " 'Ratty, you wouldn't turn back!' " recalls the time when on a snowy day my father picked me up at nursery school, assuming that my mother wouldn't be able to make it in time from her teaching job because of the snow. But as the bus arrived I spotted my mother waving to us from the other side of Central Park West; my father didn't see her, and loaded me up the steps of the bus despite my protests that I wanted to go to my mother. My frustration and helplessness as a small child failing to communicate something of great emotional importance come back with force even today when I reread those passages in *The Wind in the Willows*.

Some of the difficulty of relating the memory of childhood to what is, after all, an adult response may be illustrated by what I am able to make, and not make, of the predominance and subsequent elimination of *smell* in "Dolce Domum." Intuitively I feel that smell is an important component of the *Heimliche* and the *Unheimliche*—the familiar but private, secret, forbidden, and repressed. Ernest Schachtel has pointed out that smell is the sense in children most subject to conditioning and suppression by adults. It is closest to an animal sense, at least initially lacking in conceptual discrimination, but in a child's development in our culture it is often allied with feelings of shame, guilt, and disgust (299). It is perhaps because of the repression of the sense of smell that I have no precise memories that I can associate with Mole's smelling of his home, but retain a strong feeling that such smelling of the familiar is related to some basic childhood experiences. And the replacement of smelling by seeing as the dominant sensory activity when Mole has returned to his home is akin to a shift from early childhood to more conceptual, adult, and socialized modes of perception. Of course, how much of what I have just said is based on traces of childhood memories and how much is an intellectual construct based on reading Freud and Schachtel is impossible to determine. Such difficulties admittedly pervade all attempts at understanding affective response, but they also pervade any attempt at literary interpretation, since our perceptions are to some extent always governed by what we know.

Despite the switch from smell to seeing, Grahame does stress that Mole's return is a kind of temporary regression. Mole sees "clearly how plain and simple—how narrow, even—it all was; but clearly too how much it all meant to him, and the special value of some such anchorage in one's existence. He did not at all want to abandon the new life and its splendid spaces, to turn his back on sun and air and all they offered him and creep home and stay there; the upper world was all too strong, it called to him still, even down there, and he knew he must return to the larger stage" (58). The image of an underground home suggests snugness, the womb, and, one might think, the grave, though here as elsewhere Grahame manages to avoid even hints of death (cf. Green, Introduction, xiv); but my personal association with this feeling is the comfort and security of lying ill in bed, waited upon by adults, and more specifically in the context of my first reading being removed into a haven from troubling matters on the outside. The infirmary had for me a further attraction in that I was waited upon by a young and interesting nurse, who thus functioned for me as a mother-substitute but also was pretty enough to arouse other kinds of interest without the problems of emotional involvements with girls of my own age.

"The Piper at the Gates of Dawn," Grahame's seventh chapter, develops some of these feelings in more complex ways. As in "Dolce Domum," the theme is one of loss and restitution, but here it is a father's loss and refinding of a child, and "infants" (Mole and Rat—see below) finding a "father." Little Portly, the baby otter, is missing, and his father expresses desolation and despair to Mole and Rat. This new incident—not linked to any aspect of what continuous plot there is—allows a new emotional experience for Mole and Rat in the process of their search for the otter-child. The feelings begin for Rat with what is apparently the piping of a bird, which is for him "so beautiful and strange and new! Since it was to end so soon I almost wish I had never heard it. For it had roused a longing in me that is pain, and nothing seems worth while but just to hear that sound once more and go on listening to it for ever" (74). Mole at this point hears nothing "but the wind playing in the reeds and rushes and osiers," but Rat hears the same sound again, and "rapt, transported, trembling, he was possessed in all his senses by this new divine thing that caught up his helpless soul and swung and dandled it, a powerless but happy infant in a strong sustaining grasp" (74). Finally, as they row closer, Mole hears as well and is likewise "caught . . . up, and possessed . . . utterly." Reaching the island, the two are struck with a deepening awe, Rat trembles violently, and Mole's rapture is described at length:

Perhaps he would never have dared to raise his eyes, but that, though the piping was now hushed, the call and the summons seemed still dominant and imperious. He might not refuse, were Death himself waiting to strike him instantly, once he had looked with mortal eye on things rightly kept hidden.

Trembling he obeyed, and raised his humble head; and then, in the utter clearness of the imminent dawn, while Nature, flushed with fullness of incredible colour, seemed to hold her breath for the event, he looked in the very eyes of the Friend and Helper; saw the stern hooked nose between the kindly eyes that were looking down on them humorously, while the bearded mouth broke into a half-smile at the corners; saw the rippling muscles on the arm that lay across the broad chest, the long supple hand still holding the pan-pipes only just fallen away from the parted lips; saw the splendid curves of the shaggy limbs disposed in majestic ease on the sward; saw last of all, nestling between his very hooves, sleeping soundly in utter peace and contentment, the little, round, podgy, childish form of the baby otter. . . .

"Rat!" he found breath to whisper, shaking. "Are you afraid?"

"Afraid?" murmured the Rat, his eyes shining with unutterable love. "Afraid! Of *Him*? O, never, never! And yet—and yet—O, Mole, I am afraid!"

Then the two animals, crouching to the earth, bowed their heads and did worship. [76–77]

When Portly awakens, the "demi-god" has vanished, and the little otter searches around like "a child that has fallen happily asleep in its nurse's arms, and wakes to find itself alone and laid in a strange place. . . . till at last the black moment came for giving it up, and sitting down and crying bitterly" (78). But Rat and Mole do not weep, because they have been granted the "gift of forgetfulness" (77); they feel "strangely tired, with a lingering sense of contentment" (79), and by the end of the chapter Rat is asleep in the boat, "with a smile of much happiness on his face" (80). My adult response to this upon the first rereading was a mixture of empathy and revulsion; no doubt this is what my colleague referred to as "that awful religious stuff," with its too-obvious paralleling of Pan and Christ. The swooning worship feels a bit heavy, yet it also feels uncanny, as though I am being reminded of something once familiar but now repressed. I believe that my response at the age of ten was positive—if not to Pan himself, then to the range of emotion felt by Rat and Mole, that sense of suddenly seeing things with a new clarity, the awe at the beauty of nature (inextricable from love for and loss of the Connecticut Arcadia), but also the feeling of being completely taken care of by an adult, expressed in quite different ways in the descriptions of the baby-otter sleeping between the hooves of Pan and the other animals' rapt and worshipful submission to his power.

There is a considerable difference between the phantasized demi-god about whom Grahame wrote seventeen years earlier in his essay "The Rural Pan,"[5] and the one in *The Wind in the Willows*, for while the earlier Pan has an ephemeral quality of immanence in nature, in the novel the force is incarnated, with different results for response and for the meanings that can be extracted from the experience of the text and constructed as the author's. Three things stand out for me: the rise and fall of emotion, the lingeringly described details of Pan's muscular form, and the way the otter child is cradled between his hooves, sleeping contentedly as though he has fallen asleep in the arms of his mother or nurse. This strikes me as the embodiment of father and mother in one figure, and the animals' responses combine love for the nurturing mother (Nature—referred to as "she" early in the paragraph and described as "flushed," as though with sexual excitement) with submission to the benign, but also powerful and intimidating, father. Perhaps through an unconscious sense of this, as a child I felt (and still do feel) Mole's and Rat's experience to be intensely erotic, building up from the initial intoxications of the melody to the violent trembling at "things rightly kept hidden"—a virtual definition of the *Heimliche* and, in their being obliquely revealed, of the *Unheimliche* as well. The intensity peaks in the combination of love, fear, and worship, followed by the gradually decreasing level of emotion, to the physical exhaustion that leaves Mole "half-dozing in the hot sun," and "the weary Rat . . . fast asleep."[6] Grahame's rhetoric seems extraordinarily intense for a book supposedly "clean of the clash of sex." This is true of the description of the river in chapter 1, of this scene of "rapt" possession, and of another passage I shall discuss below.

Roger Sale has written that if you "ask any lover of the book to name the most memorable parts . . . the answer will invariably be scenes from the first half" (176), and Peter Green fully agrees with him (Introduction, xiii-xiv). This is verifiably untrue, as many readers (though perhaps not as many critics) speak of Toad as the center of the book; but it did happen to fit my own story of reading insofar as I could construct it, when I composed the first version of this chapter. At the time, I wrote that

delightful as he is, Toad just did not exercise the same magic upon me, nor does he today. Intellectually, one may perhaps identify Toad as the id, the repository of dangerous desires (Green, *Kenneth Grahame,* 282). Of the four animal friends he is the one who violates codes of behavior and even becomes an actual criminal. Yet at age ten I did not recognize such acting-out as part of myself; it was low comedy, amusing, but viewed as from a distance.

By far the most disconcerting comment on the published essay was that of a close friend, the late Branwen Pratt. Mentioning to her that I had an article coming out on *The Wind in the Willows,* I was a bit taken aback when, after having said that it was a favorite in her family, Branwen went on to assert with conviction that Toad was the *center* of the novel, the rebellious, phallic child, and that she and her children had always known that. I could only reply that I knew not all readers took Grahame's book that way, and that she should wait until the article appeared. Upon receiving the offprint, she commented that my denial that Toad had much interest for me either as child or adult was clearly a defense against acknowledging those aspects of my personality formed in the Oedipal phase—rebelliousness, aggression, and the other "bad boy" characteristics concealed behind my image of myself as a "good boy." Among other evidence for this she cited the description of myself at age four, being in effect taken away from my mother by my father, in which I mention none of the feelings of murderous rage against my father which could be inferred from the very way I describe the incident.

Branwen actually may in her bit of psychoanalysis via the mails have seen even more accurately through my unconsciously donned mask than she knew. For there was a whole side of myself as a child, especially between the ages of about eight and eleven, that I simply did not acknowledge in my reported associations with *The Wind in the Willows:* the hot-tempered, aggressive, and heedless parts of my personality. Not that I was much like the juvenile delinquent Toad resembles; but Toad's irresponsible antics may have represented a constellation of repressed wishes that were just too threatening for me to allow myself to identify consciously with him at age ten, and an awareness of which I still refused as an adult. The fact that Toad is the only character in the book who even thinks of his attractions for a woman (the jailor's daughter) also gave me some pause until I realized that any such pseudosexual interest on Toad's part is treated, with good reason, as absurd—but here again I realize suddenly that the way I put this could also refer to the absurdity of a ten-year-old boy's sexual interest in a twenty-five-year-old camp infirmary nurse.

But at the time of writing the essay, it seemed to me that the dominant affect in my childhood response to *The Wind in the Willows* had to do with loss, beginning with the awareness of separation from one's mother in infancy, and inevitably repeated in various ways—literal and symbolic—as I developed. The most conscious source of affect was, for me, that of a loss of a place that was home in a more tangible way than a series of New York apartments over the years—a home that had been periodically regained and temporarily lost with the expectation of recovery each summer, but which was sold for a pittance when I was eight (something that aroused a good deal of resentment in me against my parents). These feelings carried over into preadolescence, in the anxiety of having to make my own way with an unfamiliar group of peers, and in the mysteries of adult sexuality as well as the delights and anxieties of a potentially new kind of relationship to girls. In the latter regard, the "Piper at the Gates of Dawn" is important not because it addresses the problem of sexuality directly, but because its rise and fall of emotion, with the revelation of a mystery at the peak, approximate the feelings I was tentatively beginning to connect with becoming an adolescent. In this respect it strikes me as an excellent example of how feelings can be aroused by the indirection with which the *Heimliche* is presented in Victorian novels.[7]

Response and the Constructed Author

It is not difficult to describe how the author's personal relation to *The Wind in the Willows* might intersect with my own set of meanings and feelings, constructed from adult, and memory of childhood, response. Feelings of loss and deprivation of a loved place and the desire to escape from the city seem to have dominated Grahame's life. Having lost his mother when he was not quite five and, effectively, his father as well (since James Cunningham Grahame soon gave up the care of his young family to their maternal grandmother), Kenneth Grahame spent the remainder of his childhood in Cookham Dene, Berkshire, Cranbourne near Windsor, and St. Edward's School, Oxford, coming to love the Berkshire and Surrey downlands and the Thames Valley, as well as the still very medieval atmosphere of Oxford. It seems certain that his uncle's refusal to permit him to enter Oxford University was experienced as another loss of a place he had come to consider his own, and that London and a clerkship in the Bank of England (of which he eventually became Secretary) were antipathetic to his strongest feelings.

Peter Green sees the appearance of Pan as one manifestation of a rebellious element in Grahame's character, expressed mildly in some of his early essays; but Green takes the way Grahame deals with Toad to be a much more direct expression of his ambivalence about rebellion, since Toad the open rebel is repeatedly associated with motorcars, which Grahame abhorred, and is ultimately punished, though in another way he is ultimately triumphant, winning back Toad Hall from the rabble (*Kenneth Grahame*, 131–47). Green has nothing good to say about the Piper, deprecating him as "desexualized, paternalized" and a "projection of Edwardian ruralism, post-Beardsley social opposition, wistful yearning for conformity, an urge towards some replacement for God as a comforting Father Figure" (253). Yet I find that the feelings expressed, as they evoke feelings in me as reader, are more complex, in the vision of a masculine father, as well as a distinctly motherly one, implying a boy's feelings of longing for his mother (also present as the "flushed" [Mother] Nature) sublimated into a bisexual or homoerotic figure whose exact quality Grahame could never acknowledge directly.

Considering how concrete the details of physical description are in the text, it seems strange that a psychoanalyst such as Lili Peller could describe the form of the "Faun" (her word) as one that "barely perceived, dissolves and melts into the foliage" (427); but Peller classifies *The Wind in the Willows* as an "Early Tale" that appeals to pre-Oedipal children, and in which sex is reassuringly denied through the mask of sexually unspecific animals. I think, however, the fact that this particular children's book is read and treasured by many adults, who often first read it in preadolescence, makes a difference. What might be comforting denial to a young child may be, for one on the brink of adolescence, an equally comforting and equally disguised affirmation of sexual feelings. And Grahame is at once even more elaborately evasive and revelatory than I have yet suggested. The narrator's comment that the animals are seeing "things rightly kept hidden" sounds close to the concept of *heimlich* experiences just because things at home, private, and secret (and repressed), have a disturbing *(unheimlich)* effect when revealed in distorted or symbolic form. And the duplicity goes even further. Grahame takes the trouble to tell us that Mole feels no panic terror; yet etymologically and conventionally in English panic terror is precisely what one is supposed to experience at the sight of Pan. If the intense emotions felt by the animals contain no element of panic terror, are we to believe that they are entirely serene? This is not borne out by the actual descriptions of Mole's and Rat's reactions, and the submission to a powerful masculine figure contains an element of fear in addition to love (though we should keep its ambiguity of gender in mind).

But this attempt to explain my response to the "Piper at the Gates of Dawn" chapter and to relate it as well to Grahame's own life also involves several evasions. Most of my discussion is expressed in the rhetoric and tone of objective interpretation, as when I wrote "I find the feelings expressed in chapter 7 (as they evoke feelings in me as reader)" to stem from "the vision of a motherly father, as well as a distinctly masculine one, implying a boy's feelings of longing for his mother (also present as the 'flushed' [Mother] Nature), sublimated into a bisexual or homoerotic figure whose exact quality Grahame could never acknowledge directly." What I have done is to try to keep my approach consistent by means of the parenthetical "as they evoke feelings in me as reader," but I have made no attempt anywhere to explain why I have those feelings and instead turn to what "Grahame" could not acknowledge. And most notable is that here, as in the account of the incident of being taken away from my mother by my father, I avoid saying anything about my relationship to my father. This is not very surprising, considering that I refer to the demi-god as a "bisexual or homoerotic figure," and that I also have felt discomfort with Mole, Rat, and Badger when they take on the role of Toad's punitive fathers. Surely it is the combination of strength and lovingness in the Pan figure to which I am responding, as I at times responded to my father in early childhood; it is a response of which I have long been aware, and yet in writing about such a figure I avoided referring to these particular associations, choosing to switch from the subjective to the inferentially objective by attributing the mixed emotional qualities in that scene to Grahame's repressed sexual ambivalence.

I find it most significant that in doing so I implied a similarity between Grahame's childhood and mine, which upon reflection seems largely illusory insofar as relationships to parents are concerned. Grahame may or may not have been sexually ambivalent, but if indeed he did have an unacknowledged attraction to men it may have stemmed from his experiences in a public school, but more fundamentally from the *lack* of any father-figure in his childhood who combined qualities of authority and affection. My immediate family was unusual, especially for the late 1930s and early 1940s, not so much in that my mother was a teacher, but in that until the beginning of the war my father stayed home most of the time working as a free-lance writer. In addition, I was taught from as early as I could speak that society's casting of men and women in fixed roles was unnatural—that a woman did not have to be a housekeeper and a father be away at work, that girls could play with trains and boys with dolls. Yet for me as a small child the situation was difficult: my father was at home, but for most of the day if I demanded his attention and affection I was rebuffed; he was working. And in some ways this may have been worse for my relationship to him than if he had held a nine-to-five job.

The point of going into these details is that first of all they clarify my emphasis on the Pan-figure's function as that of a "motherly father," and second that they distinguish my response to this scene from whatever may have been Grahame's reasons for creating such a figure. The initial evasion of my own response may have been due to the pain in my feelings about my father, especially as his relatively early death still seemed fairly recent. I could go much further with my associations, including the possibility that the sense of loss of "Nature" in our Connecticut property was directly related to my much earlier sense of desolation at separation from my mother when she went back to work when I was two-and-a-half, but I think I have done enough to demonstrate the difficulties involved in attempting a full account of one's affective experiences of reading and their sources.

After my adult rereading and contemplation of my response I wanted to see whether Grahame's other works contained any elements comparable to the veiled eroticism I thought I detected in chapter 7 and elsewhere in *The Wind in the Willows.* Peter Green suggests that one can find in the earlier works more explicit and thus less powerful expressions of Grahame's impulses and conflicts which are converted into symbolic form in the later book. The rejection of adults as the lofty, uncaring, and unreasonable "Olympians" in *The Golden Age* (1895) and *Dream Days* (1898) becomes in *The Wind in the Willows,* according to Green, a symbolic affirmation of Grahame's childhood values. Green conjectures about the success of the two books of sketches about children that the fin-de-siècle temperament was ready for a revelation of the gulf between the adult's world and the child's (*Kenneth Grahame,* 162); and to some extent we are still part of that modern temperament which had its roots in late-Victorian days. But there are other themes and emphases in those sketches which can be related directly to "things rightly kept hidden," even though they are in fact expressed overtly. Nine of the eighteen sketches in *The Golden Age* and four of the eight in *Dream Days* deal with one or more of four related themes: children's curiosity about adults' love-lives; boys' curiosity about girls; children's voyeurism; and heterosexual feelings and phantasies in young boys. Indeed, the preoccupations of these sketches with such matters came as a bit of a surprise. I can give only a sampling here.

In "A Holiday" *(The Golden Age)* the narrator tells of himself as a child leaving his brothers and sisters to follow the summons of Nature, taking the "hearty wind" as his guide.

A whimsical comrade I found him, ere he had done with me. Was it in jest or with some serious purpose of his own, that he brought me plump upon a pair of lovers, silent face to face o'er a discreet unwinking stile? As a rule this sort of thing struck me as the most pitiful tomfoolery. Two calves rubbing noses through a gate were natural and right and within the order of things; but that human beings, with salient interests and active pursuits beckoning them on from every side, could thus—! Well, it was a thing to hurry past, shamed of face, and think on no more.

Yet a "magical touch in the air" causes him to regard "these fatuous ones with kindliness instead of contempt; as I rambled by unheeded by them" (14). This seems a fairly clear instance of a child, emerging from what Freudians call the latency period, resisting but having to acknowledge that love and sexuality between adult humans, as well as cattle, are normal.

The same narrator, writing about himself at an earlier age in "The Finding of the Princess" (also in *The Golden Age*), recounts an adventure on which he has set off, phantasizing finding "the necessary Princess"—necessary for a heroic adventure—and then in his rambles suddenly believing he has found her in the person of a young woman "laughingly struggling to disengage her hand from the grasp of a grown-up man" (39). He is naively open with the couple about his belief that she is a princess, and they take him into the house and give him what he considers a sumptuous meal. There is a dual perspective, for we understand that the young woman and the man regard the boy with a careless and patronizing amusement. When leaving, the child sees the couple walking with arms around each others' waists down the path, and upon turning for home he is "possessed" by a "wild unreasoning panic, and . . . sped out of the garden like a guilty thing hounded by nameless terrors" (43). That night he dreams of himself as a fish, thrusting "up a nose through water-lily leaves to be kissed by a rose-flushed princess" (44). The connections among the child's various feelings are not explained by the narrator, but even had I not known of the episode of seeing things "rightly kept hidden" in *The Wind in the Willows*, it would be difficult to avoid feeling that the sudden access of guilt and panic has to do with the boy's immediate experience of voyeurism and attendant jealousy, while the concluding incident of the dream, with its images of swimming and thrusting, and the princess's "rose flush" (seeming to anticipate the flush of Nature in *The Wind in the Willows*, as the panic anticipates the "no panic terror" of Mole) suggests an erotic as well as a fairy-tale or literary desire for the "princess."

In contrast, "The Burglars" *(The Golden Age)* is a straightforward, mildly amusing account of the group of children who are central to many of the sketches as they take the curate and their Aunt Maria, who are "spooning," to be burglars and cause them much embarrassment. The sketch opens with some speculation by the children as to just what spooning is, and Edward (the eldest) can only conclude lamely that "'it's just a thing they [adults] do, you know'" (62). Sexual curiosity is the motive force in this sketch, but the denouement is mild farce, revealing the "spooners" as merely ridiculous. The private, secret aspects of family life are here made part of the overt content and, as Peter Green suggests in general about these two early books, are thereby deprived of emotional force; and there is even more distancing in the tone of knowing adult irony from the double perspective of the narrator recalling his childhood.

The strongest instances of represented emotions are probably "The Magic Ring," one of several sketches in *Dream Days* dealing with boys' budding interest in girls and women, and "Its Walls Were as of Jasper" (also in *Dream Days*), part of whose emotional force comes—as in the case of "The Finding of the Princess"—from its lack of explanation of some of the events recounted. "The Magic Ring" is probably the most overtly erotic sketch in either of Grahame's collections. It tells in the first person of a boy's visit to a circus, during which he falls in love, first with Coralie, the "Woman of the Ring,—flawless, complete, untrammelled in each subtly curving limb" (65), and then more profoundly with Zephyrine, the Bride of the Desert, a "magnificent, full-figured Cleopatra" (70). Like "The Finding of the Princess," this sketch ends with the child dreaming, in this case of himself and Zephyrine, while the eyes of the white-limbed Coralie glimmer at them in jealous reproach. Here, we are on the verge of overt masturbation phantasies, but as in "The Burglars," the erotic is tamed by the knowing, ironic tone of the narrator. But "Its Walls Were as of Jasper" is more ambiguous and less obviously written from a dual child/adult perspective. The first-person narrator is taken by his aunt (there are no parents in these books, likely a reflection of Grahame's own semiorphaned childhood) to a large country house where he is promptly ignored by all the adults. Wandering from room to room, he comes across the library, where he takes down a picture book and, after initial disappointment that the text is in a foreign language, discovers pictures in it that mirror some of his own phantasies. The page on which he focuses depicts a wedding, and he falls into a rapt contemplation of it. But when discovered by his hostess, he is spanked soundly and then made to suffer with *The Sabbath Improver*. The nature of his transgression is never specified. Is he being punished and made to feel guilty for an indulgence in daydreaming? The spanking itself is sexually ambiguous: in the text the boy's phantasies are interrupted by his own "Ow! Ow! Ow!" and the book is "ravished from his grasp" (87) by his "dressy" hostess. Here, some kind of secret seems to exist, in the form of a missing explanation of the boy's transgression, into the knowledge of which the child protagonist is never admitted. The possibility that it might be something as simple as handling a valuable book is lessened by the fact that the child is then made to read a "moral" tome—suggesting something "immoral" about the picture book, or about the phantasies involved in looking at it: for he has been thinking about the pictured couple and how he would "at last . . . have a chance of knowing *how* people lived happily ever after" (87).[8]

In the process of constructing a Kenneth Grahame in reading his works, I have found it significant that the real Grahame at least twice took the trouble to deny that *The Wind in the Willows* contained either problems or sex (in the publisher's blurb, already quoted, and in a letter to Theodore Roosevelt),[9] considering that his two previous books were in a sense full of both: Green conjectures that these statements, "so flagrantly untrue," are an "unconscious covering-up action," a denial of latent meanings that Grahame sensed and was disturbed by (*Kenneth Grahame,* 274). Although most of Grahame's contemporaries (and possibly Grahame himself) probably would have found that description absurd, in a (barely) pre-Freudian age the defense against recognizing such content would be the very fact that the sketches are about "innocent" children, whose pains and passions could be taken as mere attempts to mimic their elders. In fact some of Grahame's first readers were horrified by the precociousness of these children and their hostility to adults (*Kenneth Grahame,* 177), indicating that such a defense (which is also built into some of the sketches by means of the ironic narrative tone) is not always a reliable one, and that a writer may cross dangerous boundaries without being aware of them. There also seems to be strong evidence of Grahame's capacity for self-deception (a trait made very clear by his thinking that his half-blind son might be accepted into the Army) and, less probably but not impossibly, a sly private sense of humor, as one surprising passage in *The Wind in the Willows* demonstrates.

At the opening of chapter 2, following Mole's ecstatic discovery of the river at the close of the first chapter, we are told that Rat has been swimming in the river with his friends the ducks, and annoying them by diving down to tickle their chins; and he has composed a five-stanza song he calls "Ducks' Ditty." I quote here stanzas 1, 4, and 5:

All along the backwater,
Through the rushes tall,
Ducks are a-dabbling,
Up tails all!

. . . .
Everyone for what he likes!
We like to be
Heads down, tails up,
Dabbling free!

High in the blue above
Swifts whirl and call—
We are down a-dabbling
Up tails all!   [12–13]

Unless one wants to posit that Grahame consciously slipped in an
allusion that would appeal to knowledgeable adults' salaciousness
while bypassing innocent children readers, this poem seems a remarkable example of Edwardian doublethink—the ability to know something and deny it to one's consciousness at the same time (but see my
comments on the intentionality of Tom Pinch's "organ" in chap. 8).
For "uptails all" has a long history as a slang expression for sexual
intercourse. The *OED* gives as its first meaning, "The name of an old
song and its tune," and one has to seek pretty assiduously in that
chaste dictionary to piece together the historically primary meaning.[10]
Even if Grahame did not know any of the several old songs that use
this phrase,[11] it is most unlikely that he did not know Robert Herrick's
poem, "Up tailes all," included in Herrick's major collection of poems,
Hesperides, and in which the meaning is perfectly clear (*The Poems
of Robert Herrick,* 263). Herrick was one of Grahame's favorite
poets, and one of the four, after Shakespeare, who led the list for
numbers of poems included in Grahame's idiosyncratic anthology of
poems for children.[12]

In its context in *The Wind in the Willows,* the double entendre
seems at first to make no obvious sense, and the phrase *can* serve
simply as a description of how dabbling ducks feed. But in relation
to my response to the earlier passage in which Mole is described as
"emancipated" because he has "learnt to swim and to row, and entered into the joy of running water," I here think of a generalized
sensuality in swimming, amounting to being touched all over one's
body (a strong association for me from childhood summers swimming in the brook), and also in boating, in the alternation of struggling against the water's resistance and submitting to its force when
drifting. Rat in chapter 2 tickles the ducks' necks in a kind of aggressive teasing of their bodies while he is swimming—itself an activity
that for him has no utilitarian purpose, but is done for the sheer
pleasure. Granted that there is not a lot else in this chapter that can

be taken as "erotic," putting together Mole's joy in swimming and boating with Rat's activities and the song he sings to the ducks, the presence of the potentially salacious allusion (which it would be for any reader who knew and understood Herrick's poem, or any of the "old songs") strengthens the likelihood that Grahame's "clean of the clash of sex" is a denial of what he uncomfortably sensed that his text might actually evoke.

And further, one can explain Grahame's making all the principal characters male, animal, and lacking in the usual animal qualities of predatoriness or sexual need as resulting from his own sense of having created some emotionally powerful and dangerous material. It seems less useful to label the animals "phallic," as Maureen Duffy does (309), than to try to evoke something of one's own sense of the peculiar atmosphere of *The Wind in the Willows,* especially in chapters 1 through 5 and 7.[13] This peculiar atmosphere seems to have given many readers some trouble (including the colleague who was offended by its religiosity) at least by the time they get to the "Piper" episode, yet both *peculiar* and *atmosphere* really denote responses to the text rather than objective qualities identifiable *in* the text. My interpretation of "The Piper at the Gates of Dawn" is in fact an attempt to come to terms with my response, and my references to other critics and Grahame's life and buried intentions are a further attempt at justifying that response as something more than purely idiosyncratic.

Sometimes considerations of the author can also function as a self-distancing device. I have, for example, wondered just what Grahame thought of Aubrey Beardsley's title page for *Pagan Papers,* which shows two strange faunlike but definitely human creatures, one, seemingly male and in human dress, looking wistfully at the other, who is naked and perfectly ambiguous sexually. There are also what seem fairly obvious male and female sexual symbols in the foliage— something about which Beardsley was hardly diffident. Certainly there is little in *Pagan Papers,* apart from three of the six pieces later reprinted in *The Golden Age,* that even faintly hints at the erotic. Beardsley indeed may have only been indulging his own preoccupations, but it is also possible that he was trying to interpret graphically what he felt was repressed by Grahame in an essay such as "The Rural Pan"—that the wish to be away from the city and for a union with nature had strong erotic motivations, and that phantasizing a "Pan" immanent in nature suggests that these were erotic, or homoerotic. The distancing or evasion here is that again I have written as though I were performing objective interpretation and placed the emphasis on what Grahame may have thought, rather than what I think or feel.[14]

Another kind of self-distancing, here motivated by the wish to make connections, to make the nineteenth-century novel seem a coherent phenomenon, is involved in my trying to place Grahame in a literary-historical context; yet it also seems to me a natural thing for me to attempt, and is related to what I have in general been saying about texts as utterance and representation. In most respects Grahame looks like something of an anomaly: a man who published in the 1890s one mild book of essays with a scandalous title page, and two best-selling volumes of sketches about childhood, and who then wrote only one more book, which in the year of its appearance evoked confusion among many of his former admirers because it was so strikingly different from his earlier work. But this last book has remained the work by which he is remembered: a book not distinctly limited to a child or adult audience, and seeming not to resemble any text that we normally think of as a Victorian or Edwardian novel. Yet that text is, as Peter Green has shown, in its own peculiar way as much a transformed autobiography as *Wuthering Heights, David Copperfield,* or *The Mill on the Floss.*[15] Each of these novels, with others of the period, resembles Grahame's fantasy-novel in that each has an overt content of propositional meaning that overlays a strong though disguised content of the forbidden. If the programmatic content of *The Wind in the Willows* might be described as the celebration of country joys and the reform of Mr. Toad, that of *David Copperfield* is that David's heart must mature from its infatuation with Dora to the true love of Agnes; but Steerforth, Murdstone, and Heep are more than hinted to be David's doubles in desire, aggression, and ambition, and there is no evidence—only narrative assertion—that David really escapes the shadows of his childhood (but see my discussion of the ambiguities and complexities of this aspect of the novel, in chap. 7).

Emily Brontë may be more elusive in her elaborate narrative layering, but the *heimlich* concerns of brother-sister love are at the bottom of the overt tale of Romantic love ambiguously and uncannily fulfilled only in death. In quite a different way George Eliot in *The Mill on the Floss* places the most private, familial matters at the novel's emotional center, and yet structures the text in terms of a moral and philosophical program that is then subverted, or at least distorted, by the wish-fulfillment phantasy of the conclusion. With Henry James the typical programmatic content seems to disappear, and phantasies of the forbidden are readmitted through other kinds of indirection—the "uncanny" mystery of *The Turn of the Screw,* the innocent viewpoint of the child in *What Maisie Knew,* and conversational and narrative circumlocution around and about the main topics in many of the later novels.[16]

Was the Experiment Successful? Was It Even an Experiment?

To bring out some of the problems with my "experiment," I quote here the concluding paragraph of the original essay, which would not have been suitable to include above.

It is not my intent to suggest that *The Wind in the Willows* is a universally serviceable paradigm for Victorian and Edwardian novels. For one thing, my rather over-simple generalizations must stem in part from my preoccupations as a critic and a person: primarily, the search for hidden meanings. But I contend that the exploration of meaning along subjective and biographical axes provides a dialectical basis for intersubjective syntheses, initially between critic and author, and potentially, if the critic's experiences bear any resemblance to others', between critic and other readers. In the area of Victorian literary domesticity, where the *Heimliche* so often masquerades as a synonym of the *Heimische,* instead of the *Unheimliche* (rather as Mrs. Rochester's sex-mad screams are for such a long time attributed to the placid and sexless Grace Poole), the approach may prove to be one of the most fruitful methods for recovering meanings that really matter to us.

First of all, why did I bother with those thumbnail sketches of an attribute I had supposedly detected in nineteenth-century novels as well as in *The Wind in the Willows?* If I were to say that in order to be published in such a journal as *Victorian Studies* I had to make claims for some broader (and Victorian) significance than a subjective reading of Grahame's novel could provide, I should be telling only a half-truth—for those generalizations, valid or not, function to give my treatment of Grahame's book a kind of authority, for myself if not for my readers. But apart from those sweeping generalizations early in the essay, the section about which I have the greatest doubts is the paragraph just quoted. And it is not the penultimate sentence with its logjam of abstract polysyllabic words that brings embarrassment now; for that sentence still seems a reasonable if awkward statement of the way I hoped in that essay, and hope in this book, to develop a model of reading within which one could construct interconnections among interpretation, the extrinsic, and the reader's understanding.

What now embarrasses me above all is the final sentence, and especially the final word: "us." To substitute "me" for "us" would not have been candid, because at the time I wrote the essay I believed (despite any protestations to the contrary) that other readers *should* find important the same things I did. It is clear that this critic in some sense "made the meanings" of his entire essay. So what was the "experiment," and where did it go wrong, if it did? The experiment was in general terms an attempt to develop through a concrete example the model of interconnections in reading mentioned above, by placing in juxtaposition a set of responses, which were "the meaning(s)" of Grahame's novel to me, with their autobiographical associations and with facts about Grahame's life and other writings, and to see what then emerged. But there were several preconditions essential to make the whole thing possible, including the fact that Peter Green's biography of Grahame did not hide any of the more disturbing details of its subject's life. It was also helpful that, although not overtly a Freudian, Green took *The Wind in the Willows* to be a symbolic utterance of Grahame's internal conflicts and repressed phantasies. I might have worked some of this out for myself, but Green provided a shortcut. And of course had I not been predisposed to find latent meanings in narrative, not only could the essay not have been written, but I probably would have had no sympathy whatever for Holland's or Bleich's approaches to response, which are heavily influenced by psychoanalysis.

Nonetheless, I still believe it was an experiment of a sort—perhaps as close as one can get to the experimental in reading, apart from empirical surveys of groups of readers. Given the nature of an intrapsychic process that only finds form and expression in the act of utterance (lecturing first, then writing, in my case), I'm not sure one can talk about success or failure. I produced *something,* which a number of professional acquaintances claimed to like, and about which others had some reservations. One correspondent, while envying me for getting into print before he did with what he called "autobiographical criticism," questioned heavily the proportion, even the presence, of any statements that purported to be objective fact, such as my whirlwind tour of Victorian novelists and use of the "facts" of Grahame's life; but I'm afraid I shall never be able to meet his rigorous standard of writing consistently in a subjective and autobiographical mode (I have some doubt that this is possible for any critic). Apart from Branwen Pratt's skillful targeting of my evasion of my relation to Toad, a former student's criticisms were perhaps the most disturbing: he asked why my childhood associations were of any more significance or interest than stock sentimental responses to Grahame; to which I can only reply that the particularity of my associations, even though they are obviously nostalgic, should free me of the charge of stock-response—but that judgment is up to my readers.

A possible lesson in methodology that one may take from this all is that, as I have said before, reports of responses and associations are always selective, and no one will give or is capable of giving a complete or verifiably accurate account of either; yet is not selectivity an inevitable feature of all literary criticism? But this experience also taught me something else: that an introspective and retrospective response approach to interpretation is in no way like a psychoanalysis. Without the process of transference, by means of which I might have again lived through the feelings of being, so to speak, a Toad, my basic responses to *The Wind in the Willows* have not changed. The most moving sections are still chapters 1 through 5 and 7 (Toad largely dominates chap. 6); and part of the reason for my not wanting to deal with the last half of the book is that I feel uncomfortable with Rat, Mole, and Badger when they become stern, punitive, and even vengeful authority-figures in their attempts to stem Toad's scapegrace behavior. And I can't help hoping that the narrator's statement that he was truly an "altered" Toad somehow isn't true—especially as "altered" can mean "castrated" (it would be nice to think that Toad could wink at the reader as the narrator says this).

At least one other question may remain insufficiently answered. What is the point of referring to the author and trying to figure him or her out, when it is hard enough to describe and account for one's own responses? I think that for me and for other readers who cannot be satisfied with works of literature taken as autonomous, the situation is fairly straightforward: if we encounter a literary text that is emotionally powerful and in some way enigmatic (and these qualities often go together), then we find ourselves asking, "What kind of person could create such a marvelous and puzzling thing?" I certainly find myself asking this question about Grahame, Carroll, Thackeray, Dickens, Hardy, Austen, and Emily Brontë, as well as a contemporary such as Maurice Sendak. It is in this way that the "author," or "authorial intention," however one wishes to conceptualize it, becomes part of the motivation to understand.

6 · Alice as Self and Other(s)

Self

When first considering writing about Kenneth Grahame I felt certain that *The Wind in the Willows* had been of much more importance to me as a child than had *Alice's Adventures in Wonderland,* whose appeal I even claimed in print had been primarily intellectual rather than affective. As I shall explain, this was a defense against acknowledging deeper reasons for my never having written anything about *Alice.* The immediate motivation finally to do so was an incident at a conference on theories of reading, where a colleague and I had the unusual role of presenting in the form of duplicated handouts a number of response papers on *Alice's Adventures in Wonderland* by our students, with only the briefest comments possible because of time limitations. At a subsequent panel on the "readings" that had been presented, including the ones we had distributed, the discussion of our pedagogical approach soon deteriorated into a squabble between on the one hand, two eminent critics, and on the other, a group of graduate students and feminist and reader-response critics. The two luminaries dismissed student responses as being of no use or interest, and one of them accused us of being "romantic, democratic, and egalitarian," while some of the graduate students in particular asked whether that position reflected a "refusal to share power with the young"—a question not calculated to promote serious discussion. Thus my original purpose in writing about *Alice* was to define a context in which our students' papers and our approach would demonstrably have some value.

But I had already been wondering why, having taught Carroll's Alice books for many years, and being involved in psychoanalytic criticism, the theory of the grotesque, and Victorian illustration, I had never even tried to write anything about them.[1] For in spite of my disclaimer, I really knew that *Alice's Adventures in Wonderland* had been as important in my childhood as *The Wind in the Willows*. The stories of reading that follow can, like what I have written on Grahame, be considered to constitute an experiment in the sense that they add up to a process of discovery whose results were not fully predictable at the outset. The goal of this process in regard to *Alice* is not only to demonstrate further a method of interpretive reading through response, but to address the larger issues of the social process of becoming aware of the responses of other readers and what kinds of intersubjective understanding it can produce, as well as the relevance for reading of conceptualizing of the author's relationship to his text.

At times I have felt that not even trying to write about either of Carroll's masterpieces until my late forties represented a personal failure. In teaching the books I never had lacked for things to say (and it has been especially necessary to have things to say because a large proportion of students are initially nonplussed, if not repelled, especially by the first of the two Alice books). The major factor in my "failure" seems to have been that the previously unacknowledged intensity of my involvement with *Alice* when I was a child created a feeling that I could not enter the "adult" world of Carroll criticism. This recognition grew gradually, from the time I began to teach *Alice's Adventures in Wonderland* by means of reader response; I came to realize that I had as a teacher been treating Carroll's text as a structure of determinate meanings, and that since my interpretations were ultimately based on response, I had been evading not only an epistemological problem but my own difficult relationship to the book, to Carroll, and to Alice, whoever she might turn out to be.

I recall reading *Through the Looking-Glass* rather more frequently than *Alice's Adventures in Wonderland* in childhood, and even adolescence. It has been remarked by Donald Rackin, in an article subtitled "What's So Funny About *Alice in Wonderland?*" that for many children the disturbing material greatly outweighs the humor, and this is borne out by the reports of many of my students who have read it in childhood (although such a group is now very much in the minority, it seems). I do not mean to imply that I was turned off *Alice's Adventures in Wonderland* by its frightening aspects, but rather that I found reading it a much more involving emotional experience than that of reading *Through the Looking-Glass,* to which I felt I could turn for some fun. This again is a difference in response to the two books that has been reported to me by some students. So, as I discuss *Alice* here, I will have little to say about the wit and the play of language which I can appreciate as an adult; for me as a child, at least, the book's meanings had so much to do with serious aspects of my own life that the humor largely passed me by and perhaps will never be the dominant element in my appreciation of Carroll's achievement in that book.

In the cooperative venture of the response classroom, some students have been able to produce more coherent, interesting, and convincing response papers on *Alice* than I. The challenge thus became to find out what would happen if I considered anew and at length, taking student responses into account as well, my response to and understanding of the book. It is notable that most critics have tried to find (or create) a set of fixed meanings, whether these have to do with unconscious symbolism, existential significance, or the position of Alice in relation to the narrator's (and thus, supposedly, "the reader's") attitude. James R. Kincaid, whose essay I find one of the most stimulating just because it corresponds so little to my own experiences of reading *Alice,* argued in 1973 that while most critics assume that we are supposed to identify with Alice, a good deal of aggressive irony is directed by the narrator against the small protagonist, that her prudishness, priggishness, and unthinking acceptance of predation and the deaths of others often make her the butt of jokes perpetrated by the narrator—jokes that she of course fails to understand.[2]

While many of the professional psychoanalytic readings of *Alice's Adventures in Wonderland* seem to exemplify the application by specialists of a preconceived system in the interest of their specialty,[3] Kincaid's and other nonpsychoanalytic readings usually seem to express personal responses, unacknowledged as such, and couched in the rhetoric of objective interpretation. I take Kincaid's essay as a prime example in part because of its apparent goal of revealing a serious limitation in the work of practically all other critics, and thus claiming for itself a special truth-value. Yet Kincaid repeatedly refers to "the reader" in making his points, as if to imply that all readers experience (or *should* experience) the text in the same way. In apparent contrast the more recent essay by Donald Rackin does acknowledge that the reader is a multifarious creature: the child who, like as not, is terrified by Carroll's book; the adult who can detect the humorous, loving, but sometimes ridiculing tone in the narrator's comments about Alice; and "the adult reader as child," who remains a child in what is "perhaps our deepest part," and who shares Alice's and the child reader's fears and anxieties even if Carroll manages to evoke "laughter to dispel [the novel's] own best (and worst) insights" (6). Yet underneath this apparent acceptance of a variety of readings, Rackin still seems to believe that there is a fixed way in which each of these generalized readers responds, and his generalizations do not touch upon the variously disturbing or liberating aspects of the text for individual readers.

While a search for correct meanings or responses may be futile, there is a good deal to be learned about *Alice's Adventures in Wonderland* from readers' self-aware accounts of how they read and respond and why they think they read in a particular way. Of course the word *about,* here as elsewhere, is problematic, because it implies the existence of meanings independent of readers; but on the other hand we only learn *about* texts through reading them, and even if the understanding thereby attained is individual, it may alter over time through the reader's changing life experiences, including the experience of hearing the responses of other readers. In proceeding to describe three of my students' stories of reading *Alice's Adventures in Wonderland,* and my own, I assume that meaningful representations of childhood and adult reading experiences can be achieved by concentrating on affects and associations. Granted that such representations can only approximate the actual reading process, which remains past, selective, private, subject to the distortions of memory, and impossible to verbalize completely, they are the only means we have to communicate about our reading. Further, as I have tried to do with Grahame, I shall treat as part of, rather than obstacles to, the fullest description of my own reading of *Alice* all those things that have accreted upon it since my first acquaintance with the novel at the age of six. Awareness of criticism, biographical information, and others' responses all have contributed to the palimpsest that makes up my story of reading *Alice's Adventures in Wonderland.* The possibility that this subjective palimpsest has some intersubjective relation to, as well as clear divergences from, other readers' experiences is what gives potential value to such a demonstration.

I first discuss three student response papers, two of which suggest just how difficult this book can be for young readers, and a third, which gave me my first clue as to how I might actually join the ranks of *Alice* critics. The complexity of childhood and sometimes later experiences of reading *Alice's Adventures in Wonderland,* and the difficulty of reconstructing them, can be seen in one student's response paper that on the surface looks wildly idiosyncratic, even incoherent. Jane, a woman in her mid-twenties from a village in industrial Scotland, associated the fancy lettering (visible in Tenniel's illustration) of "DRINK ME" on the bottle in the opening chapter with the calligraphy of an art teacher in her school, a man who gave parties for the students, and who turned out, in this woman's words, to be a "dirty old man." Astute questioning by a classmate evoked a further chain of associations from lettering back to the bottle and thence to drunkenness, connected specifically with memories of her grandfather coming home drunk on Saturday nights, yelling and cursing. I undertake this kind of questioning myself only if something leads me to think it will be acceptable as well as productive; from my position as teacher, however egalitarian I may try to be, it is more likely to be intimidating, and students usually take it more easily from their classmates. Although Jane was not able to analyze her response much further than this, I (silently) inferred a link between drunkenness, violence in a family member, and fear of adult sexuality, in particular of an adult—the art teacher—loved in childhood who is suddenly perceived as dangerously sexual in one's adolescence. There seemed also to be a general fear of a loss of control, whether in herself or in others, for she further associated *Alice* with her own childhood nightmares of falling interminably and of changing in appearance, as well as the prevalence of child-beating in her culture, which she connected with the Duchess's beating of her "little boy." She also referred to the Duchess as a "pervert" who approaches Alice sexually in chapter 9.

It seems that this student, who remembered hating *Alice's Adventures in Wonderland* as a child but claimed to have grown to like the book, could not organize or analyze her reconstructed childhood reading and associations because so many aspects of the rereading experience evoked material too disturbing for her to objectify it in any but a fragmentary way. I would say on the basis of other student responses to *Alice* and my own struggle in attempting to piece together my childhood reading of the novel, that although the details are particular to Jane, such a problem is fairly common and signals an inhibition about dealing directly with one's relationship to the text. Indeed, I have never taught Carroll's *Alice* to a class in which more than twenty percent of the students did not find the book bewildering, disturbing, or incoherent—and this has been true even of some who had read the book in childhood. The search for an understanding of my response through associations has been as difficult and painful as I imagine it would have been for Jane had she made a similar attempt. My own parallel childhood fear of losing control, specifically of saying the wrong thing in company, comes to me vividly as I read *Alice's Adventures in Wonderland* in the present, and Alice's growing and shrinking seem to include both the mystery of the other—how *does* a girl grow and change?—and my own child-body under fear of various kinds of loss of control.

More recently, I received a response paper based on a rereading of both of the Alice books from a student (the "Marian" of chap. 3) who, though she had read the novels as a child, thought that they had not made much impression on her (a fairly typical memory, I have found). And Marian had, like so many others, considerable difficulty describing her response, and indeed initially claimed that she did not have one at all. Yet she knew that she had *some* feelings about the books, and instead of trying to argue that the novel is incoherent or that Alice is nothing like a real child, as some of my students do, she pursued them:

1. In reading the two novels I clearly recognized a perpetuating pattern of domination, oppression, confusion, struggle, contempt, rejection, repression, fear, and anger—a typical range of emotions, in fact, of a child (or person?) who struggles to sort out, understand, and assert himself in an "adult" world, at once hostile, oppressive, and intolerant. The pattern is clearly one I experienced as a child. And so I ask, do I then identify with the character Alice? I think not, for my response came not as a series of specific images or memories of myself as a child. Rather, the reading of the novels activated a general and complete *feeling*—a dull and heavy recognition so much a part of me that it went nearly unnoticed. Alice, in fact, seemed somewhat incidental. She seemed, as did the other characters, two dimensional and no more or less unpleasant and irritating. I find this interesting since I undeniably see connections between Alice and my own role as a child. Before I proceed I must pause and readdress the idea that I rejected this response, seeing it as having little value in the first reading. I would argue here that in fact I placed a significant value on it and that the *nature* of this recognition resulted in its being rejected—or suppressed. Upon a second reading this fact became apparent and I explored it thus.

2. A significant point about my second reading is that I could not seem to recall any details from the first reading. There was just an overriding impression of an unpleasant and bizarre string of disjointed and distorted images. Surprisingly, the second reading seemed far less so, and consequently far less disturbing. Somehow I seemed to resist it with less vigour. Still, my "monitoring system" was again hard at work, my notes reflecting a series of detailed and organized patterns. And, again, midway through the second novel I found myself wondering why I was not responding—why, in fact, I seemed to be responding even *less* than in the previous reading.

3. Having grown quite frustrated and curiously exhausted in my reading, I left the text, opting for a mid-afternoon snooze, hoping for renewed insight. Here a very interesting thing occurred. As thoughts of the novel played in my mind, I drifted into a dream in which, to my surprise, I was surrounded

by a number of people in my life, namely my mother, my sister, my grand-mother, and my aunt. I don't need to work too hard to discover what they all had in common—each has an undeniably dominating nature to which I have been subjected numerous times. In this dream I witnessed my aunt, who was involved in an uninterrupted self-dialogue, yelling directions, orders, and insults to her four young children, all having to do with getting ready for a meal: "wash your hands—did *you* wash your face?! . . . what's *that* on your dress - sit up straight, I said!! Don't laugh so at the table, it's not *done!*" In the background the others carried on a similarly argumentative commen-tary on this event. Removed until this point, I somehow observed this from my room upstairs, and as I did I experienced an all too familiar sinking sensation. The knot in my stomach tightened and I felt trapped. Inevitably the procession, children and all, moved into my cloister, bearing down on me with renewed passion. Standing about me they showered me with orders, insults, and accusations. I, feeling dwarfed by their anger could get not a word in despite repeated effort.

I awoke in some confusion. Realizing my dream, I was amused that the novel had found its way into my dreams. Still resisting the obvious links between my own experience and the novel, so repressed that they could be acknowledged only in a dream, I read on. And when I had finished I sat and fretted at my lack of response. Again and again I asked myself why I wasn't responding. Then, suddenly hearing the defiance of my own inner dialogue, the question began to form—am I simply not responding or am I refusing to respond to my response? And here I suddenly connected my resistance to the reading of the novel with the notion of a possible resistance to my own personal history.

4. I sat for a time and reflected upon responses I had had prior to this reading of the texts. It occurred to me that my only memory of the novels before this adult reading was as a child who refused to explore Alice's world. What little experience I did have with it was decidedly negative. I realize now that I came to the novels this time with an attitude of resistance and a type of defensiveness. My past experience with the novels indicated I had viewed them with a "closed mind," for time and time again I had been introduced to the texts, and time and time again I had resisted and rejected them.

5. But the workings of the mind *cannot* be "closed." They can, however, be suppressed and so, if I suppressed any responses as a child, the question is *why?* What caused me to resist this text at so young an age? The answer which suggests itself implies that I have recognized in this novel a certain reality. I wonder if, as a child, I had identified with Alice. Of course I cannot answer this. I only wonder, if I did, why I did not delight in Alice's being able to live out her feelings and likewise, why—if this pair of novels *does* reflect my past—as an adult I cannot delight in it? I believe the answer lies in the depth at which such associations lie within me, and in the knowledge (both then and now) that rationalization cannot explain away the complexity of human behavior and the despair at its duality. I believe that upon realizing

this reality I chose, then and now, to ignore it and thus in essence, willed it out of existence.

6. Here then, at last, I can see a direct and painful link between my reading of the novels, my past, my present, and my failure to respond to my response. I find exposed my childlike fears, insecurities, sorrows, and vulnerabilities. Beneath that is exposed the awareness that dominance and oppression are today, as then, non-negotiable facts of life. Even deeper still is the reality that there *is* an identification with Alice. This notion is at once so repelling that again the mind snaps shut, for such an identification presses upon me the realization that I share in the oppressiveness, the mercilessness, of the human race.

7. Perhaps the greatest disturbance of all in this novel-response is the simple fact that I *did* refuse response so strongly. My conscience speaks to me, asking in a very small voice (not unlike that of the gnat), have I become complacent? Have I become indifferent or immune to the perpetual oppression/repression cycle which is life itself? There is no response, only, again, a wave of panic.

By a failure to "respond to [her] response," Marian clearly refers to the fact that although the Alice books aroused strong feelings in her, she was for almost two weeks unable to acknowledge or concentrate on those feelings as significant, and certainly unable to search her own past for associations that might have revealed the sources of the feelings. Only the dream, whose form seems to have resulted from certain passages in the two books in which Alice is either criticized or threatened, but whose actual content came directly from Marian's own experiences with certain family members, freed her from the defensive denial of her affinity with Alice, although ultimately her position in regard to *Alice's Adventures in Wonderland* and *Through the Looking-Glass* remained one of resistance to their particular meaning for her. Few students have been willing to explore their initial revulsion from *Alice* to the extent that such a cognitive (if not affective) turnaround occurs—far fewer, interestingly enough, than the students who have gone through the same process of denial and recognition with *Wuthering Heights*. Marian's recognition, which came to her slowly and painfully, was one that she did not really want to have and is still uncomfortable with.

Most exceptional, however, is Maureen's paper, one among a very few similar ones over the years that have reported finding *Alice's Adventures in Wonderland* actually a positive force in the reader's life and have helped to move me towards an understanding of the importance of *Alice* for myself as a child. Maureen's paper on *Alice* was, in its assuredness and coherence, in notable contrast to my own attempts up to that time to deal with the novel, Carroll, and Alice.

Describing *Alice* as her very favorite book since the age of six, Maureen was certain that she identified with the protagonist, and in a particular way. "With the exception of the pig-baby and puppy," she writes, "I responded to even the animal characters as being Alice's elders, and the theme behind many of my associations is 'child in the adult world.'" And many of the conflicts she describes have to do with both her sense of identity and place in the world, and with problems of language, understanding, and communication. For example, the experience of reading about Alice's "circular conversations with the caterpillar" evoked memories of "being unable to control conversation to [her] own advantage," as when an admission of being tired meant she had to go to bed, but equally an assertion of feeling energetic meant she was *over*-tired, "and it was still time for bed."

Some of Maureen's understanding of Alice's feelings of not fitting in stemmed from a strong conviction in childhood that her perceptions were right, combined on the other hand with an insufficient comprehension of cause and effect, which led to her frequently being told that she was wrong: "Thus, I became angry when someone said that it was going to rain, for I had seen it rain soon after such remarks often enough to assume a causal relationship. So certain was I that my views were valid, I could not understand why I should keep them to myself." This tendency apparently often led to scoldings for being too outspoken—perhaps Alice's major transgression in Wonderland. And this young woman seemed to see herself even at the time she wrote the paper as being rather like Alice, observing and yet separating herself from others' alienating modes of pseudocommunication, which she compares with the way Wonderland characters interact in only "a random way, soliloquizing to one another."

Maureen was very articulate on paper, but still unsure of her ability either to communicate to or understand others, and reported consciously using a defense of intellectuality to cope with relationships. And much as she loves *Alice's Adventures in Wonderland,* even her most positive description of response in the paper she wrote on *Alice* has its negative aspect. Alice's question, " 'Who in the world am I?' " spurs the memory of a childhood experience of "the sudden awareness of, and revelling in, the fact that *I AM*. I remember wondering why I lived in my body and whether I could live in someone else's body." Yet she also finds it "ironic, and somewhat disturbing that I strongly identified with a girl who, suffering from distorted long-term memory and body-image, and who lacks a self-image in her fantasies, would clearly have a severe identity problem in her conscious state." One could substitute "dreams" for "fantasies," and "waking" for "conscious," but this would be a distortion of what Maureen wrote; and I suspect that she used "fantasies" specifically because of her own rich, conscious phantasy-life. I do think that by referring to Alice's lack of a "self-image in her fantasies," Maureen intends lack of *consistent* self-image, something she may have felt about herself. Yet there also seems to be an element of defense, by distancing, against recognizing this, in the pseudoclinical language in which she writes about Alice. Be that as it may, the coherence of Maureen's paper depends upon her ability to relate her own response to *Alice* as both child and adult reader to her personal experiences, and to define both Alice *and* herself as victim of and yet superior to the irrationality of the "adult" world (a world she had only recently entered when she wrote the paper).

What I have just written is, of course, an interpretation of a text (the response paper) and author (Maureen), without the benefit of any independent empirical verification. As such, it is subject to the limitations of any close, "objective" reading of texts, except for the special circumstance that "child in the adult world" is also a substantial theme in my own attempt to describe and unearth the sources of my own response to *Alice;* and to some extent Maureen's paper in its assuredness and coherence made it possible for me to attempt to write about some very personal aspects of my responses to Carroll's book. I consider this to be an instance of how objectified and communicated literary response can lead other readers to greater understanding in their own terms. If the incident at the conference referred to at the beginning of this chapter was my immediate motivation for trying to deal with *Alice* and response, Maureen's paper was more important in opening the way for me. Interestingly, one thing present in many student accounts that was missing from Maureen's was any expression of fear; despite her adult reservations, expressed only at the end of the paper, she describes her long familiarity with *Alice's Adventures in Wonderland* as predominantly life-enhancing, in part because she sees Alice as managing to hold on to a sense of identity which, like her own, feels threatened.

In considering my own story of reading *Alice's Adventures in Wonderland,* it seems from the first incident, the descent down the rabbit-hole, as though like Maureen I identify strongly with Alice's intensity of purpose. And her motivation through curiosity together with her speculation about coming out in the "Antipathies" recalls a theme of much discussion in childhood: if you could dig down through the earth, would you come out in China? In turn, this question was related to the way my childhood friends and I "dug" a great deal to find out just what things were like in the lives of adults, in particular the nature of sexuality and of that "other," the female. And although I would not have understood the pun as a child, "Antipathies" also evokes a major theme that I did respond to: hostility and aggression as they relate to repeated frustration of purpose. Again, while in some contexts a failure such as Alice's with locks and keys might be perceived as sexual, in Alice herself such a failure provokes a more general cycle of frustration, leading to either rage or success, but with the frustration repeatedly returning in some other form.

A related matter in the early chapters is a fear of loss of both verbal and physical control, a loss experienced intermittently by Alice, and by me, as stemming from sources both internal and external. Anxiety about saying the wrong thing in company (even though I might use the same words without anxiety when alone with my parents) amounted to a fear of myself, and often resulted in an inner fury at the irrational rules of adults—a fury that in turn may have increased the tendency to say the wrong thing. It feels very much as though some such circular process is going on in Alice, that her inability to understand the alien creatures leads to frustration, to anger, to the "accidental" dropping of words frightening to the mouse and the birds, and to the involuntary "wrong" recitation of innocuous moral poems in aggressive parody versions. In turn, Alice fears this mis-speaking, this loss of control over herself, as she fears the loss of physical control reflected in her various changes of size. It is this kind of memory of childhood anxieties about loss of verbal or bodily control and the frustration stemming from them that puts me at odds with Kincaid's attribution to Alice of stuffiness, excessive prudence, callous egotism, ruthless insensitivity, and "instinctive rudeness" (97); for Alice and I are in several kinds of danger from within and without, and this establishes my identification with her so strongly that I can ignore the narrator's sarcasm toward her—if, as Kincaid claims, it is actually there—or, alternatively, can hear in the narrator's voice that irrational and inimical adult world. (My very reference to sarcasm results from having read, and being half-convinced by, that claim in Kincaid's article; but actually I hear the sarcasm more strongly in James Kincaid's voice as critic when reading his essay than I do in the voice of Carroll's narrator.)

If the first two chapters arouse associations with anxiety about loss of control and frustration with adult irrationality, the third and fourth evoke another childhood phantasy: the wish to rebel against the rules that govern that mysterious adult world. I relate the caucus-race to the unpredictability of those rules, my dislike of competitive games, and in the present, my resentment that I am compelled by regulations to give grades to students much as Alice gives a thimble to the Dodo, which he returns as her prize—for I give them an empty symbol of what is already theirs (their writing and verbal contributions in class) in return for their sticking to *my* rules. Such associations place me strongly on Alice's side, and thus her "accidental" reference to her cat Dinah at the end of chapter 3, which routs the offensive creatures, becomes a delightful way of turning upon frustrating and irrational authority figures, although Kincaid takes it as evidence of Alice's inherent unpleasantness.

Following these patterns of response established by/for me in reading the early sections of the novel, Alice's giantism and her resultant imprisonment in chapter 4 have to do not so much with birth, growth, and sexuality as with a continuation of her struggle against the "adults"—a conflict in which she is temporarily triumphant in kicking poor Bill the Lizard up the chimney and then for once controlling her size. (Here as elsewhere *symbolic* in the usual sense does not seem to be quite the right word for designating the kind of response I have, the meaning I construct, for throughout *Alice's Adventures in Wonderland,* even though the details seem alien on the surface, the emotional experience feels strong and immediate.) The difference between my childhood and adult responses may be analogous to Freud's distinction between *heimlich* and *unheimlich* sensations—the first familiar but secret, the second a surprised recognition of the returned repressed.

Certainly the caterpillar's advice, "Keep your temper," capsulizes a significant aspect of the connection between my life and personality and Carroll's fantasy world. Alice's response to the caterpillar is almost to *lose* her temper: "'Is that all?' said Alice, swallowing down her anger as well as she could" (chap. 5, 41). My sense of the caterpillar's advice is that this is what parents, teachers, and bureaucrats have done to me over the years—given confusing or useless advice that makes me furious with frustration, and then told me (directly in childhood, more subtly later on) to keep my temper; and most of the time I swallow it down, with all the immediacy of physical feeling that this metaphor implies. Thus where Kincaid sees the Alice with a serpentine neck (chap. 5) as a cruelly naive child who disregards the pigeon's sensitivity on the subject of eating eggs, I see that pigeon as another in the series of adults who confront Alice, and whose manner of arguing is both illogical and intimidating.[4]

The violent language of the Duchess to her baby is more of the same insanity of the adult world, and the absurd rules at the Mad Tea Party are both an example of institutionalized adult irrationality, and the inversion of a particular fear of mine from childhood. While Alice is frustrated by the lack of food and the mad rules, at school I was afraid of being forced, by a rule without any reason I could discern, to eat foods I detested. Because this was so crucial an anxiety in childhood, I turn at this point to the Mock Turtle and Gryphon chapters (9 and 10) of *Alice's Adventures in Wonderland,* which evoke for me a complex of associations, as school, food, and death are linked sequentially, and thus associatively if not logically. Kincaid deals with Alice's visit in those chapters to the Gryphon and Mock Turtle by contrasting the gruesomeness of Alice's involuntarily parodic recitation, " 'Tis the Voice of the Lobster," which he says moves from the "mutual joy" of creatures sharing a pie to the horror of the panther eating the owl, with the "wild comic victory over death" that has preceded it in "The Lobster-Quadrille" (97). One may choose to believe that every time Alice recites a poem and the words come out both wrong and aggressive she is expressing her true (and, according to Kincaid, nasty) nature; but how one judges (responds to) the function of these unwilled acts in context is another matter. Kincaid is repeatedly moralistic and scolding about Alice's supposed aggressiveness, but as I have read such passages since childhood, with an increasing ability to conceptualize my responses, Alice is mystified and frightened by what seem alien words in her own mouth and intimidated by the seemingly powerful "adults" in such scenes who are quick to point out her errors.

Furthermore, to read "The Lobster-Quadrille" as a definite "victory over death" feels so contrary to the meaning I have always taken from this poem that it would seem that how one understands it depends on subjective assumptions. Kincaid's understanding seems to result not only from the structure of oppositions he has set up in his article (nasty Alice vs. the narrator and the delightful Wonderland characters), but possibly from a wish that this be the meaning. Such a wish for a positive meaning is something I can understand, as I have always found the poem disturbing, always seen the "beloved snail" as a small child, and the whiting, who thus addresses the snail, as an adult, a parent. The second stanza ends with "Would not, could not [join the dance]," a clear refusal (and "turn not pale" implies a refusal motivated by fear), while the third and final stanza ends at best ambiguously with the same question—"Will you, won't you?"— as the first (chap. 10, 90). The entire poem recalls to me the false reassurance of a parent trying to get a child to do something he's afraid of—perhaps my own father trying to get me to jump into the water or roller-skate, with the resulting noseful of water or bruising fall, leading to my frustration and rage. Another reader might understand the poem as symbolizing a parent urging a child into maturity and giving *genuine* reassurance, but for me this quadrille is a dance of fear and death, not convincingly qualified by any reassuring message, religious or otherwise (such as "the other shore" referring to the afterlife), and I think my associations from childhood are what determine my reading it this way. (I no longer believe as I once did that "The Lobster-Quadrille" has a straightforward semantic meaning equivalent to the way *I* happen to read it.) It would be interesting to know how Kincaid read this poem as a child; but as it is, his published reading has no authority but that of assertion.

This response of mine to "The Lobster-Quadrille" is reinforced by a more complex set of associations with the Mock Turtle's song, "Beautiful Soup" (chap. 10, 95). If as a child I didn't understand exactly what mock-turtle soup was, I did assume that the Mock Turtle was singing about something in which *he* could be cooked, and yet that his emotions were ambiguous, combining a sorrow at the inevitability of death with a seemingly contradictory sorrow at being denied the glory of being cooked into a beautiful soup, along with perhaps a third meaning of wishing to regain the lost experience of eating that lost soup—something I would now explain, "objectively," as an infantile separation anxiety. I could not have verbalized these feelings as a child, but the profound disturbance and fascination aroused by the poem suggest that I constructed something like them preverbally.

Yet another more personal meaning of soup, however, also linked it with death. For about six years, beginning at the age of five, I had a strong aversion to soft or liquid foods and would gag if required to taste them. I am uncertain about the source of this aversion, but an incident from about age three may be relevant. Having been swung around and around by the arms by my father after supper and then lying in my crib, I found that a half-solid, half-liquid substance was coming out of my mouth uncontrollably. The connection between my father's causing external and internal loss of body control and soft food substances may explain both the fear of gagging and especially of vomiting later on—a fear that was for a time stronger than that of death—and the uncanny feelings I have always had about "Beautiful Soup." The further fact that I was most often forced to eat those objectionable foods at school relates to the Mock Turtle's description of life at school in the sea, giving his chapters a special kind of affective unity for me.

These associations may cause some readers to think, "Do we really need to hear about Steig's fear of vomiting? Isn't that kind of association so utterly personal as to be too idiosyncratic to be worth including, as few if any other readers will be able recognize themselves in it?" I certainly hesitated about including it, although it seems to be a common childhood anxiety related to eating, the topic and the affective center of "Beautiful Soup." And it seems important to include at least one example of the way in which affective responses to literature can have strong connections to bodily sensations as well as to "mental" feelings and thoughts. I do not know whether any other readers have understood "Beautiful Soup" as I have even in a more general way, but even if the circumstances surrounding my childhood memory of the poem are different from those of most other readers, I find within the text itself a strong ambiguity of reference: Why should a mock-turtle be weeping at the song and thought of a beautiful soup? What I have done above is to summarize how and why that ambiguity affected me—how, so to speak, it was filtered through my affective and perceptual systems.

Chapters 7, 8, 11, and 12 continue the main plot from which the Gryphon and Mock Turtle are something of a digression, though they are not a digression from the book's mode or mood. These are the chapters in which Alice gradually gains some self-confidence in her dealings with the odd and alienating creatures of Wonderland. She is still threatened, though for me less by " 'Off with her head!' " (which she dismisses with, " 'They're only a pack of cards, after all. I needn't be afraid of them!' " [chap. 8, 72]) than by the frustration of the croquet match and the excessively affectionate attentions of the Duchess. The croquet match seems to parallel my childhood awkwardness and lack of understanding of the rules of games, while the Duchess is a virtual portrait (both in words and in Tenniel's illustrations) of a late great-aunt of mine, one of those relatives whose love may be genuine but is highly unwelcome because of the overbearing ways in which it is expressed. Thus I identify with Alice's revulsion at the Duchess's arm around her waist and feel reassured by the Queen's otherwise imaginary power when she gets the Duchess to run away in fear of decapitation. No one ever helped me out of the grasp (which could be physical or verbal) of that aunt, about whom I had nightmares when very young, and so I find Alice to be for at least one time in her adventures specially protected by one adult and thus triumphant over another.

In the concluding chapters I am fully with Alice in her accession to a still greater self-confident power over the Wonderland creatures.

She scarcely seems threatened by the craziness of the trial (although its foreshadowing of Kafka is present to my adult consciousness[5]); her attitude is now distant and contemptuous. Yet when the playing-cards commit their one act of violence against Alice, she gives a scream "half of fright and half of anger" (chap. 12, 109), something that, if one added, "but also of fascination," could stand as a motto for my response to Carroll's text, especially as a child. If there was and is any laughter, it is evoked more by a relief at Alice's overcoming fear and danger through anger and aggression than by the delightful puns and other kinds of word-play.

Other(s)

Thus far I have been concerned primarily with a responsive reading based on identification, but there is another possible dimension of response to *Alice's Adventures in Wonderland* which has never turned up in my students' response papers, with one minor exception. If for both male and female readers the character of Alice may be the central *subject* of the reader's experience, a phantasy self, she may also be an *other,* an object of both wonder and desire, especially for male readers. Only one male student, so far, has reported this kind of response, and it was not articulated beyond a recollection that in reading the book as a child he had thought Alice a "neat" girl whom he would really have liked to know. My childhood imagination was probably as much visual as it was verbal, and although I might have found some small amount of attraction in Tenniel's prim and rather rigid-looking Alice, in fact I grew up with Arthur Rackham's Alice, who still has for me a much more believably female figure and face, and whose age seems to vary between six and eleven, something appropriate for the interest of a boy reader during approximately that age-span. It seems likely that Rackham's illustrations helped me better to visualize Alice mentally than Tenniel's could have done, and it is also likely that I drew a connection between that Alice and an Allison (with the appropriate upper middle-class English accent) who, at eleven, I fancied was my first real childhood love. But earlier and later, among a few women's names that have since childhood produced a very special feeling, the name *Alice* holds pride of place. This is undoubtedly due in part simply to frequent reading of Carroll's book, but there was also a real Alice with whom I attended school from age seven to eighteen, and who was as little like Tenniel's Alice as imaginable—a dark-haired tomboy whose straightforward personality seemed, unlike those of other girls, to undergo little change in adolescence. I don't think I ever longed for her, being entranced periodically by more conventional incarnations of young woman-hood, but she was always in the background of my consciousness, and in some vague way I always considered her to be an ideal, waiting for me in the wings if I ever wanted her—not as much like Agnes Wickfield as like the woman with no damned nonsense about her (and I am aware of the implications of thus comparing myself to David Copperfield and Edmund Sparkler).

The name *Alice,* then, produces its effect by melding in my imagi-nation these two seeming opposites. I say "seeming" because Carroll's Alice, in her ability to stand up to adult nonsense, has something of the strength of personality I saw in my real Alice. And as I have read more about Carroll, a third Alice has in recent years come to occupy a place in this composite phantasy and thus in my experience of Carroll's text. According to Jean Gattégno, the fictional Alice "must certainly be dissociated from Alice Liddell" (26), a point asserted rather than argued. Carroll wrote to Alice Liddell Hargreaves in 1885 that "my mental picture is as vivid as ever of one who was, through so many years, my ideal child-friend. I have had scores of child friends since your time, but they have been quite a different thing" (Carroll, *Letters* 1:561). This sorts ill with Gattégno's remark that "Carroll's fondness for her did not survive the writing of *Alice*" (27). There is no empirical way to test either Gattégno's assertions or the veracity of Carroll's professing at age 63 the continuation of a special feeling for Alice.[6] But Carroll's remark, even if its sincerity can be neither proven nor disproven, is important for understanding my response to the female character as an object of desire.

As I have already argued in chapters 2 and 5, biographical details can become part of the reader's consciousness and have a significant effect on response, and thus on the meaning of the text for that reader. Most of the students in my children's literature course are women, and, as I have said, their relatively infrequent positive re-sponses to the fictional Alice have treated her only as subject—a phantasy version of themselves—and never as a potential object of desire. For this reason they tend to consider the feelings of the histor-ical author towards the real Alice to be at best irrelevant, and at worst—because of his voyeuristic photographic pursuits—repugnant. The negative responses by women to Alice herself do, however, have the quality of treating her as an object, an other, in the form of "That's not *me,*" though this often seems to be a kind of defensive denial. But as a boy and a man, I have found it impossible not to respond to Alice (the fictional one, first of all) as a potentially desirable and sexual being, as well as to Alice as myself, a generalized, genderless child. And further, I cannot separate the knowledge of the historical Carroll *or* Alice from the fictional Alice and must assume that if Carroll was "in love" with his real Alice, the fictional one is to some extent a phantasy version of Alice Liddell. Yet there is a further complication in that to a degree the "real" Alice herself seems to have been in part a phantasy of Carroll's, the "ideal child-friend." And to the extent that it all remained in phantasy in the sense of never being acted upon, Carroll's "love" is also a phantasy (but really my construct as I attribute it to Carroll), which makes it no less real as a feeling in Carroll.

Many of Carroll's letters make evident the presence of a sexual, and also a sadistic, component in his devotion to young (and some older) girls—though always in a joking form, with much reference both to kisses and to what terrible fate awaits a child who does not answer a letter from him.[7] But what ultimately makes vivid to me Carroll's love for his own image of Alice Liddell (and thus the character he created for and from her) is a single photograph, the frequently reproduced one of Alice dressed as a beggar-maid, taken when she was six or seven, about which I would have some hesitation in saying openly that it is one of the sexiest Victorian pictures I have ever seen had I not checked to find that male colleagues share this reaction.[8] Nowhere in Carroll's portraits of young girls with which I'm familiar is there any child as beautiful as Alice Liddell, and in the beggar-maid photograph this beauty takes on a special quality. Of all those children she is the one with the most open, most direct expression: eyes that look out at the observer with absolute candor. While it is Carroll who posed Alice in a seductive stance and who dressed her in rags revealing much flesh, it seems to be the young child's own preternatural combination of innocence and womanliness that makes the total effect possible. Placing this against Carroll's last portrait of Alice, taken when she was eighteen, produces a vivid contrast.[9] Most of Carroll's portraits of adolescent girls suggest (mendaciously or not) placid souls, but this one of Alice presents a radical transformation from childhood: a face distinctly troubled, with no hint of the open, trusting, and yet somehow seductive look remaining. It is as though Carroll's words in the introductory poem to *Through the Looking-Glass* about the "bitter tidings" that "Shall summon to unwelcome bed / A melancholy maiden!"—words that could refer to both the marriage and the death bed—were embodied in the posture and expression of the eighteen-year-old Alice Liddell, again posed by

Carroll but surely contributing something of herself to the nature of the image, as in the earlier portrait.

The palimpsest of my reading experiences thus includes a link with Lewis Carroll in what I imagine to be his love of the real Alice, something that has caused me to recognize the way in which my relationships—both real and phantasied—over the years to girls and women as the desirable but ultimately unfathomable other, have been objectified in the totality of my readings of *Alice's Adventures in Wonderland*. And thus the beggar-maid and the troubled adolescent have become part of my perception of and response to Carroll's text. This link between Carroll and myself is of course a mental construct, and I might further conjecture that my taking "the author" more and more into account in recent years derives from an unwillingness to give up either the author-as-father or my own father-as-author, the latter having the double meaning as author of myself and professional writer, a career in which his success ended when I was about the age Alice is supposed to be in Wonderland.

Does this kind of reading differ in fundamental ways from those normally practiced? James Kincaid's essay on *Alice,* if outwardly more conventional, seems as idiosyncratic to me as this chapter doubtless will to him. Perhaps the main differences are, first, that I have not attempted a reading that is supposed to account for the text's unity in terms of a single aspect of meaning, and second, that the affective and associative bases of my reading are specified. The ultimate question is whether literary interpretation as it continues to be practiced yields up understanding in ways fundamentally different from the kinds of processes I have been detailing. Nonallegorical fantasies such as the Alice books only more obviously require the reader to supply his or her sense of coherence and significance to disparate textual materials—that is, texts like *The Wind in the Willows* or *Alice's Adventures in Wonderland* do not give us the comfort of an illusion that they are somehow direct representations of life. But it is questionable whether more "realistic" novels (such as *Mansfield Park, Jude the Obscure,* or *Sons and Lovers*) necessarily constrain the reader more by supplying more coherence, rather than, like fantasy novels, requiring the reader to supply his or her own.

III · LIMITS OF SIGNIFICATION

7 · *David Copperfield*'s Plots against the Reader

This and the four chapters to follow focus on several specific factors in the process of reading and understanding: how readers deal with textual indeterminacy; a reader's attitude towards the author/narrator as a creator of character and manipulator of plot; the setting by the reader of limits to possible signification; and literary influence as a pathway towards literary understanding. In most respects the general concerns of earlier chapters continue here: what happens when a reader confronts a text, how meaning or understanding are generated or constructed, what role affective and associative response play in the reading process, and, as always, what role the extrinsic plays in response.

Although it would be imprecise to say that meanings are hidden in most nineteenth- or early twentieth-century novels if this is taken to mean that the authors consciously intend to conceal something that actually "exists" behind the text, there are some novels in which this actually seems to be happening. In *Wuthering Heights,* while Emily Brontë may be thought to have concealed something in failing to reveal Heathcliff's parentage, his whereabouts during his absence, and the source of his money and gentlemanly appearance upon his return, there is no basis for assuming that she "knew" (conceptualized) these facts in any more detail than a reader can know them. But there have been, long before the modernist or postmodernist novel, writers who seem to be experimenting consciously with narrative techniques so as to complicate and confuse for the reader the process of construing meaning (by *construing* here I mean specifically what a reader does when he or she posits an author and tries to find an intended meaning).[1]

In the history of the English novel *Tristram Shandy* is the obvious case, but *Bleak House,* with its two narratives, one personal and limited in viewpoint, the other omniscient and panoramic, is one instance of a Victorian experiment of this sort, while another is *Vanity Fair,* whose narrator seems to take on various personalities, and even at one point to become a character in the story. But readers of these two Victorian novels can for the most part acquire some sense of a consistent tone or tones and a definite set of values: one is able to conceptualize an "author," if to do so should happen to be a part of one's normal style of reading. Despite the trickiness of narrative technique, we become aware of something or someone we may denote as "Dickens" or "Thackeray," even if different readers' actual conceptualizations of these "authors" may vary considerably. But there is at least one nineteenth-century British novel in which the novelist seems deliberately to elude being conceptualized, to be continually in hiding, behind the multiple narrators who by their very multiplicity make the satisfactory delineation of a consistent viewpoint, of meaning itself, difficult or impossible. Such characteristics make James Hogg's *The Private Memoirs and Confessions of a Justified Sinner* (1824) one of the most frustrating of premodernist novels in English. It is of special interest for the problem of the relations among author, text, and reader because of how it seems to convey an author's conscious intention to elude the reader's attempts to understand his intention, his meaning. Unlike Emily Brontë, Hogg seems *deliberately* to be hiding meanings.[2] In reference to the way Wolfgang Iser expands the concept of concretization of places of indeterminacy (Ingarden) into a theory of indeterminacy as the *main* force that motivates a reader to construe meanings,[3] one might call the ambiguities and uncertainties of Hogg's novel "determinate indeterminacies." As Iser describes the process, "by reading we uncover the unformulated part of the text, and this very indeterminacy is the force that drives us to work out a configurative meaning while at the same time giving us the necessary degree of freedom to do so" (*The Implied Reader,* 287).

As by *determinate* I mean intended by the author, from the reader's viewpoint one might instead call these "places" in Hogg's text "indeterminable determinacies"—that is, uncertainties through which the author intends to invite but ultimately frustrate the attempt to "work out a configurative meaning." Thus I find myself unable to talk about meanings in Hogg's novel without referring to the author and his intentions and to the process of reading; this may in part be caused by my predisposition to think such matters important, but one important qualification is that with Hogg I get the sense that the author is busily attempting to confuse me, and so his presence comes to feel inescapable. From the outset, this author seems to have taken great pains to create simultaneously an illusion of the authenticity and a sense of the unreliability of the fictional documents his "Editor" presents us with. He even goes so far as to suggest the unreliability of a character named James Hogg, who has attempted to mislead this Editor as to the location of the grave of the justified sinner, Robert Wringhim Colwan—an unreliability in apparent contrast to the straightforward Editor, the bluff chap who purportedly wrote the first part of the book and found and published with it the second part, which contains the Memoirs and Confessions found in the suicide's grave. Hogg in real life actually published in 1823 in *Blackwood's* a letter describing the opening of the grave of a suicide and, as happens in the novel, finding the corpse remarkably preserved. Part of this letter is then reproduced in the novel when the "Editor's Narrative" resumes after the "Memoirs," and we then discover that the corpse is that of the justified sinner.[4] Any reader who is not taking this novel as a genuine historical account will realize that Hogg is having some fun with the question of textual authority, but the narrative becomes serious enough to exceed any such "fun," and to give the reader more than one moment of pause.

It may seem improbable that Hogg should want the reader to believe that he is a liar, but someone surely seems to be. For it becomes clear from the novel's first page that we can never be certain what is meant "really" to have happened in the novel's action, as we not only get different views of the same events, but are initially addressed by a narrator (the Editor) who is himself clearly uncertain about the facts. Indeed, we could even conclude that there is no "real" action, that the entire text is a "place of indeterminacy." And my experiences of reading the *Justified Sinner* suggest that Iser is right insofar as he identifies indeterminacies (or "blanks") as one force that can motivate a reader's attempt to establish meaning; for no matter how frustrating it may be, I do find myself returning to Hogg's novel as if a detective to an unsolved murder.

Indeterminacy is established in Hogg's first paragraph, as we are told that what the Editor is about to relate is based only on tradition, apart from the one known fact that the laird, George Colwan, inherited in 1687 his family's lands and property. Even the traditional belief that the laird was wealthy is qualified by the phrase, "or supposed to be so," while his wife—whom he marries "when [he is] considerably advanced in life"—is referred to as "the sole heiress and reputed daughter of a Baillie Orde, of Glasgow" (1). The Editor as narrator does not continue to qualify in this way every supposed fact, which would make the text unreadable, but uncertainties crop up repeatedly in this narrative, in the "Memoirs and Confessions," and in the two in relation to one another. Who is the actual father of either of the laird's supposed sons—Colwan himself, or his wife's pastor, Robert Wringhim? Is the mysterious Gil-Martin an incarnation of Satan, a double of Robert Colwan, or even a reincarnation of his murdered brother, George? All these possibilities are implied, and the questions are never answered.

Plots

I have thus prefaced my chapter on reader-narrator-author relations in *David Copperfield* with a brief discussion of what I consider to be intentionally hidden (or intentionally indeterminate) meanings in Hogg's bizarre novel, not because I think Dickens does something very similar, but rather because I have come to feel more and more that certain less consciously created aspects of indeterminacy in *David Copperfield* are among the most interesting features of that novel, those that most tend to motivate interpretive reading. Both my fascination with and my hostility to the author when I read Hogg are based on the feeling of being deliberately manipulated by that author into searching for a "reality" that cannot be found.[5] In reading Dickens's novel, however, my hostile response and urge to interpret stem from a more complex set of qualities. I had considered titling this chapter "Violence in the Author," "Plotting *David Copperfield*," or even "Surprises in Reading and Teaching." Such a lack of decisiveness originates in the conflicts in my thoughts and feelings about Dickens's "favourite child," conflicts that in turn are partly related to my awareness of a strong division among critics as to how to think about the structure of *David Copperfield,* in particular of how they respond to the meaning conveyed overtly by the protagonist's movement from the condition of the "undisciplined heart" to what is presumably a "disciplined" one in his second marriage, to Agnes Wickfield.[6]

As happened fortuitously during a semester in which I was for the first time using a thorough reader-response approach in teaching *David Copperfield* among other Dickens novels, I was invited to devise and deliver a paper at a conference session on "Violence in Dickens," *and* to contribute to a Modern Language Association volume on teaching *David Copperfield.* My first thought about the conference invitation was, "That's not my area—and anyway, violence bores me." But almost immediately recognizing this dismissive reaction as an evasion, I resolved to consider just what in Dickens felt violent to me and soon realized that each time I had finished rereading *David Copperfield* it had felt like the most violent novel in the Dickens canon, even if after David is caned by Murdstone there may be infrequent acting-out by characters of violent impulses, and long stretches of text that seem calm, joyful, even idyllic. Clearly, there was something problematic about that generalized description of my response to the novel. As it turned out, that sense of violence has a good deal to do with the novel's structure and its narrator's didactic interpretations of his own past life, both of which I feel in some ways to be "plots" against the reader as well as some of the characters. In particular it has to do with the question of the "undisciplined heart" and the credibility of the resolution of the story in David's marriage to his "good angel," Agnes. But the nature of the indeterminacy I was reacting to in *David Copperfield* became clear only through some of my women students' response papers, and subsequent discussions, as the class became something of a feminist training-ground for me.

But violence first, feminism afterwards. The explanation of what I mean by a sense of violence as an element in the experience of reading *David Copperfield* must begin with the paradoxical observation that one of Dickens's most overtly violent characters, Quilp in *The Old Curiosity Shop,* does not feel violent to me, for I identify with and even love him for his antic energy and his defiance of the legal profession, domesticity, and sexual purity (Nell)—indeed of "normal" morality. Nor does it seem that Quilp feels violent to himself, as, for example, Jonas Chuzzlewit does after murdering Tigg. And thus I find myself defining violence as a matter of someone's feeling violated, feeling violent (and thus guilty), or both. David as the hero of his own story, and thus of mine as I read and actualize his, is the most obvious object of violence, and yet David as narrator and Dickens as the author who controls the plot are perpetrators of violence within the story-line, and thus against me as reader.

Perhaps the most salient fact about my story of reading David's story is that for many years I felt doubtful about the way psychoanalytic critics have labeled the triangular relationship between David, his mother, and Murdstone as Oedipal, for although I could see this abstractly I clung to a utopian belief that Dickens was depicting a special and contingent rather than a universal pattern: Murdstone is after all an especially violent and tyrannical stepfather and husband,

and to label the triangle Oedipal seemed to be to rob it of its particularity. With a different stepfather or his own father, I reasoned, David could have had a fundamentally different kind of childhood, and a less neurotically fraught process of maturation. Only in attempting to write about my sense of violence in the novel did I realize that I had been resisting seeing Murdstone as an aspect writ large of my own loving, liberal father, and it was with a shock of recognition that I suddenly found I had to acknowledge that the undefined uncanny feeling I always got from Murdstone was after all directly related to my childhood. Becoming a father myself, and recognizing the excessive demands I sometimes made to, and the occasional feelings and even outbursts of rage against my sons led me to associate Murdstone's posing of impossible sums to David with my own proud father's excessive expectations and resultant disappointments with me (my mother in the background, like Clara Copperfield, trying ineffectually to smooth over the conflict). So although my feelings about David Copperfield had not changed, I now accepted as the source of an uncanny sensation previously based on a subconscious familiarity the almost literal Oedipal triangle in the Murdstone household and the way in which it is paralleled with several other symbolically Oedipal triangles—a structure that I had earlier considered excessively schematized by psychoanalytic critics. I now took the consideration of those triangles as a possible way to get at the nature of my problematic sense of the novel as predominantly violent.

This newly awakened and vivid level of response constitutes part of what is a personally constructed subtext, not a set of "meanings" I claim to be objectively present at or beneath the novel's surface. Perceiving (constructing) this subtext has led to my noticing other instances of seeming violence. For example, even before Murdstone appears in the text, while David seems to remain in a paradise with Peggotty and his angelic but also sexually provocative mother, David as narrator uses violent language that foreshadows what will soon be happening to David the character. He describes his falling asleep in church, falling off the pew-bench, and being carried out "more dead than alive" (chap. 2, 64); it seems hardly accidental that in Hablot Browne's etching depicting this scene, "Our Pew at Church," the supposedly paradisiacal setting has already been invaded by Murdstone, who is sitting across the aisle from the Copperfield pew, looking hungrily at Clara Copperfield.[7] Within two further chapters the illusory nature of that paradise becomes apparent, and overt, active violence occurs not only in Murdstone's caning of David, but in David's biting him, which seems to David to justify his stepfather's rage and produces the hero's first feelings of guilt.

But by chapter 9, a kind of *narrative* violence begins to be perpetrated, as David's mother and her Murdstone baby—the one concrete bit of evidence to David of her sexual betrayal—are killed off, an event that, in the light of later events that parallel it, reads like an act of vengeance against both the treacherous mother and the stepfather who has invaded David's imagined paradise. While I am not suggesting that David as character is responsible in any literal way for his mother's death, the temporal sequences of events surrounding this and subsequent triangular relationships create in me the feeling that someone's will is responsible. Literally of course it is the will of the novelist, but David's being hero, narrator, and putative author of his autobiography displaces that sense of responsibility and willing of events in the process of reading to some uncertain locus among Dickens, David as author/narrator, David as character, and myself as reader, character, and storyteller actively constructing meanings while identifying with some aspects of David's experience.

Tracing the other love-relationships involving David makes Clara Copperfield's death seem in retrospect even more like an event willed with relish. It is not uncommon for readers to find that Dickens is somehow manipulating a plot to achieve ends (and endings) that fulfill a didactic and emotional purpose, and which feel as though they are forced, that they do not occur, so to speak, naturally. One need cite only the apparent death and resurrection of Rose Maylie *(Oliver Twist)*, the turning over of Esther to Woodcourt by John Jarndyce *(Bleak House),* and the manipulative scheme set up for Bella Wilfer's moral improvement *(Our Mutual Friend)*—but every reader will have his favorites. Such narrative strategies are the privilege of an English novelist writing in Dickens's era, and he is far from being the only one who can be said to use them (think of the convenient death of George Osborne in *Vanity Fair*, or Jane Eyre's happening to come upon the cottage of her cousins when she is in danger of dying of starvation and exposure), but in no novel of the time do I find more such manipulation than in *David Copperfield,* to the extent that it begins to feel as if the author is committing violence against the characters and against me as reader. One way of conceptualizing this aspect of narrative plotting might be to see such events in terms of Mark Spilka's notion of "projective fiction," whereby external events mirror the protagonist's phantasies and wishes (see *Dickens and Kafka: A Mutual Interpretation*); but ultimately I find this concept too unsettling, and I cannot allow my experience of the novel to become so de-centered that there remains no "real" character but the protagonist.

While on an overt textual level the bad stepfather can reasonably be blamed for the death of David's mother and infant half-brother, the matter of responsibility becomes increasingly equivocal as David's relationships to females follow one another. "I told Em'ly I adored her, and that unless she confessed she adored me I should be reduced to the necessity of killing myself with a sword" (chap. 3, 87). On the basis of childhood memories I can feel the emotional reality of this love, although it seems for David at this point to function as much as a refuge from the stresses of growing up as it does as a potentially sexual love. Someone is protesting too much in reporting that David "loved that baby quite as truly, quite as tenderly, with greater purity, and more disinterestedness than can enter into the best love of a later time of life, high and ennobling as it is" (chap. 3, 87). I would suggest that Emily's full story amounts, among other things, to a statement that she must be subjected to the violence of an abduction, desertion, and disgrace because she both fails to duplicate David's mother sufficiently—being too independent (see Emily's behavior to David in chap. 10)—and yet duplicates her all too well by growing up and betraying David's love. And the two interveners between Emily and David are punished as well. Ham first suffers through loss of Emily, and then drowns. Steerforth functions ambiguously as the invader of David's second illusory paradise—the Peggottys' home—as David's surrogate with Emily, both as seducer and scourge, and as a betrayer of David who loves him; and thus, in his drowning with Ham, he is punished as another victim of the novel's vengeance.

One may not normally think of David's marriage to Dora as being sullied by violence, but it is there that manipulation of plot—Dickens's violence against character and reader—reaches its peak for me. First of all the obstructive father, Mr. Spenlow (rather like the Linton parents in *Wuthering Heights*), is rapidly dispatched after he opposes David's love for his daughter. But the more important variant of the phantasy of the father-mother-son triangle places two Davids at two points in a triangle. The first David is the *naif* who falls in love with the coy but ultimately submissive replica of his mother (and, as his "child-wife," of the "baby" Emily as well), while the second David is the intervener who becomes a reincarnation of Murdstone, in his attempt to form Dora's mind. While he soon realizes that Dora's mind is already formed and tells us that their second year of marriage was very happy, his wish to violate her personality is almost immediately transferred to the plot, as we are told after a series of complaints about something missing in the marriage and about his own "undisciplined heart" that "as that year wore on, Dora was not strong" (chap. 48, 766). The scene is set for her death, seemingly caused by her miscarriage, which is presumably another example of her incompetence as a wife.

Except insofar as their marriage is dependent on the death of Dora, David's and Agnes's relationship as young adults does not involve this kind of violence by the plot against the characters and the reader, but it is replete with another sort of violence. For David and Agnes are part of a triangle that brings out our hero's most overtly violent feelings and actions since his biting of Mr. Murdstone. My subtext here is the way in which identification, revulsion, and rage develop and combine in David's attitude towards Uriah Heep. It has become almost a critical commonplace that Uriah represents to David repressed aspects of himself—his sense of social inferiority, ambitions for success, and ambivalent feelings of lust for and hatred towards women. Harry Stone has explicated most fully the significance of the biblical allusion to King David and Uriah the Hittite: in the Second Book of Samuel it is *David* who lusts after and indeed seduces Uriah's wife, Bathsheba, and who in response to Uriah's refusal to sleep again with his wife and thus cover up the king's responsibility for her pregnancy sends him to the front line of battle, assuring his death:

Yet the differences between the Biblical story and the novel are striking. In the Bible, David is sinful, Uriah innocent. In *Copperfield,* David is innocent, Uriah sinful. This strange reversal . . . suggests Uriah's role as David's darker self. For if the two are one, the reversal is not so strange. Then Uriah can personify David's most aggressive and covetous thoughts—which, in fact, he does. In the Bible, David's sinfulness is open, in *Copperfield* it is repressed and objectified in Uriah. [222]

Note also that God punishes King David through the death of his and Bathsheba's first son, something of a parallel to the fate of David Copperfield's unnamed half-brother, which I suggest is a punishment for Murdstone and for David's mother as well.[8]

If Uriah is the intervening figure in the triangle that includes David and Agnes, a substantial part of Uriah's potential threat depends upon David's inability to acknowledge any of his own sexual feelings for Agnes. It is as though David (and Dickens) can imagine Agnes as a sexual woman only in terms of violation. Uriah thus must be made an extreme grotesque, most obviously in order to give David and the reader immediate reasons for regarding this potential lover, not consciously acknowledged by David as a rival, as a potential and repulsive violator. But at a crucial point David suddenly recognizes his own violence and thus his affinity with Uriah: after striking Uriah he says, "I felt only less mean than he. He knew me better than I knew myself" (chap. 42, 687).[9] More importantly, it is as though Uriah holds the secret about Agnes, as implied in the way he smacks his lips for her, and underscored by the possible biblical allusion to the lamb, metaphor for the very sexual Bathsheba. If Agnes's sexuality was unimaginable to David, to Dickens, and to their original readers, it has, rather paradoxically, been no less so to those twentieth-century male critics, such as Chesterton, James Kincaid, Robin Gilmour, and myself, who have tried to debunk her status as "the real heroine" (Dickens's own designation in his memorandum to himself in the process of writing the novel).[10] But in reexamining my responses I have realized that, given that it is she whom the hero ultimately marries, I had always wanted to believe in Agnes's sexuality but could not and had blamed Dickens for this, rather like a young boy who blames his father for keeping the mother to himself. Yet there is a direct personal association more specific than this. Just as David is upset by Daniel Peggotty's report that Emily is getting to be quite a woman (chap. 10), and as later David is unable to acknowledge anything but brotherly feelings for Agnes, whom he has for years called "sister," I refused for several years in early adolescence to believe that a girl two years older than I, who had been my closest companion throughout my earlier years (the "J" referred to in chap. 3), was sexually active.

Plots Unraveled

It was teaching *David Copperfield* through reader response, however, that led most directly to my questioning of previous readings of the novel in which I had equated the coquetry and flirtatiousness of David's first three female loves (Clara, Emily, and Dora) with sexuality, and Agnes's placidity and honesty with a repellent "purity." It is not, as I see it now, that Agnes is the problem, but rather that David is; and not because of his "undisciplined heart," but because he divides women into the sexual and the pure, and thus is goaded to violence by the hint that Uriah, with his capacity for stimulating grotesque phantasies of sexual violation, is truly the first to "know" Agnes as neither David the character, nor David the narrator, or perhaps even Dickens the author is ever able to do. As I have already indicated, one of the things that has happened repeatedly in teaching through reader response is that students will, in considering and objectifying their own responses, present ways of looking at a work that depend upon their individual experiences, and which yet at the same time seem to have the power to open up a whole new vein of possibility in reading for others. Before I began teaching in this way I had developed for *David Copperfield* a standard line of interpretation, which tended to inhibit students' ability to develop their own readings without either echoing mine or relying excessively on published criticism. I could speak interestingly on the autobiographical elements, the child's point of view, and the pattern of sexual triangles in David's development. With Dora and Agnes I rejected the didactic reading and declared Agnes not a "flat" but a hollow character, an abstract ideal rather than a real woman; the latter role I assigned to Dora.

Having decided to stick strictly to a reader-response approach, I gave the students a detailed assignment that asked them to choose some aspect of the book that they felt to be in need of interpretation, to offer their own, and to connect that interpretation to their responses and the associations that might explain those responses. I suggested a number of possible areas, such as family and marriage, David's relationships to women, David as reliable or unreliable narrator, and the child's view of reality, but students had the freedom to choose any other aspect of the novel. In the intervening two weeks while they struggled through the novel and prepared to write their papers, we talked about the autobiographical aspects and about my own distributed response paper. The latter included a reconsideration of my earlier attitude to Murdstone in relation to my father (discussed above), and of my earlier labeling of Dora the "real woman," which I now suggested had been self-deceptive, saying that in condemning David (and Dickens) for "murdering" Dora with a wish, I was possibly repressing memories of my violent feelings towards a coquettish girlfriend whom I had allowed to drive me to both fury and misery for two years in adolescence. Yet I insisted that the one figure about whom I could not revise my attitude was Agnes, because I could not believe in her as a character but saw her only as Dickens's (or David's) middle-class, middle-aged phantasy: the pure, self-effacing woman who has really loved one all her life. I am not to be the hero of my own story here and offer this partial summary only to indicate how I encouraged the students through example to be thoughtful in analyzing their responses and open and trusting in presenting personal material to a group of strangers. As I have said in earlier chapters, it would be naive to deny that my paper had some influence on how the students wrote theirs, but insofar as I can judge from the result, the influence (as with my paper on *Wuthering Heights*) was more in topic than in content of responses, for the students were certainly not too intimidated to describe responses widely different from mine.

As in any response classroom, a certain number of the students were initially uncomfortable with the approach. I prefer not to assert the weight of authority to shame such students into performing "correctly," and I find that even those papers that express some discomfort bear on the question of response and allow for the clarification and development of what a student may have only faintly suggested in the paper. Perhaps the best instance of such a paper is the one by the young Scotswoman which I summarize in chapter 6, but near the end of this chapter I shall give an example of how unrevealed autobiographical details may come out in classroom discussion to everyone's enlightenment. First I want to summarize a few of the fullest and most detailed papers on *David Copperfield* and our discussion of them, however, in order to show further what a shared response method can accomplish not only in developing self-understanding, but in creating critical insights that open out new views of a work.

The question of Dickens's women, as might have been anticipated from both the way I had presented my responses and the predominantly female enrollment in the course, was most frequently chosen as a topic. But most of the results were quite unexpected. Many factors besides the questions the instructor may raise initially can influence the way students write response papers. One woman, Billie, made her paper available to us somewhat ahead of the deadline, and it clearly affected some subsequent contributions. On the face of it this paper by a student in her late thirties was unsophisticated and sentimental. It seemed to take straight what are often thought of as the most "Victorian" values apparent in Dickens's overt intentions. Billie, a devout Catholic, had no difficulty with the marriage to Agnes as the ultimate, believable, and desirable goal of David's development, and she set up a dichotomy between the "spiritual" and "sensual" sides of David's relationships to women, claiming that the pre-Murdstone "Edenic" world, with Clara Copperfield "like the Virgin Mary . . . young, innocent, and fair," is regained only with Agnes. But the paper's dominant theme was family problems, with David's unhappy childhood, the financial difficulties of the Micawbers, Emily's desertion of the Peggottys, and Mr. Wickfield's alcoholic grievings serving as examples. For this student the two themes intersect in David's marriage to Dora, whom she sees as eliciting from

David a sensual response rather than a spiritual one, and thereby trapping him into an unsatisfactory marriage; in contrast Agnes, in appealing to his spiritual side, offers David a more meaningful and more enduring marriage.

Without the personal associations described in this paper it would have been difficult to tell how much of Billie's interpretation involved stock responses and how much was a genuine exploration of her experience of reading. This student's father, like David's, was absent in her early childhood, and then his place was taken by a stepfather by whom she felt rejected—like David she felt there was one appetite too many at the table. Her education was interrupted after high school, when she had strongly wished to go to university, and her early married life was full of financial difficulties as well as conflicts with relatives. It appeared that her unquestioning acceptance of David's marriage to Agnes had much to do with the development of her own life toward a current feeling of fulfillment and stability as a wife, mother, and successful university student. In reading David's life story, Billie found so many striking parallels to her own that other questions became unimportant. The main difficulty members of the class found in the paper was Billie's distinction between the sensual and the spiritual, but in discussion it became clear that this dichotomy had resulted from a somewhat unreflective use of terms, which had trapped her into seeming to deny the presence of sensuality in successful marriages. Indeed, she was visibly embarrassed when this was pointed out to her and took pains to clarify her intention. (Interestingly, Billie was the student who, at the beginning of the course, seemed to be the most resistant to my approach, expressing grave doubts and anxiety about writing on her responses, primarily because it would prevent her from relying on published criticism to frame her arguments; yet she turned out to be the most productive writer in the class, most able to relate interpretation to response and to explain response on the basis of detailed associations.)

This student's way of combining a literal or even "Victorian" reading with genuine self-reflection seems to implicate teachers of literature, and perhaps of Dickens in particular, in a situation rarely acknowledged in Anglo-American criticism or theory but given some attention in West Germany. Dieter Richter has called it *"the contradiction between institutional reading and private reading,"* referring to the problem of students reading "differently than teachers wish"—that is, not reading critically but instead participating in "sympathetic, vicarious identification with texts" and thus developing "something on the order of a double reading morality: in the reading institutions they behave like critical readers, once outside of them they behave quite differently" (31, 36; emphasis in original). Richter blames this problem on the tendency of teachers to encourage students to treat the literary work as a distanced object instead of taking into account the kind of elective reading students do and using the individual experiences of such private reading as a starting point from which to explore social and cultural values.[11] I can imagine a paper like Billie's being strongly criticized as naive by some of my colleagues, but unless one takes off from such a point, as Richter suggests, and builds upon the work the student has done (instead of just giving a low grade), nothing is really accomplished except perhaps that the student learns to write in a way that embodies the teacher's values instead of her own.

An initially inexplicable response by another student emerged when I again raised in class the question of Agnes Wickfield's credibility as a character. Surprisingly to me, Joan, whom I had thought the most self-consciously feminist student in the group, in discussion strongly insisted on the reality and solidity of Agnes as a character, though at first she could give no explanation of why she responded that way. But when we had her paper in hand the basis of this response became clear: Joan identified strongly with Agnes, not because of the aura of the angelic and of "stained-glass windows" with which David surrounds her, but rather because she saw Agnes's lack of assertiveness in her love for David as analogous to a trait of her own in adolescence. Neither popular nor considered pretty when she was in high school, Joan had always been the one to whom boys came for "understanding"—usually of their problems with other girls. She acknowledged that to some extent her acting as consoler was a conscious strategy to attract boys, but remarked wryly that it never worked—they always went off with the girls who could successfully play the baby-doll role, which she connected with Dora. This set of associations opened up a possibility I had never considered: that while Agnes is from David's point of view a confidante and guardian angel, someone whom he could not (as he says) love as he had loved Emily or Dora, from Agnes's point of view the matter might look quite different. Dickens does not give us the psychologically complex character constructed by Joan out of her own experience, since he shows us Agnes only through David's eyes (though, as I have suggested, with a hint of a different view through the lustings of the grotesque Uriah), but Joan's strong conviction that Agnes is more than an abstract ideal enabled me for the first time to imagine psychological processes within a character whom I had previously felt to be virtually missing from the novel. But the word *imagine* is crucial— for what I actually was enabled to see was how a woman might conceptualize Agnes differently from a man, how she might better be able to fill in the "blanks" of indeterminacy from her own experience. The substance of the character within the text is still indeterminate, lacking in concreteness for me, except to the extent that I now can feel as though there is something in Agnes just beyond my field of vision which I can *almost* see.

In class discussion this insight, or construct, of Joan's caused David's credibility as narrator and the adequacy of his understanding of himself or another, whether Dora, Agnes, or Steerforth, to be called into question. And two other papers by women students took up the more general but related question of the paradox that while the female characters are seen only from a limited masculine viewpoint, they are more complex and interesting than the males (totally contrary to the received—and generally male—wisdom about Dickens's women). Chris in her paper felt especially incensed by the treatment of Emily, who is defined by the males solely through her function for men—her status changing, after she succumbs to Steerforth, from that of an adored child and young woman to a kind of "neuter" (Chris's word), a woman for whom a husband or another lover is unthinkable. The argument that this was a standard Victorian attitude did not soothe this student's irritation; and she traced her own anger back to adolescence, when "peer pressure makes it clear that a girl's social, and by inference, other worth as a human is directly related to her desirability by males." This perception, response, and association led Chris to question David's narrative reliability and to express a wish for Agnes to be more than what David tells us: an angel who "cannot be sexy in David's world." Chris also picked up on the reference to Betsey Trotwood as "masculine," pointing out that Betsey "does not need the male counterpoint as others do, in order to be 'valid.'" This point in turn aroused an association with her father, who had wanted Chris, the second of three daughters, to be his "boy," and although she herself did not make the connection, it seems likely that this memory aggravated her resentment of David's (or Dickens's) limited vision of women.

Rosalyn's paper on this general topic, written partly in response to Billie's, was the only one that saw some positive worth in Dora, on the subjective ground that being childlike is an important trait of Rosalyn herself, especially as a reaction against her strict German upbringing. She wondered whether the problem with sensuality in the novel is not that it is false but that it is, for David, dangerous.

More aware of depth psychology than the other students, Rosalyn was able to make use of psychoanalytic concepts in a way that demonstrated an understanding through her own experiences. She was thus able on the basis of considerable self-awareness to be more open to and less critical of David's shortcomings. Indeed, this student saw something of herself not only in Dora but in Steerforth (the need to dominate) and in Rosa Dartle (a tendency toward depression and self-destructiveness when she felt bereft of love). And she was more clear-sighted than I and most of the students about Clara Copperfield, whom she described as calculating and manipulative— something I had always sensed but never acknowledged, perhaps being too committed to the schema that identified Clara, Emily, and Dora as the sexual women in David's life.

Some of the men in the class had more difficulty connecting their responses to personal associations; but there was one paper and subsequent discussion that is worth summarizing, in part because it aroused great laughter, but primarily because it illustrates how a seeming resistance to revealing personal details can lead to significant results in subsequent discussion. Almost the whole class was quite definite that David's problems with Murdstone were entirely that cruel stepfather's fault, but one man went so far in the opposite direction as to insist that Murdstone's hostility towards David was justified. His paper gave no clue as to the origin of this response, and we were all puzzled until some probing caused the crucial fact to emerge: this man had had a close relationship with a divorced woman which had broken up because of her young son's insurmountable hostility towards his mother's lover. A certain amount of hilarity arose from this revelation, but none of us dismissed the response as idiosyncratic; as with the sudden insight into the potential psychological depth of Agnes, we now saw the relationship between David and Murdstone from the stepfather's viewpoint.

If the class and I learned anything "about" the novel from all this, it was perhaps that the way Dickens restricts the point of view to David nonetheless implies other realities as other characters might see them, which can become part of an individual's total understanding of a book even though that reader can construct these only on an inferential and inevitably subjective basis. It is important to stress as well, in relation to this particular class, that although reader-response theory and teaching have often been said to fragment reading into a series of discrete, individualistic positions, leaving no way to take social and cultural factors into account, a variety of such factors are implicit in the students' papers: for example, the extent of the continuity of Victorian values and the reason that his women characters are a "problem" for modern readers of Dickens both can be discussed as social and cultural as well as personal topics. This experience required me to at least reconsider, and in some respects give up, the way I had for years been reading *David Copperfield*. The feeling of someone's violence against Clara, Emily, and Dora, and thus against the reader, remains and if anything is reinforced by my new view that David is not only "blind" to Agnes's feelings, but unable, in part because of Dickens's own limitations, to empathize with women's behavior and motivations—his mother's, Emily's, or Dora's. But I have had to alter my easy dismissal of Agnes as an empty character, and my belief that David or Dickens shows us little or nothing from her point of view suddenly has become a matter of paramount importance in my reading of Dickens, for among other things it has caused me to realize that I have always read him from a distinctly "male" position, and that what lacked reality for me does not always do so for women readers. In a sense this may be the most radically subjectivist chapter in the present study. For while I cannot claim that what Joan perceives about Agnes is actually *there,* in the text, I also cannot free myself from the feeling that Joan's construction of Agnes in terms of her own experiences is truer to "Agnes" than either David or Dickens have been.[12]

8 · The Intentional Phallus in Dickens and Hardy

The purpose of this chapter and the next is to demonstrate how the boundaries of possible signification for any reader are related to what that reader assumes is possible in a particular historical period, and equally to how he or she conceptualizes the author. A concern with the limits of signification indicates a need on the reader's part to stabilize response by setting boundaries around the range of referentiality the author could have *intended*—the last word here meaning not necessarily what is planned consciously so much as what is within the range of possible recognition by the author as present in his or her text. Such limits, and the authors to whom they are applied, are necessarily conceptualizations, not hard facts.

One editor among the several who rejected the essay on which this chapter is based wrote that while he agreed with my argument, such intentionalists as Hirsch had already had their theories of interpretation conclusively refuted. That comment seemed inapt because I believed I had presented the beginnings of a new way of looking at the relationship between intention, interpretation, and response, and because I did not in any case see the essay as an attempt to refute Hirsch, but rather one to show how "extrinsic" knowledge or a conceptualization of authorial intention might be used in the actual process of reading literary texts.

Although the idea for the pun in my chapter title was proposed by a colleague, probably as a joke, it seemed so fitting that I wondered why I had not thought of it. Freud writes of the supposed uncanniness of the female genitals that whenever a man dreams of a place or a country and says to himself, when he is still dreaming: "this place is familiar to me, I've been here before," we may interpret the place as being his mother's genitals or her body. In this case too [of men who say there is something uncanny about the female genitals], then, the *unheimlich* is what was once *heimisch,* familiar; the prefix *"un"* . . . is the token of repression. ["The 'Uncanny,' " 245]

This is surely in part the bias of a male writer, and if for a man the penis is not uncanny, it is surely the most familiar *(heimisch)* and private *(heimlich)* of his possessions; and it is something we would presumably not expect to find revealed or referred to directly in the text of a Victorian novel. If deemed present by a modern critic, it would have to be in some figurative form, and this presence as well as other sexual content could not, according to the conventional critical wisdom, be conscious to the Victorian author or reader. At a conference about two years before *Validity in Interpretation* was published, and at which Professor Hirsch introduced his distinction between meaning and significance (something then unfamiliar to me and to most of the audience), I raised the question of how that distinction would apply to the case of sexual innuendoes in *The Old Curiosity Shop.* For in the early chapters the demonic dwarf Quilp makes what seem to be sexual overtures to little Nell, offering to marry her when his present wife is dead, calling her " 'cherry-cheeked, red-lipped' " (chap. 6, 93), " 'chubby, rosy, cosy,' " and leering at what he calls the " 'capital kiss' " her grandfather gives her " 'just upon the rosy part' " (chap. 9, 125). Quilp also calls her a " 'fresh, blooming, modest little bud' " (125), implying early puberty. I asked Hirsch whether those critics who had stated that Nell was a sexual being, in spite of the way Dickens's novel seems to emphasize her purity, were dealing with an element of the novel's meaning, or its significance. He replied that such an inference of an undercutting of the novel's overt meaning could only be part of the significance attributed by a critic, and not the meaning.

I must infer (assuming that I remember correctly an incident from two decades ago) that this answer was based on an assumption, rather like David Bleich's about *Vanity Fair,* that one can be certain that Dickens did not intend to convey any such implication, indeed could not have imagined such a thing, since for him Nell represents the essence of presexual innocence, while Quilp's leering advances are evidence of that dwarf's evil nature. In *Validity in Interpretation* Hirsch attempts to confront the problem of unconscious (or "subconscious") intention:

> If a text has traits that point to subconscious meanings . . . these belong to the verbal meaning of the text only if they are coherent with the consciously willed type which defines the meaning as a whole. If such meanings are noncoherent with the willed type, then they do not belong to the verbal meaning which is by definition willed. As soon as *unwilled* meaning is admitted, then anything under the surface of the vast sea could be considered part of the iceberg, and verbal meaning would have no determinacy. [54]

I have difficulty with the concept of "willed type," and in particular with how one knows what is "willed" if it is also "subconscious." But I can see how one might argue that the verbal, or original, meaning of *The Old Curiosity Shop* cannot be that Quilp undercuts the ideals that the novel seems to profess; and one could go further in adducing the horrible, lonely death of Quilp as structural evidence of the novel's "willed type," its propositional meaning. From this perspective all of the modern readings of Quilp as demonic representative of vitality, savaging the ideals of the respectable characters, would be in Hirsch's terms opinions about the *significance* of what Dickens wrote in relation to a modern view of Victorian society, which is based on a particular concept of, and way of valuing, conscious and unconscious forces in man. Unless one can demonstrate that Dickens himself was expressing that view of the human condition and of human sexuality, such readings cannot be said to deal with meaning in Hirsch's sense. If my account is accurate, Hirsch was at that conference rejecting an instance of, and in the passage just quoted, rejecting a broader form of, deconstruction before the term was even familiar (indeed, known) in the English-speaking world; for several critics in the 1960s had already in effect argued that *The Old Curiosity Shop* deconstructs its own overt meanings.[1] And if this range of signification is said to be impossible for Dickens, such a judgment must be based on certain prior assumptions about the range of signification that *is* possible for him, and perhaps for all early and mid-Victorian authors. Yet such an assumption has no force but one of the assertion of a commonly held belief (or what used to be one).

In order to clarify the issue, before continuing with *The Old Curiosity Shop* I turn to a passage from another Dickens novel which illustrates in a parallel way the problem of distinguishing what Hirsch calls "verbal meaning" or "the author's meaning" from what he calls "significance." The example is from chapter 24 of *Martin Chuzzlewit,* published three years after *The Old Curiosity Shop.*

> It must be acknowledged that, asleep or awake, Tom's position in reference to this young lady was full of uneasiness. . . . When she spoke, Tom held his breath, so eagerly he listened; when she sang, he sat like one entranced. She

touched his organ, and from that bright epoch even it, the old companion of his happiest hours, incapable as he had thought it of elevation, began a new and deified existence. [340]

Reading this passage out of context, a post-Freudian reader is likely to be struck by a sexual pun remarkable for the thoroughness with which it is developed. And, when thus considered out of context it would not seem to be, in Hirsch's terms, "coherent with the willed type" of the novel. But *in* context it is perfectly coherent with the novel as a whole: Tom Pinch is in love with Mary Graham, and although he has earlier been depicted as virtually asexual—the village girls come to their windows to throw kisses to him because there was "no harm" in Tom Pinch (chap. 5)—now not only has Mary thrown a new aura around his musical organ, she has also caused him to feel a desire resembling none of his previous feelings. This produces the guilty dream that "he had betrayed his trust and run away with Mary Graham," who is his friend Martin Chuzzlewit's betrothed (chap. 24, 340).[2]

This set of feelings is consistent with the idea that Tom's sexual organ is now elevated in a way unfamiliar to him, and furthermore Tom's playing his musical organ is carried through as a central trope right to the closing page of the novel, in connection with the memory of his "old love" (chap. 54, 715).[3] Thus what seems to be an unconscious meaning is coherent with the "willed type" of the entire story of Tom Pinch's hopeless love. But need such a meaning have been unconscious? At one extreme of a spectrum of possibilities, it might be maintained that Dickens was so careful to avoid any sexual explicitness, in part for fear of losing his audience, that the apparent pun must be pure accident, something that twentieth-century academics might pruriently giggle over but that is simply not *in* the novel. A more moderate view is that although Dickens did not consciously intend such a pun, the words took the form they did because of Dickens's repressed awareness that Tom is experiencing a sexual awakening; such a position is of the sort often taken in the past by psychoanalytic critics of Victorian novels, who assume that sexual meanings must be unconscious in a respectable Victorian writer. At another extreme would be a view that until recent years no Dickensian would have accepted: that Dickens was fully conscious of and amused by the pun, but assumed that the average reader would not notice it, although it might constitute a private joke between himself and some of his more sophisticated readers.

There is no way to resolve this as a matter of objective fact, and the range of possible views of a double meaning in the passage suggests how difficult it can be to apply Hirsch's theory of willed verbal meaning, and especially of unconscious meaning coherent with the "willed type" of the work, to a particular textual situation. Our only basis for determining how we understand the text is one or another set of a priori assumptions about Victorian novelists and sex. And it is difficult for me to understand why it would be more presumptuous to assume that Dickens was aware of the pun he had created than to assume that it was either unconscious or accidental. We simply cannot know on the basis of any verifiable hypothesis, although one may suggest that Dickens was no fool and was well aware of the role of sexual desire in life and love. Meaning and significance, whatever the theoretical distinction between them, do not help here as practical guides to understanding. If any letter of Dickens's was extant which expressed horror at the accident or amusement at what he had got past his readers, that would be a piece of extrinsic evidence establishing the status of the apparent pun as verbal meaning, and in such a case, *pace* Wimsatt and Beardsley, the author's comment on his own work would have verified his meaning.

In the absence of such evidence, one might suggest that a consciousness of the pun is improbable because we find no such puns or other sexual explicitness elsewhere in Dickens's novels, so that the passage in *Martin Chuzzlewit* must be an isolated, and thus unimportant, instance. We can turn back to *The Old Curiosity Shop* to see whether this really is a persuasive argument. Seemingly there are no sexual puns in anything Quilp or the narrator of the novel says, and certainly there is nothing as striking as "she touched his organ." Yet several critics have pointed out that there is an equivocal meaning to Quilp's keeping his wife awake all night, until the end of his cigar glows red, especially as this follows upon her challenge to her ladyfriends that " 'the best-looking woman here couldn't refuse him if I was dead, and she was free, and he chose to make love to her. Come!' " (chap. 4, 76); and that when Quilp dispossesses Nell of her bed, "throwing himself on his back . . . with his pipe in his mouth, and then kicking up his legs and smoking violently" (chap. 11, 140–41), we may have sexually symbolic actions, if not verbal puns.

The relevance of this material (I should be begging a question were I to call it evidence) is that for a reader so disposed it tends to confirm the likelihood of Dickens's intention to give comic, and thus subversive, sexual overtones to Quilp's approach to Nell, and that, in relation to the passage from *Martin Chuzzlewit,* it strengthens the probability of Dickens's awareness of sexual innuendoes—an awareness that, if not fully conscious in the novelist at the time of writing, is not something one can confidently call repressed and purely symbolic in form, as in Freud's "dream-work," which disguises a reality too anxiety-producing to be confronted directly. Indeed, Tom Pinch's dream just prior to the description of the elevation of his organ (however one understands that) is one of guilty and implicitly sexual wish-fulfillment rather than elaborate symbolic dream-work.

If we accept Hirsch's definition of valid interpretation as the probable meaning inferred according to a willed type or "intrinsic genre," of the two instances from Dickens that of Tom Pinch seems more solidly verifiable as meaning. For it is undeniably part of Dickens's intention to present the character as sexually and emotionally immature, and as developing a whole new set of feelings owing to his attraction to a beautiful young woman. At the novel's close, having lapsed back into his role as a wise and holy fool,[4] Tom is seen playing his organ, explicitly a compensatory activity for not getting Mary. Dickens certainly also intends to suggest that Tom has reached a kind of ideal spiritual state, and yet because he cannot omit the pathos of Tom's memories of Mary or the substitute gratification of his organ, the narrator's peroration may strike one as special pleading: a use of rhetoric that sounds as though it doesn't even convince the speaker. And, if we infer a discomfort in Dickens with his own language here, why is that not a part of the authorial meaning? While he may not have set out to express discomfort, intention surely resides in what one achieves rather than in what one meant and to some extent failed to do. But here I begin to make what I consider the unavoidable link between the inference of intention and the effect of the text for a reader.

As I understand Hirsch's scrupulous attempt to develop a coherent model of meaning, he tries to avoid the error of placing all meaning in the author's mind (where no interpreter could find it), by locating meaning in an unspecified place between the author's mental and verbal acts and the actual text in its totality. This suggests that meaning is not coterminous with the work: it is an aspect of its verbal structure whose interpretation must precede any explication of the work's *significance* in relation to anything outside itself. But how can a reader infer meaning without constructing signification and thus, in Hirsch's sense, significance? The danger in Hirsch's concept of meaning and significance is that it will reduce all meaning to the propositional, the "message," a danger he seems quite aware of in his later writings. Even in his own demonstrations of how to read for propositional meaning, he as often as not fails to convince one that his theory when put into practice produces something closer to the "author's meaning" than what other interpreters have achieved (for example in his comparison of his own reading of a Wordsworth poem with previous ones [*Validity*, 227–30]).

I think the only basis for drawing a line between meaning and significance in the matter of Tom Pinch, between organ = only a musical instrument, and organ = musical instrument and phallus, is one's own particular set of assumptions about Victorian sexual attitudes and, more specifically, taboos that may have dominated Dickens as a novelist. It does have to be said, however, that a reader of *Martin Chuzzlewit* who did not know that Dickens wrote the novel in the early 1840s, or who was unaware that overt sexual puns would never appear in books published at that time by respectable publishers, might well miss the uncertain status of that "pun," and simply assume that it *is* overt; such a reading would be inadequate, and this is another instance of literary understanding depending, to a degree, on what the reader knows.[5] Assumptions about the range of possible signification cannot lead to decisive conclusions, and this may be especially true in those areas of literature and of human experience, such as sex and aggression, which may produce anxiety and around which some of the debates about the boundaries of meaning, unconscious meaning, and significance tend to revolve. Hirsch gingerly approaches this issue in mentioning the Freud-Jones readings of *Hamlet* as an Oedipal drama, but backs off with a number of (to me) obfuscating "ifs"; he does, however, grant that the fact that Shakespeare is a pre-Freudian does not preclude the possibility that an Oedipal interpretation is valid (*Validity*, 122–26).

Part of the difficulty seems to reside in one's sense of cultural history and of past attitudes towards sex and aggression, and I shall turn presently to a third, more complex literary example of how both this difficulty and the concept of the author operate in the process of interpretation. But first I want to stress that when I argue for the probable manifestness (but not the fully conscious intentionality) of sexual meanings in passages from Dickens, I am thinking of them as historically, and not anachronistically, present. When we have a question of implied rather than simple lexical meaning (if there is such a thing), the question of historical validity will be the more difficult to resolve.[6] No general supposition about what the average contemporary reader of Dickens would have understood can lead to a "correct" conceptualization of authorial meaning; but one may consider the possible secondary lexical meanings in their literary and historical contexts. Thus, Quilp calls Nell "cherry-cheeked," and "cheeks" was used to refer to posteriors as early as the mid-eighteenth century; "part" might refer euphemistically to "private part[s]" from Middle English onwards; and "organ" at the very least has as one of its meanings in Dickens's time as in ours a functioning part of the body. But it is the context, not the lexicon, that makes credible the suggestion of probable sexual meanings: Quilp's direct, if parodic, advances to Nell and his wife's acclamation of his irresistibility, and Tom's frustrated desire for Mary. Mark Spilka has suggested that Quilp is a symbolic phallus (in "Little Nell Revisited"), something more conjectural than the question of individual verbal meanings. The possibility of the author's fully conscious awareness of sexual content becomes considerably stronger, however, when we recall that in the novel's originally intended conclusion Quilp was to be revealed as the former paramour of the "Dragon," Sally Brass, and progenitor of the tough little girl whom Dick Swiveller names "the Marchioness." And Dickens chose to make Quilp a Punch-like figure, thus implying a connection with the long-popular tradition of the dwarf, and Punch in particular, as the "little man," or phallic symbol.

The existence of Dickens's original text making the parentage of the Marchioness explicit (and once one knows this rejected portion of text one starts to find lots of hints of it in the published text) suggests another potential means of recovering—or, more precisely, conceptualizing—intention, and thus placing but also widening the boundaries of signification: namely the examination of the process of composition when multiple versions are extant. Although the availability of such revisions and multiple versions may not be a typical situation, the use here of a more extended example may serve to illustrate some of the ways in which intention, meaning, and response can be seen to be interrelated. The process of composition, like the intention in the author's mind prior to or while writing, is not identical with the text, and thus when we look at multiple versions we are looking at the detritus of history. The individual versions, like biographical data, remain disparate in themselves, and a meaning that is overtly present at one stage but missing at another does not, or so it normally is assumed, become part of the second text once we know about the first. The author has, after all, willed the omission of this semantic element. And yet only for those textual critics who privilege the author's final text as the best one does the earlier version remain merely a key to the process by which that final text was arrived at. If we do not take this latter position, what functions might multiple versions have in the process of coming to understand a text?

My example of an instance in which the relations between the meanings of various versions of a text, the "author's meaning," and the reader's understanding become truly problematic (which I take in present usage to mean interesting) is the first meeting between Jude Fawley and Arabella Donn, constituting the bulk of book I, chapter 6, of *Jude the Obscure*. Before the first bound edition was published Hardy had bowdlerized this scene and much else for serial publication in *Harper's Monthly Magazine,* and subsequently reviewers of the book edition singled out the unbowdlerized version of this chapter for special attack, which is probably what led Hardy to revise it for the 1903 Macmillan edition.[7] In the first case, the serialization in *Harper's Monthly Magazine* (titled *The Simpletons* in its first install-ment and *Hearts Insurgent* thereafter), the alterations to crucial parts of the text are extreme and in some ways absurd and were committed by Hardy to satisfy J. Henry Harper's sense of his readers' delicacy. But in the second case (1903) Hardy was attempting to satisfy the objections against his supposed bad taste and pornographic tenden-cies in the first book edition of book I, chapter 6, without totally violating his artistic conscience. The 1903 alterations to this chapter remain essentially the same in the 1912 Wessex edition and thus are apparently enshrined as the author's definitive intentions.[8]

My purpose in looking into these three versions of Jude Fawley's sexual awakening is not in order to establish a definitive text, but to demonstrate how each represents different ways of expressing, or avoiding expressing, a certain set of meanings. My argument is that Hardy's fullest artistic intention can be thought of as existing prior to or outside of the three versions of the episode, and as being expressed more or less completely in each; and thus that a compari-son of the three can lead to a plausible understanding of that, so to speak, transcendent set of meanings. But in the process of this expo-sition I shall suggest that such a conceptualization of authorial inten-tion is inevitably an act of the reader, and that therefore intention is objectified only in the reading experience and in communicating the nature of that experience to others.

The variations among the three versions of book I, chapter 6, have to do with Hardy's treatment of the curious missile thrown at Jude by Arabella, which awakens him from his dreams of scholarly and priestly achievement into the world of sexual passion. In all three versions the missile is thrown, and in all three it is possible to infer that it is a pig's penis. In the first book version (based on the full manuscript that Hardy initially altered only for Harper) great comic play is made with this item: it is described as a limp piece of flesh hanging over the rail of the footbridge upon which Jude and Arabella meet, and at which both of them stare without full consciousness of its significance as they talk. At the end of the episode Arabella's two friends laugh uproariously at the fact that the couple were conversing with this object between them. In the 1903 edition all references to the pizzle are omitted after it is thrown and Jude asks the girls which of them threw it.

Although Hardy asserted that the serial version did not represent his artistic intentions, the changes he made in this particular chapter for *Harper's* are surprisingly limited, and since they were made in order to reduce overt sexual content in a text appearing in a family magazine, they are important as an indication of just where Hardy believed that content to be detectable. Although crucial parts of the the plot of *Jude the Obscure* (as before it, in the serial version of *Tess of the d'Urbervilles*) are in this version mangled beyond belief to protect the cheek of the young person from blushes, in the pizzle-throwing scene all of the references to the item on the bridge-rail, as well as the hilarity of the girls, are left in. What has been changed, first of all, is the initial denomination of this item as "the characteristic part of a barrow-pig" (1896, 38). In the serial it becomes "a piece of flesh, portion of a recently killed pig" (*The Simpletons*, installment 1, *Harper's Monthly Magazine* 90 [December 1894]: 79). In *both* the altered versions, however, Hardy omits the information that Arabella herself had just cut this part from the carcass of the pig—and this is the only important omission from the first book version common to the serial and 1903 versions. The relevant passage in the first book edition begins, "She was a complete and substantial female human, no more, no less; and Jude was almost certain that to her was attributable the enterprise of throwing the lump of offal at him, the bladder from which she had obviously cut it off lying close beside her" (1896, 39). In the 1903 and subsequent editions the "enterprise" becomes that "of attracting his attention from dreams of the humaner letters to what was simmering in the minds around him."

What did Hardy think he was doing in making the changes for *Harper's*? Evidently he felt that the phrase "characteristic part of a barrow-pig" was a key to the identity of the particular part, since a male pig might be said to be "characterized" by his penis. Without this identifier, and with a much vaguer phrase, presumably the more innocent urban readers of *Harper's* could take the part to be some other item that is "useless" except for greasing one's boots—a point Hardy makes in all three versions. Having eliminated the direct implication that the part is a pig's pizzle and the pig itself a previously castrated boar (the meaning of "barrow-pig"), Hardy apparently felt free to leave in the serial's text the comically suggestive elements of Jude's and Arabella's encounter on the bridge, while nonetheless removing any suggestion that Arabella herself had cut off the "portion of a recently killed pig." It is tempting to wonder whether Hardy here is having a bit of fun with his readers' capacity for suppressing their own naughtier intuitions (as Dickens perhaps is in chap. 24 of *Martin Chuzzlewit*), or was simply uncertain as to what constituted objectionable content; but the omission of the nature of Arabella's specific role as pork-butcher in this passage is another matter.

In what we may call the original version (the first book edition), because it is the one upon which the alterations were performed, we find certain actions described. Arabella throws the characteristic part of a castrated pig (penis without testicles) at Jude; and it is a part that she has herself amputated from the already mutilated boar. They then meet on the footbridge and carry on a conversation of a fairly bland sort, but whose underlying sexual tension is comically objectified in their subconscious awareness of that piece of flesh dangling over the rail. In the 1903 version and later, however, although the "characteristic part" is present, and the term "barrow-pig" is used, the fact of Arabella as amputator is absent, as are all other references to the pizzle. We may conjecture about Hardy's attitude towards his readers that when confronted by a presumably naive, periodical-reading audience and prudish publisher, he saw the main problem as eliminating any easy identification of the "part," and perhaps avoiding making Arabella too coarse. When faced with the task of toning down the sexual implications of the whole episode for a more educated, book-reading public, he left in the identification but dropped what many reviewers had objected to as the coarseness and vulgarity of the humor surrounding the object identified, and eliminated as well Arabella's role as amputator, which might also contribute to a sense of her coarseness for that more elite audience.

He thus changed the tone and emphasis and, I would argue, the meaning to a degree. Taken together, however, these variants bring into focus an implied meaning more generally pervading *Jude the Obscure*: that Arabella is, through her sexuality and aggressiveness, an emasculator. In compromising between artistic integrity and audience placation in the 1903 revisions, Hardy simply toned down this implied meaning without eliminating it. Applying (as I understand it) Hirsch's concept of "willed type" or "intrinsic genre" as a key to probable meaning, one may say that the genre of Hardy's *original* version of the episode is a partly symbolic or emblematic mode; in this mode the pig's penis is not an incidental detail that could have been anything else, and its meaning is only made somewhat more abstract in the 1903 changes. The emblematic meaning of the doubly emasculated boar, similarly, is played down in 1903 but not eliminated, and Arabella's connection with the fate of the boar is still compounded in the later conflict with Jude during the pig-killing episode that ends their marriage.

Although D. H. Lawrence claims with some indignation that Arabella's connection with pigs is tendentious, a way for Hardy to discredit Arabella by connecting her sexuality with "low" animality (*Study of Thomas Hardy*, 489), another and perhaps dominant association with the pig in this novel is with the male, and of Arabella with the symbolic castration of the male. In the pig-killing scene (book I, chap. 10) the quarrel is between Jude, who wants to kill the pig—if it must be killed at all—quickly and mercifully, and Arabella, who wants to let it bleed to death slowly. On the surface this is a conflict between Arabella's materialistic practicality (the meat will be "blooded" and sell for less if the animal is killed too quickly) and Jude's perhaps overidealistic humanitarianism. But on another level Jude is identified with the pig, as he earlier identifies himself with rooks and worms, and later with a trapped rabbit. And so, as Arabella is a killer of pigs, she is a destroyer of men: she stifles Jude's ambitions temporarily and prevents his ever achieving them; she marries Jude, leaves him, remarries another man, and at the very end remarries Jude, an act that leads directly to his death.

Where, then, in dealing with literary understanding, can one draw a useful line between meaning and what Hirsch calls significance? I seriously question that one can, for two reasons. In interpretation a "meaning," if it is not to be simply a restatement (that is, a quotation or paraphrase) of what is in the verbal text, cannot be separated from other elements in the work— something Hirsch is careful to emphasize in his stress upon coherence. And the revealing of an "original meaning" or "authorial meaning," though it may (as I hope I have demonstrated with the three pig's pizzles) be based on various kinds of information extrinsic to the text, also involves a number of subjective factors, the most important of which is the reader's conceptualization of an author. The nature of this conceptualization will depend on so many variants of reading style among individual readers that any claim for the "most probable" meaning can refer to no more than what a defined group of readers *believe* to be the most probable limits to signification.

For me as for many critics today it is more interesting to consider how readers arrive at meanings than to try to dictate how one *should* arrive at meanings. What has happened to me as reader as a result of learning of these instances of authors revising their texts is that such extrinsic knowledge as that of Dickens's original intent and Hardy's textual alterations becomes a part of the palimpsest of my understanding when I read *any* version of these texts. What I am saying is that matters external to a text do affect one's reading of it, but that "the author" ultimately has no existence except as a reader conceptualizes him or her; this may be done entirely from within the reading of a text (and thereby sometimes may result in historical or biographical inaccuracies), or with the additional factor of extrinsic knowledge (historical, biographical, or textual), but in either case the process is essentially subjective even though one retains a sense of the text as "other."

So, to return to the title of this chapter, who put the intentional phallus there? In the case of Hardy, it would be difficult to deny that a penis is thrown at a man by a woman; but whether that pig's pizzle is also a phallus, that is, symbolic and of importance for the novel's structure of meanings, and if so, just how, is an open question for the reader. And in the case of Dickens, the question is equally open: In *Martin Chuzzlewit* there is an organ "elevated" by love and sexual desire, and Dickens put it there; but is it a phallus? In *The Old Curiosity Shop* there is a little man, full of mysterious energy, leering over a young girl—and Dickens put *him* there. But how "organ" and "elevated," "rosy part" (among other ambiguous terms in Quilp's leering overtures to Nell) and his Punch-like qualities are taken is again dependent on the reader's assumptions and style of conceptualizing both authors and meanings. And so the phallus as a symbol of the penis, the male, or more generally the erotic, though made potentially available for the reader by an act of the author, is really available only as something the reader *may* construct. And whether the reader will be motivated or not to construct meaning in a certain way depends upon the limits of signification, the possible range of the conceptualized author's meanings, in the reader's mind.

9 · Making *Mansfield Park* Feel Right

If all narratives could be assumed to "mean" in the same way, as, for example, paraphrasable didactic statements, autobiographical allegory, or mimetic representations of reality, then the problem of literary understanding would be infinitely simpler. But even within a single genre such as the novel, the modes in which signification may be perceived to occur are many and varied, while there is also inevitably an interrelation between the way meaning can be said to emerge and the reader who construes/constructs that meaning. Yet readers and perhaps critics in particular tend to have individual predilections for reading the meanings of all works in more or less the same way. Thus one may read the major nineteenth-century novels as primarily didactic, confessional, mimetic, mythic, or self-deconstructing with varying degrees of strains on one's ingenuity, and on the credulity of those who read differently. There may be a sense of security to be gained from adopting a single style of reading, or, if one's loyalties to some interpretive system or ideology are strong enough, from reading according to one basic set of analogies, usually assumed by the critic to be truths. As should be evident from other chapters in this book, I myself tend to "discover" certain kinds of meaning and to pass over others, finding ways to debunk overt propositional meaning by valorizing elements in a text that I think act counter to the didactic meaning or "message"; and even the initial construing of propositional meaning is guided by my style of reading, and thus should be called constructing rather than construing. Yet whether I am constructing an overt propositional meaning or its subversive opposite (also propositional), ultimately I not only cannot know how close to the author's consciousness or feelings *either* aspect of these meanings may have been, but I cannot know whether my reading is not after all idiosyncratic, a going "outside the text" to "make up" meanings of my own; for the ability to persuade others remains the only available kind of verification—and a shaky one if *verification* is used in its strict sense.

One aspect of my motivation to search for hidden, subversive meaning is my rejection of unity as a criterion of value; this may be simply another part of the rebellion against the New Critical precepts I imbibed as an undergraduate, or such a rejection—which is certainly not peculiar to me—may result from my particular position in history, culture, and social class. The rejection of unity is a recent phenomenon, and unity itself was a culturally derived aesthetic criterion rooted in history, rather than a transcendent one. Thirty years ago in a book on "literary openness" Robert Martin Adams attempted to oppose to the criterion of unity a concept of "open form," but it was claimed by him only for certain works. Defining literary form as "a structure of meanings, intents, and emphases, i.e., verbal gestures," Adams is concerned to demonstrate that some literary works include "a major unresolved conflict with the intent of displaying its unresolvedness" (13). This sounds quite like what Mukařovský calls "intentional unintentionality—devices that affect the viewer as a violation of semantic or semiotic unity and which the originator has consciously introduced into the work for this purpose. Unintentionality, thus becomes, in fact, a formal device" ("Intentionality," 105).[1] It is notable that although many of Adams's literary examples are from fiction, he cites not a single nineteenth-century English novel, but rather takes all instances from the modern novel and what he sees as its precursors, narratives by Cervantes, Swift, Stendhal, and Flaubert. Such an exclusion may be merely contingent (the nineteenth-century English novel not being Adams's field), but I think it more likely that it stems from his insistence on the *intent* to display unresolvedness. For in general the plots of the Victorians and pre-Victorians such as Austen at least seem to be intended to effect a resolution of conflicts and contradictions, while a few novelists such as Sterne or Hogg (in *A Justified Sinner*) would seem to be repeatedly demonstrating the irresolvability of their narratives, and announcing the impossibility of ascribing conclusive meanings to them.

But in recent years it has become something of a critical project to uncover such qualities in Victorian novels. Thus, Barry Westburg finds that *Great Expectations* is a "confession about fiction-making," rather than about life (185), and Peter K. Garrett in *The Victorian Multiplot Novel* argues that the plots of such writers as Dickens, Thackeray, Eliot, and Trollope present multiple perspectives that, when their significance is properly understood, make it impossible to assign a single dominant meaning. *Mansfield Park* does not have a multiple plot, but nonetheless it seems to me in some ways as "open" as any story by Kafka, especially if I take the multiplicity of interpretations as one guide to openness. As I argued in chapter 2, the dominant motivation behind criticism is the need to clarify and stabilize one's relationships to texts that are in some way disturbing or puzzling. One way to do this, indeed, is to conclude that certain texts—intentionally "open" works, multiplot novels that seem to be striving for resolution, or such a heavily plotted novel as *Great Expectations*—actually revel in their own openness, undermine their own drive to resolve themselves, or are really *about* themselves.

No critic I have read (and I do not mean that there might not be one) has claimed for the problems of reading *Mansfield Park* a solution of this kind. And although there are other literary works whose published interpretations range over so broad a spectrum that they seem to present a series of mutually contradictory positions, among nineteenth-century British novels *Mansfield Park* has a special status in this regard. Historically, the vexation with Jane Austen's novel seems to stem mainly from the failure of its heroine, Fanny Price, to exhibit any of the sparkling qualities of an Elizabeth Bennet or an Emma Woodhouse, and from a related sense that Austen has somehow thus betrayed her readers and herself. It has provoked among modern critics a wide range of judgments that at their extremes are polar opposites: among others, that the novel represents Jane Austen's failure of nerve, the abandonment of her ironic vision; that it is the central work of her *oeuvre;* and that it *is* fundamentally ironic. *Mansfield Park* is thus particularly useful in an attempt to consider the question of how and where the limits of signification are placed by different readers.

I include later in this chapter an account of how I have found it possible both to explain my original discomfort with Austen's most problematic work and to accommodate it as a novel worth both rereading and teaching. This accommodation did not develop in a vacuum, nor is it a final one, for the *Mansfield Park* debate continues, and each critic gives me a different perspective on the novel, which I may or may not be able to incorporate into my own reading. There is no doubt that discomfort or a much stronger kind of negative response has been reported by many critics, although usually in the rhetoric of objective interpretation. If we wish to talk about the constraints the text imposes on interpretation—and most reader-response theorists agree that there are constraints, even if the degree of concern with them varies—we must first recognize that even if one can say that the constraints are somehow in the text, any given reader will select only those that suit what Stanley Fish would call the reader's "interpretive strategy," Norman Holland the reader's "identity theme," and David Bleich, perhaps, the reader's sense of self and affective associations. I myself prefer a more neutral designation such as the reader's style of reading. The question, as Jonathan Culler reminds us, of what, in the development of literary understanding, is textual constraint and what is individual response (and, it should be added, selection or emphasis) is not answerable with certainty. One reader may feel strongly constrained by the text of *David Copperfield* to think of the relationship between David, his mother, and Murdstone as Oedipal, while another might think of that as an imposition of meaning on the text, and stress instead the fairy-tale morphology of the cruel step-parent and the child's running away from home to seek his fortune. Judgments of *Mansfield Park* have been substantially more polarized than that hypothetical example.

Lionel Trilling has described the reader's problem with *Mansfield Park* in relation to Austen's other novels most cogently. "No other great novel," he writes, "has so anxiously asserted the need to find security, to establish, in fixity and closure, a refuge from the dangers of openness and chance. There is scarcely one of our modern pieties that it does not offend" (210). Moreover, it "seems to controvert everything that its predecessor *[Pride and Prejudice]* tells us about life" (211). Yet for his own reasons Trilling wishes to save *Mansfield Park* as a masterpiece; and to this end he begins with the drastic strategy of dismissing the heroine as one with whom it is difficult to be sympathetic and then goes on to read the novel less as a representation of character and society than as a dramatized utterance that uses the depiction of society to make certain propositional points. But these points are not didactic in the usual sense. Trilling does not see *Mansfield Park* as a moral or cautionary tale, a consciously intended lesson. Rather, he constructs as its author a Jane Austen who is an agent of what he calls the "Terror of secularized spirituality" (230), under which every individual is to be judged not on the basis of actions, but according to his or her internal spiritual condition in a secularized world. Thus Trilling's Austen scores off Mary Crawford for the pure "style" of her being, her lack of any principle of "sincerity" (220), just as the Price family of Portsmouth is condemned as vulgar for their lack of interest in Fanny. Trilling himself seems to me ambivalent about the Austenian vision of society that he has inferred (or constructed): to some extent he seems allied with his Austen in passing judgment on the spiritually less adequate characters. But at the same time he expresses discomfort with this alliance, and to retain his judgment that *Mansfield Park* is a great novel it seems he must find that this terrifying vision is undercut by an ironic one, which turns out more than a bit surprisingly to be the vision of an ideal state of existence in the reconstituted household at Mansfield Park as embodied in Lady Bertram, a vegetable-like creature who is "safe from the Terror of secularized spirituality." And thus the irony of Trilling's Jane Austen is directed against her own criteria of personal adequacy, in admitting indirectly her own dream of a blissful existence "unconscious to the demands of personality," a dream that, according to Trilling, "speaks to our secret inexpressible hopes" of shutting "out the world and the judgment of the world" (230).

Trilling's is one of the most ingenious attempts to save *Mansfield Park* from its detractors (and from the critic's own doubts), and it also seems a very personal one: it is as though Trilling is speaking his own "secret inexpressible hopes" for an unjudged, unharried, and conflict-free existence. Marvin Mudrick is more straightforward in his judgment of the Jane Austen who wrote this novel, and his chapter on *Mansfield Park* remains the most energetic account of a reader's negative response to it. Referring to the principle of "freedom" that he considers *Pride and Prejudice* among other of Austen's novels to espouse, Mudrick says that "in *Mansfield Park,* Jane Austen abridges this freedom for the first time. The individual can no longer act without locating himself. Place and group have, indeed, become central: the individual faces, not a choice of action, but a choice of allegiance; and the action of the novel is a collision of worlds" (155). Although this sentence is couched in objective terms, the extent to which Mudrick is writing about his own response becomes clear in several of his remarks on Austen's heroine, Fanny Price. Thus, "We never take the author's word for Fanny. The surface is there: humility, shyness, unfailing moral vision; but behind them we feel something persistently unpleasant—complacency and envy, perhaps; certainly an odd lackluster self-pity" (161). Mudrick does not trouble to outline his critical principles, and within his chapter on *Mansfield Park* he shifts back and forth between assertions about "we" or "the reader," and a mode of objective interpretation, usually designating Austen as the one who is to blame for the novel's deficiencies. This is a kind of shifting that, if perhaps less common today, can still be found in critical studies of literature and for many critics seems the natural way to write.

But what kind of discourse do we have when two ways of locating signification—in "the reader" or in the text and novelist—are thus employed almost indiscriminately? That is to say, what are the statements about, and are they all about the same object, or does the object shift with the rhetoric? I would venture to say that, at least in the case of a critic like Mudrick who writes with a fine and evident passion, the object is indeed the same: not the literary text, but the critic's response to it. The fact that the particular response is presented as the one that all readers have, or *should* have, does not alter the matter. Critical writing is always an attempt at persuasion, and the reader of Austen and Mudrick is free to compare his or her own response with the critic's and accept as much of it as matches or clarifies what that reader has already felt or opens up a new area of response. This is perhaps all the objectivity that criticism can claim; but there have been enough reactions to Mudrick (or to others who read *Mansfield Park* in a similar way) which attempt to refute his argument on objective grounds, that I think a bit more attention to the details of his reading style (or "critical strategy") is in order.

I have earlier cited Morse Peckham's definition of authorial intention as that constructed "historical situation" to which the reader looks in order to know how to respond when he or she is uncertain of the "appropriate verbal response." And although one's impression of Mudrick as critic may be that he is little plagued by uncertainty, I suggest that something like what Peckham describes happens more than once in the course of Mudrick's chapter on *Mansfield Park*. For example, when Mudrick says, "The thesis of *Mansfield Park* is severely moral: that one world, representing the genteel orthodoxy of Jane Austen's time, is categorically superior to any other. Nowhere else does Jane Austen take such pains to make up the mind of her reader" (155), this assertion *could* be an inference from the novel of the author's conscious intent. Yet the very image of Austen taking "pains to make up the mind of the reader" indicates that "Austen" here is a construction by the critic of the author's intention for the purpose of justifying the critic's feeling of annoyance at her, his feeling of being manipulated by the novel towards certain beliefs— manipulation and beliefs that he locates in "Jane Austen." And in order to justify his resistance to that manipulation, this critic constructs not one but two Jane Austens: the authentic one, whose proper mode is irony and who is much like Mary Crawford, and the one she has become when she is writing *Mansfield Park* because "under such social and personal pressures [as her family's view of her as the 'type of Christian womanhood'], which must have become more insistent as she saw herself year after year less likely ever to disavow them, it is easy to believe that Jane Austen felt obliged to produce a work of uncompromising moral purpose, whatever the bent of her taste and imagination" (172). And the supposedly authentic Jane he decides to associate with Mary Crawford, bringing them together by an act of imagination (172).

> However deliberately, Jane Austen is attacking much of herself in the image of Mary Crawford: the attack is on the most earnest ethical gounds, and fixes the tone of the novel; and the consequence of the attack is an aesthetic failure. We return, then, to the system, the enclave of conformity, which triumphs over Mary in the novel, but which Mary triumphantly survives as a living figure; just as Jane Austen survives the wreck and oblivion of her closed society. [170]

There is indeed considerable evidence extant of resemblances between the actual Jane and her creation, Mary Crawford. Austen's letters are full of Mary's kind of skepticism, irony, and the seeing of other people as "wrong," and Mudrick himself makes this point (169). The description of Austen surviving "the wreck and oblivion of her closed society," however, does not have a very clear referent (surviving in what way—in the immortality of her works, which do include *Mansfield Park*?). It could be an anticipation of the opening of Mudrick's next chapter, in which he insists that "*Emma* is a throwing off of chains. . . . Its surface is, in fact, unmarred by a trace of self-justification, ill humor, or backsliding into morality" (181)—in other words, that Jane Austen "survives" in writing *Emma*. Yet when one recalls that a significant part of the narrative structure of *Emma* is given over to its heroine's reform from egotism by the agency of, and her ultimate marriage to, none other than a Mr. Knightley, this seems less a literary analysis than a thankful sigh of relief for the return of Austen's irony, as though bands around the critic's chest are loosened when turning from the conclusion of *Mansfield Park* to the opening chapters of *Emma*.

I by no means intend to ridicule Mudrick's criticism; as one who has had what seems to be a typical (and not just a male) response to Fanny Price, it is gratifying for me to see Mary Crawford thus justified, to see Fanny properly disparaged, and to be told, in essence, that we ultimately need not bother about *Mansfield Park* because in it Jane Austen deserts her true, ironic vision. Yet it is something of a paradox that there seems to be a substantial agreement between Mudrick and critics who attempt to justify *Mansfield Park* on the basis of its mature and sophisticated moral vision: for all of them believe that the didactic and moralistic content of that novel is central to Austen's intentions and to the novel's success or failure. It is just that they make very different judgments of the value of that content in relation to Austen's other novels. Alistair Duckworth, for example, finds that we must "see Fanny . . . as the representative of Jane Austen's own fundamental commitment to an inherited culture—not merely to the 'ceremonies of life,' but to the 'conduct . . . the result of good principles' . . . , to a social order founded in religion, which the country house can in fact embody, but which, more importantly, it can be made aesthetically to represent" (73). And he therefore takes *Mansfield Park* to be central among Austen's novels. It seems clear that Mudrick could never accept the notion of the centrality of the novel, nor that of Austen's "fundamental commitment" to such values, but he would almost certainly agree that Austen intentionally embodies such values in *Mansfield Park*.

But what could Mudrick, who seems to believe that he is interpreting objectively, say to Stein Haugom Olsen's rebuttal of Mudrick's supposedly incorrect reading of *Mansfield Park* and, in particular, of the character of Mary Crawford? Olsen quotes Mudrick's remark that "we observe Mary as impatient with dullness, evil, and pomposity, but good-tempered, affectionate, intelligent, kind" (Mudrick, 165; Olsen, 138) and follows this by quoting two passages from Austen's novel. The first describes Mary's "ill-will" towards Sir Thomas Bertram, who has made it clear that Edmund is to become a clergyman in the parish of Thornton Lacey, and the second describes Mary's apprehension about visiting her relations (her half-sister, Mrs. Grant, and her clergyman husband) in the country. The first is supposed to prove that Mudrick is wrong about Mary's good temper, and the second, about her capacity for affection. Of the second passage from *Mansfield Park* Olsen says that it

neatly juxtaposes the attitude of the two half-sisters. . . . It is observed unobtrusively of Mrs. Grant that "she had always loved" Mary. About Mary nothing is said except about her manoeuvering to avoid being exposed to a "style of living and tone of society" which she would not be able to tolerate. The reader is discreetly informed about Mrs. Grant's affections for her half-sister, and if Mary were really affectionate, this would be exactly, one would think, the kind of situation in which it would be appropriate to inform the reader of her affection as well. Instead, the author shows Mary's affection as thoroughly subordinated to her self-interest. . . . So Mudrick's description "affectionate" is clearly inadequate judged by this passage, which occurs as soon as Mary is introduced to the reader. [139]

Allowing that Mary's self-interest is emphasized throughout *Mansfield Park,* knowing how subtle the barb of Austen's irony can be one might question whether Mrs. Grant "had always loved" Mary, or whether she thinks she *should*. Mrs. Grant is considerably older, and one might expect that the half-sisters barely know one another.

It is often possible to find "evidence" in Austen's text (or in any narrative) which can prove any point that is not too outrageous. And I think Mudrick's real point about Mary is made elsewhere than in the passages quoted by Olsen: since Mudrick believes that Mary is a part of Austen, he attributes the seemingly negative aspects of Mary's personality to Austen's self-rejection, her intermittent conservatism; and he can argue that Mary *is* genuinely affectionate in her love for Edmund even though he is to become a clergyman. It seems to me clear that Olsen does not take Mudrick on his own ground, but abstracts from his argument those details he finds useful to demonstrate how an interpretation can be "incorrect." And it is worth noting that Mudrick's sentence begins with "we observe," suggesting, as much of Mudrick's rhetoric does, that he is talking about his own response—a response that suggests a latent novel with Mary Crawford as protagonist lying beneath the surface of Austen's didacticism and rigid moralism. But because Mudrick does not employ such a concept as that of manifest and latent meaning, he is forced ultimately to see Austen's apparent failure of irony and her submission to conventionality as *the* meaning of *Mansfield Park,* and thus to reject the novel as a failure.

Avrom Fleishman, writing fifteen years after Mudrick, puts the central problem for readers of *Mansfield Park* in this way: "Was she simply reflecting the prevailing social and economic constraints on individual freedom; was she defending or attacking the class system which enforced those constraints?" And he goes on to say that "the latest Austen critics [and this allusion includes Mudrick] have entertained no such doubts and have decided boldly that she was a conservative" (11). Today this is no longer quite the case, as we shall see. Fleishman claims to read the novel by means of a "multi-perspectival criticism" (ix), and to me his most original contribution to the *Mansfield Park* debate is to see Fanny sympathetically though critically, claiming that she "is presented as an inextricable knot of moral idealism and self-protective egoism, and—to convince us of the binding power of the knot—we are struck by the directness with which a high moral standard is put in the service of self-protection" (78). In other words, Fanny uses her "high moral standard" as a way of coping with a threatening world, so that she has a psychological presence and is not merely a spokeswoman for Austen's assumed conservatism. As Fleishman puts it earlier in his study, "Fanny is presented not as a paragon of virtue but as a weak woman with self-defensive and self-aggrandizing impulses who, because of her economic dependency and her social inferiority, is forced to adopt what Alfred Adler has called a feminine, submissive style of life" (45). So, while the typical reader may feel discomfort or something stronger with Fanny, we should see her irritating qualities as psychological defenses (see chap. 4, above, for similar critical justifications of another supposed paragon of female virtue, Esther Summerson in *Bleak House*).[2]

An issue raised in Fleishman's monograph, though it is not stated explicitly by that critic, may in fact be the central problem of interpretation of or response to *Mansfield Park:* what the novel is *about.* It is one thing to say that we may reasonably infer in reading the novel its author's sympathy with Fanny Price and her belief in the rightness of how things work out in the end, but quite another to say that the text is "about" its own surface moral system, as I think Duckworth does. For what a novel is about for a reader is to some extent a function of what that reader finds himself or herself paying attention to. As I read *Mansfield Park* I find it necessary to consider the novel's discursive meanings as well as its effect on me, but to resist being trapped into an excessive respect for the coherence of the author's apparent overt intentions. Recently and within a single volume *(Jane Austen: New Perspectives),* three critics have seen Fanny Price quite differently. Margaret Kirkham sees her as representing Austen's rational, Wollstonecraftian feminism and being intended by Austen as an ironic trap for the reader, in that there are many hints that she is *not* the conduct-book model such characters as Henry Crawford consider her. Marylea Meyersohn finds Fanny "a center of nonenergy," who "solves the dilemma of self-expression through the mode of passivity—in Austen's words, by resisting 'the temptation of immediate pleasure' . . . in our words, by the deferral of gratification" (224). Nina Auerbach describes Fanny as tying Austen to the Romantics by the virtue of being a kind of Frankenstein, who must "make" her "malleable" world, while Mary Crawford, rather than Fanny, is the figure closest to a Mary Wollstonecraft in her ability to feel "sisterhood" with other women. Thus while one of these feminist critics champions Fanny, one finds her powerful and perhaps repulsively fascinating, with Meyersohn's response somewhere in between. Auerbach sees Fanny as the "conqueror" of her world by means of her isolation (218), and its moral arbiter as a result of the loss of fixed values in that world. The larger theoretical question implied by the existence of all these (and other) seemingly contradictory readings is what constraints the text, *Mansfield Park,* places upon inferred signification—or whether it is possible to draw fixed boundaries for such constraints.

Of the interpretations I have summarized, only Margaret Kirkham's really diverges from the others in its understanding of Austen's propositional meaning. Hers is the only one to claim that Fanny Price is not what she seems to be, that Austen is trapping the reader by a kind of disguised irony; and because of its range of interpretive interest and its originality, I shall discuss Kirkham's argument at the end of this chapter. All the others, with the possible exception of Auerbach, seem to assume that the novel is strongly didactic and moralistic, and the differences in their readings seem to have to do with how they respond to and evaluate what they perceive. The issue seemingly in dispute among the critics of *Mansfield Park* comes down to something not really a matter for debate that can ever end in a logical termination: How does one accommodate Austen's seeming change of vision and tone, her abandonment of irony, with the Austen one knows from her other novels? For some, like Mudrick, rejection of this novel becomes unavoidable, while others either try to accept its values, see it as something other than an expression of values, or, like Kirkham, prove that its values are not what most readers have thought.

What I find most interesting is the fact that so many critics have found it difficult but necessary to come to some kind of terms with *Mansfield Park* (including even rejection, or identifying Fanny as a Frankenstein *and* a "monster" [Auerbach]), and usually with the author as she is seen to embody or express herself in this novel; as one of my students has remarked, one feels motivated to make this novel "feel right." The source of the continuing interest in attacking or defending *Mansfield Park* has been, I surmise, a tremendous emotional appeal that has perhaps not been adequately described on the basis of the questions critics have asked and tried to answer—which is to say, such critics have not adequately defined the novel's emotional power for *me,* though some of them have certainly described their problems with it at length. Since I am one of those readers who finds *Mansfield Park* particularly disturbing in the context of Austen's other novels, who finds a "different" Austen in it, I begin my attempt to communicate what seems special about it by describing not how I read its predecessor, *Pride and Prejudice,* with which it is so often unfavorably compared, but its successor, *Emma.*

Despite the prevalence among formalists—among whom I would include Murray Krieger and Wolfgang Iser, as well as Iser's mentor,

Roman Ingarden—of the belief that there is a "correct" kind of aesthetic experience, any narrative plot (and especially those concluding in a marriage) can have appeals other than what is usually accepted as aesthetic or literary. The most complex novel, even *Crime and Punishment* or *The Golden Bowl*, can be experienced on the same level as a soap opera or melodrama, with tremors of delight when Raskolnikov and Sonya are finally united, or joy at Maggie Verver's triumph in winning back her husband. Indeed, it seems likely that some such affects form part of most readers' response to plots, however much aestheticians and critics assume that there is an objective difference between texts that themselves operate primarily on the soap-opera level of affirming comforting phantasies and those that offer complex insights. On the basis of my own response, I think it likely that many readers of *Emma* feel a glow of warmth when Emma and Mr. Knightley finally declare their mutual love, and one could go further and argue that *Emma*, in both abstract plot and concrete texture, appeals to a basic childhood phantasy of winning love no matter how badly one may behave. The novel's ability to evoke such phantasies is not necessarily a negative quality, nor is the reader who feels them necessarily an inferior reader.

But for me as reader, *Emma* is much more of an overt psychological portrait than *Mansfield Park* as it is concerned with the self in its striving for security, and with that self's defenses against acknowledging its relative helplessness in a world governed by creatures of a different gender. The paradox for Emma is that despite her striving for independence, her self draws sustenance from that restrictive external world, and it is a world to which she must adapt in order to survive. We may like or dislike the kind of accommodation Emma ultimately has to make, but it seems to me that the novel's plot does represent such a process of accommodation. At the beginning of *Emma* we are introduced to a young woman who is experiencing the first of a series of events threatening her accustomed power within her small society, the departure into marriage of her indulgent surrogate-mother, Miss Taylor. Although Emma continues to dominate her valetudinarian father, this is far from enough to sustain her inner security. But each successive attempt at strengthening her self at the cost of others results in another threat to her self-esteem, as her patronage of Harriet Smith leads to the courtship (which she wilfully misconstrues) of Emma by Mr. Elton, whom she has intended for Harriet, and which is offensive both for reasons of social class and because she has sworn she will never marry—likely a defense intended to sustain her independence, but also perhaps to protect her from the fear and mystery of adult sexuality. Emma's half-pretended flirtation with Frank Churchill lays the groundwork for her humiliation in regard to the talented and envied Jane Fairfax; her insistence that Robert Martin is not good enough for Harriet leads to the latter's aspiration to become Mrs. Knightley; and worst of all, Emma's cruel remark to the voluble Miss Bates—stemming from her need to feel and assert her superiority over others—earns the severe disapproval of Mr. Knightley, the father-lover figure for whose favor she has unconsciously been laboring all along. (Note that I am not inventing the character's "unconscious"; Austen is quite explicit about the sudden awareness on Emma's part of previously unconscious feelings and unconsciously motivated behavior when she recognizes her love for Knightley upon Harriet's revelation of her own marital ambitions.)

The denouement of *Emma,* which finds the heroine giving up some of her self-absorption to share love with another, could be seen as analogous to a hard-won therapeutic breakthrough. Or alternatively, one might read all of this as exemplifying the predicament of an intelligent and spirited woman who can find no place in her limited, patriarchal society to develop her potential, and whose adaptation to that society is a sad but necessary compromise. But whether one reads *Emma* as a story of successful development of personality or as one of a pathetic submission, my basic point remains the same: the novel traces the process of adaptation of a woman to her world.

In the outline of its plot alone, *Mansfield Park* is a very different novel. While in *Emma* the protagonist is socially an insider (to the extent that a woman can be in Austen's society) who must painfully give up some of her sense of individual specialness, in Fanny Price we have a protagonist introduced into an even narrower society from the outside, and the burden of the story is the gradual and difficult process of adaptation of some of the powerful figures in that society—and the failure of others to adapt—to *her.* To say with approval that Fanny's virtues are Austen's values, and bring about the transformation of Mansfield Park to its proper condition (the position of Alistair Duckworth, among others) is really different only in emphasis and value-judgment from the observation that the novel depicts Fanny's frighteningly relentless march to a position of dominance (Auerbach, among others). This claim of a basic similarity of critical positions may seem peculiar, given the extremeness of Auerbach's conception of Fanny as monster and the fact that she describes Fanny's modus operandi as an "elevation of one's private bad feelings into a power alternate to social life" (210); but I suggest that to call Fanny "a silent, censorious pall" (210) is only a different *judgment* of Fanny as the novel's (and Austen's) standard of moral conduct. Thus while to a critic such as Duckworth, the direction and conclusion of the novel seem right and just, artistically successful in part because they express Jane Austen's most deeply held values, I find that I can only accept *Mansfield Park* by taking it to be, in contrast to *Emma*'s mimetic story of ego-development and individual adaptation, much like the dramatization of a fundamental wish-fulfillment phantasy, with an obvious analogy to the Cinderella myth.[3]

If for Nina Auerbach the novel's dominant theme is the malleability of values and Fanny's resultant power to "make" her world, for Duckworth it is "ground," as in "the ground of Jane Austen's being"—a ground not threatened by anything below its surface. For Trilling, the most important concept is the judgment of the quality of self, while for Mudrick it is the repressive moral code to which Austen sells out in *Mansfield Park*. For me, the most important thematic words are perhaps *fear, revulsion,* and *power,* and the most important dramatized experience that of being an outsider in one's family, and coming to dominate it. I find I must ask myself what the meaning is for me of a story of a timid, fearful girl's coming to live in a great house where she is regarded as an outsider and appreciated only insofar as she is useful, and her developing into the *most* regarded, the only one, as Edmund Bertram says, who has been right all along.

This plot resembles nothing so much as a version of Freud's "family romance," wherein the child, in phantasy, is transported from its actual, inevitably unsatisfactory parents to a noble or royal family, its "real," much more pleasing, and totally accepting mother and father.[4] Fanny's developing the conviction that *Mansfield Park* is her real home, and her passive but ultimately successful desire to be accepted as the daughter of the house, for me give the novel the feeling of a drawn-out attempt to make the phantasy of the family romance come true. And Fanny's violent emotional reaction to her natural parents when she is sent away from Mansfield Park to Portsmouth (significantly, as a punishment for disobedience, for not being passive and submissive enough—in a particular sense, not feminine enough) reads like a dramatization of the negative half of that phantasy ("my parents are not my *real* ones"). The novel goes even further than this in enacting the family romance, for not only is Fanny ultimately accepted as a Bertram in her marriage to Edmund, but her enemies within the family (Mrs. Norris and Maria) are, analogously to the harsher versions of the Cinderella story, driven out, while her own two original siblings, William and Susan, move in as replacements (the obverse of what happens at the outset in "Cinderella," where the new family uproots the heroine). And according to the narrator, "Fanny was indeed the daughter that [Sir Thomas] wanted" (book III, chap. 17, 431).

I may seem to be suggesting that *Mansfield Park* is a kind of right-wing soap opera that champions the strength and triumph of female submissiveness, or a Cinderella phantasy establishing the inevitable victory of the mistreated but uncomplaining child. But the emotional impact of the novel is too strong, and the intensity with which various phantasies are explored too great in the dramatization of Fanny's experiences, to allow me to make that kind of dismissal. There are throughout explicit and implicit expressions of revulsion from the physical, the sexual, and the body and, in some of the descriptions of Mary Crawford and in Edmund's reaction to her, an association of physical vivacity with questionable virtue. Such revulsion can be seen as early as chapter 1, when Mrs. Norris is described as telling Sir Thomas and Lady Bertram "in an angry voice, that Fanny [the mother of Fanny Price, the heroine] has got another child," and later in the contrast between Mary Crawford's physical agility and need for strenuous exercise and Fanny's relative physical weakness and need for quiet (although see my summary of Margaret Kirkham's reading, below). And revulsion can be detected most surely in Fanny's "horror" and "stupefaction" at the "horrible evil" of Maria's running off with Henry Crawford:

She passed only from feelings of sickness to shudderings of horror; and from hot fits of fever to cold. The event was so shocking that there were moments when her heart revolted from it as impossible—when she thought it could not be. A woman married only six months ago, a man professing himself devoted, even *engaged,* to another—that other her near relation—the whole family, both families connected as they were by tie upon tie, all friends, all intimate together!—it was too horrible a confusion of guilt, too gross a complication of evil, for human nature, not in a state of utter barbarism, to be capable of! Yet her judgment told her it was so. [Book III, chap. 15, 402]

For a reader such as myself, who is concerned about the relation between Jane Austen and Fanny Price, a passage such as this one raises difficult questions. Is this Austen expressing her own feelings, as we might expect if we agree with those critics who consider Fanny her author's spokeswoman, or is there some degree of distance between Fanny's revulsion and Austen's attitude? Given the fact that Jane Austen could joke in her letters to her sister Cassandra about local marital scandals, it would seem that even if Austen shares the moral judgment regarding Henry Crawford, Fanny's is the particular reaction of a young woman who is directly and emotionally involved with the personages of the scandal. Most significant is the fact that Fanny has just begun to feel an attraction to Henry, who has been pursuing her so resolutely—for *she* is the "near relation" (of Maria) to whom Crawford has professed devotion, and it is as though terrible feelings of guilt are assailing her for that attraction, as well as a guilt for feeling disappointment that he has turned to Maria.

Fanny's reaction is so strong, and the emphasis on the violation of "intimate" family ties so dominant, that I must agree with Fleishman that "suggestions of incest . . . lurk in this passage" (65). But there is a further dimension to the implication of incest (or rather, the incest taboo), for it is one of the first subjects discussed by any of the characters in the novel. When it is being considered at Mansfield Park whether Fanny should be taken in by the Bertrams, Sir Thomas thinks of his sons, and of the possibility of "cousins in love," but Mrs. Norris—from beginning to end the epitome of deficient insight—reassures him:

"You are thinking of your sons—but do not you know that of all things upon the earth *that* is the least likely to happen; brought up, as they would be, always together like brothers and sisters? It is morally impossible. I never knew an instance of it. It is in fact, the only sure way of providing against the connection. . . . The very idea of her having been suffered to grow up at a distance from us all in poverty and neglect, would be enough to make either of the dear sweet-tempered boys in love with her. But breed her up with them from this time, and suppose her even to have the beauty of an angel, and she will never be more to either than a sister." [Book I, chap. 1, 4–5.]

It seems more than a coincidence that both Mrs. Norris, the novel's wicked stepmother villain if anyone is, and Fanny, the Cinderella and moral angel of the book, should both use the same word—"impossible"—in reference to acts of social and sexual transgression that are symbolically and affectively, if not literally, incestuous. Given the fact that most of the novel takes place in between these two passages, it may seem unlikely that Austen was consciously drawing a parallel between these two seemingly antithetical characters. Yet at the same time it is hard to believe that Austen was unaware of the dramatic irony of Mrs. Norris's assurances, since she undoubtedly planned from the outset that Fanny was to marry one of those "dear sweet-tempered boys." For the thrust of the novel seems to be towards the "sister" (as Edmund calls Fanny) overcoming by force of consistent rectitude the barrier of habit and unconscious incest taboo (which

Mrs. Norris, and thus Austen, seems well aware of) in Edmund's view of her as only a younger sister. Seen from its center of consciousness in Fanny, the novel's scheme appears to be an extended phantasy not only of the family romance, but of infantile megalomania and brother-sister marriage.

Since I have already suggested that *Mansfield Park*'s primary method is the dramatization of phantasy rather than that of the *Bildungsroman*, the novel of development,[5] it may appear a contradiction to speak of Fanny as though she were a realistic character. In her moments of strong emotion—when she is forced to visit her natural parents, as well as in her reaction to the perfidy of Crawford—she becomes much closer to three-dimensional, but the contrast between this novel and *Emma* remains, for Fanny is not changed except perhaps in self-confidence by the novel's end; she has not learned anything, there is no significant self-development; it is rather her own circumstances and the other characters that change. But in Fanny's uncharacteristically intense reaction to the adulterous elopement the smoothness of the Cinderella phantasy's unfolding is suddenly disrupted, and depths are partly revealed. Fanny's reaction is so violent, physically as well as mentally, that it seems almost irrational; and one explanation could be that she is shaken by a revelation of her own guilty wishes that her enemies in the family should be overthrown.[6]

Some of the above is unavoidably cast in the language of objective interpretation and based on psychoanalytic assumptions, but I make no claims for its objective validity. Like all the seemingly objective interpretive statements in this book, it is, rather, an account of how I have tried to come to terms with my own responses. Since my political-aesthetic values are not far from Mudrick's, I have needed some way of understanding why I can't simply reject *Mansfield Park* in spite of my awareness of reasons for admiring Austen's creation of the rebellious and spunky heroines of *Emma* and *Pride and Prejudice* more than I do her Fanny Price. But in conducting this self-serving operation, am I simply ignoring the problem of signification? At what point do any of the meanings I have put forth (and those of other critics I have cited) leave the realm of possibility as part of the novel's signification, "the author's meaning"?[7] Is Alistair Duckworth simply the most commonsensical of critics who have written on *Mansfield Park,* in that he finds no subversion by Austen of conservative values and attempts to place the novel in its historical context? If we note the subtitle of his book, "The Improvement of the Estate," and just how much in discussing *Mansfield Park* he stresses the symbolic importance of "improvement"—claiming, for example, that both Mr. Rushworth and Henry Crawford can be identified as violating Austen's own "grounds of being"—we may ask whether this emphasis, like many of the others I have summarized, is not motivated by more than a wish to find "the original meaning"—motivated, that is, by personal assumptions and values.

Surely there is something tendentious, even inherently contentious, in an attempt to enshrine what long was one of Austen's least-regarded novels as central to her canon; and surely it is a process motivated in part by a wish to show that most previous critics have missed the point. Of course, ultimately I cannot be certain what motivates anyone, except perhaps myself and occasionally some of my students, to read *Mansfield Park* as he or she does. My point is just that there are always motivations; interpretation is never a pure search for the truth, and always contains a degree of the subjective. And the need to make the book "feel right" clearly has led critics along surprisingly various paths. To some extent my own attempt has been motivated by the need to absolve Jane Austen from the charge of aesthetic failure, but that could not have occurred had I not felt a fundamental power in the novel. (Of course the "Jane Austen" I refer to is the one I construct from my knowledge of and response to her works, and each critic has his or her own Jane Austen.) How one reads the consciousness (or the unconscious) of the author must to some extent be seen as a function of the critic's presuppositions about art and life, about where and how meanings exist. But I do not intend to present a vision of a set of solipsistic critics, each taking a unique position; for the overlapping among critics of *Mansfield Park* is considerable, although I certainly feel more affinity with Marvin Mudrick and Nina Auerbach than with Alistair Duckworth. Something of the same wish as mine and others' to justify Austen seems present even in Nina Auerbach's dour essay, which claims that "Fanny is Jane Austen's most Romantic heroine, for she is part of a literature newly awakened to ancient forms and fascinated by the monstrous and marginal. In the subtle streak of perversity that still disturbs readers today, she shows us the monsters within Jane Austen's realism, ineffable presences who allow the novels to participate in the darker moods of their age" (213).

It seems to me at least as presumptuous to assert that the didactic meanings critics have approvingly or disapprovingly attributed to *Mansfield Park* express Austen's values and beliefs most truly and fully, as to claim that the novel is "about" incest taboo and family romance, or that Fanny Price is an analogue of Frankenstein and his monster (see Auerbach, 210, 218). These are the meanings we as individual critics believe we find, but largely construct as we read and reflect on the novel. I would wager that any man who went (as I did) through an adolescence fraught with sexual frustration because his female peers were too pure and too coy is likely to sympathize with Henry Crawford, and to find Fanny Price particularly irritating; Nina Auerbach's reaction, on the other hand, seems to be based on her finding Fanny to be a creature who exercises power through her very isolation, who has no need for "sisters" (219).

In the past I have even ventured to suggest that Fanny's name has emblematic and contextual significance—that her fanny is available only at a price, and that when one looks at the number of exiled and miserable creatures at the novel's close, this price has been high. Even Sir Thomas must acknowledge his moral inferiority, and Edmund go through a humiliating period of contrition for his attraction to the vivacious Mary Crawford. This only half-jocular point of mine has been somewhat weakened as a discovery of hidden signification in Austen's text by my learning, through Margaret Kirkham's essay, that Fanny Price's name is the same as that of the heroine in Crabbe's *The Parish Register,* part 2, "Marriages," who refuses to marry Sir Edward Archer, an "amorous knight," and settles instead for a youth of her own class. According to Kirkham, "Crabbe's Fanny Price is a refuser of the captive-captivate game; Austen's is shown as unfit, by her nature, to become a commodity in the marriage market, though capable of paying the price of enduring wrongful abuse and misunderstanding, which secures her 'right to choose, like the rest of us' " (241) Yet Crabbe's Fanny has her own ambiguities: this "lovely" and "chaste" young woman gives as her reason for refusing the knight her wish not to rise above her mother's estate in life; only then is the "youth" mentioned, "Who to the yielding maid had vow'd his troth." Thus the emphasis appears to be on not rising above one's station, rather than on free choice of a mate. And while Crabbe's Fanny Price may be chaste, she is also "yielding." In any case, I am no longer as convinced as I was when I first read Kirkham and had looked into *The Parish Register* that my pun is necessarily a complete imposition on Austen's text. Granted, Austen took the name from Crabbe and did not initially choose that name because of the pun but rather because of the parallel in the stories between Sir Edward Archer and Henry Crawford as potential seducers into marriages that on the woman's side would give the impression of being motivated by dreams of wealth—what Kirkham calls the marriage market. But I suspect that she also was more likely than Crabbe to have been aware of the possibilities of such punning.

There is yet another side to my response to Fanny, that harsh judge of parents, both real and surrogate. As a parent myself, I am aware of the terrible judgments one may receive from one's own children; although my sons may aver that my wife and I are "great parents," I know that I especially, as the father, am subject to scrutiny and potential disapproval whenever I take even a small misstep in my behavior, and I relate this to the "Terror of secularized spirituality" that Trilling writes of. Ultimately, however, analogously to Trilling's attribution to Jane Austen of an ironic dream of safety from the world's judgment of one's being, I want to find authority for what I have "discovered"—the undermining of Austen's surface meanings—in the author's intentions. In order to do this, I must assume that intention transcends conceptual meaning and includes all those things uncovered (but not necessarily consciously discovered) by the author in the process of writing. A real Jane Austen who became fully aware of all the meanings I have adduced which seem subversive of the surface moral structure of *Mansfield Park* is unthinkable; but a Jane Austen who writes a long novel that remains in every way within the limits of her society's overt moral code is to me equally unthinkable— that is, a Jane Austen who seems right only to those, like Duckworth, who profess to be fully contented with the dramatization of that moral code as an adequate artistic vision for the author of *Pride and Prejudice* and *Emma*. My Jane Austen only once in her novels dreams a dream of achieving power, recognition, and social and sexual fulfillment through the exercise of superior virtue—a kind of virtue rarely apparent in her gossipy, often catty letters, but which, as Mudrick suggests, was increasingly attributed to her by her family.[8]

Thus the crucial issues about *Mansfield Park* range over the matter of the didactic strain (certainly present in the novel) and whether it represents artistic failure, is central to Jane Austen's vision, or some third possibility; the ironic, and where to find it (and as we shall see, Margaret Kirkham's attempt to find irony still retains a sense of didacticism—that of feminism); and what I place under the rubric of the domestic and the uncanny, the *Heimliche* and the *Unheimliche*. Among Austen's novels *Mansfield Park* gives the greatest attention to such *heimlich* (domestic, familial, private, secret) matters as the claustrophobic atmosphere of the Park, the torments of a child who feels an alien in two family homes, the problem of sibling rivalry, and the scattered outbursts of concern with such forbidden subjects as adultery and (symbolic) incest. But the *Unheimliche*, or uncanny, if not always distinguishable from its supposed antonym, seems present in the way the Cinderella legend is handled: the way in which unstated guilty phantasies of triumph over the wicked stepmother and the unkind sisters actually come true (and the defeated "sisters" include a direct sexual rival for Edmund's love in the person of Mary Crawford). Above all, Fanny's horror in her reaction to Henry Crawford's perfidy suggests a response to feelings that are not really new, but have been repressed and are now suddenly called up again by their embodiment in real events. For Fanny by this time has been pining after Edmund, and a wish to run away with *him* cannot have been far from consciousness, while the attraction to Henry she has begun to feel introduces another dimension of guilt. There is sexual misbehavior in *Pride and Prejudice* (Lydia's elopement with Wickham), but although Elizabeth feels great shame there is nothing like the reaction of Fanny, and the matter is distanced by Mr. Bennet's defensive sarcasm.

It is difficult for me to imagine how, in writing a novel about a child growing up *en famille* as an alien, Jane Austen could have retained the dominantly ironic vision of her other novels, and it is for me the oppressive family ambience of the novel and the focus on a wronged child who becomes a more than vindicated young woman that give *Mansfield Park* its special power. One need not like Fanny or even feel that her triumph is a victory of the most deserving to appreciate how the most restrictive moral code may be employed in the service of strongly forbidden phantasies. The superego is, after all, closer in its irrationality and uncontrollable power to the id than to the ego. But what I have just written describes only my own way of coming to terms with that novel. It is not a denial of the value of any other critic's reading, but following an attempt to explain what those critics are doing, a presentation of my own approach and conclusions.

Margaret Kirkham's truly original essay on *Mansfield Park* is implicitly concerned with questions of constraints on signification, and thus on the reader's understanding. Kirkham claims to have found an authorial intention and an objective set of meanings that have been missed by all previous critics. In direct opposition to those who find Austen to have abandoned irony as her literary mode in this novel, Kirkham argues that irony,

far from being suspended in *Mansfield Park,* is turned upon the reader. We are given a heroine who, in some respects, looks like an exemplary conduct-book girl, but this is deceptive. Fanny is not a true conduct-book heroine and, insofar as she resembles this ideal—in her timidity, self-abasement, and excessive sensibility, for example—her author mocks her—and us, if we mistake these qualities for virtue. [231]

Kirkham, like Fleishman, also perceives Fanny's weakness and seeming passivity as the result of emotional damage caused by the denizens of the great house.

At Mansfield, the somnolence of Aunt Bertram, the sadism of Aunt Norris, and the false regard for wealth and status of Sir Thomas Bertram, his elder son, and his daughters, have all combined to ensure that Fanny's mental and physical health are put in jeopardy. She has not a strong constitution, but she was not as a child devoid of normal impulses to an active life. . . . Fanny, in her early years at Portsmouth, was important as "*play-fellow*" as well as "instructress and nurse" to her brothers and sisters. . . . Fanny's excessive fragility of body and lack of self-confidence are the result of inconsiderate, and sometimes humiliating, treatment by her illiberal, selfish aunts, but it has not quite stamped out of her an impulse to life which is to be seen in her continued love of dancing. [237–38]

It is important to be reminded that Fanny's seemingly negative qualities are not necessarily celebrated by Austen, and Kirkham has done a further service to *Mansfield Park* criticism by offering convincing evidence that in Austen's time the weakness and passivity of someone like Fanny was often experienced by actual men as a sexual stimulus (she does not offer a psychological explanation for this, but it is not difficult to think of one).

Perspectives and facts like these open new windows on *Mansfield Park,* and another fascinating historical detail brought out by Kirkham is that the legal judgment in 1772 that an Englishman who had bought a slave abroad could not own him in England was called the "Mansfield Judgment." Kirkham offers some convincing evidence of the probability that Austen knew of this, and goes on to argue that

through her title, the making of Sir Thomas a slaveowner abroad, and the unstated question of Miss Fanny, *her* moral status in England is implicitly contrasted, yet also compared, with that of the Antiguan slaves. . . . Slaves have masters but cannot truly be said to have a country, since they are neither protected by its laws nor accorded those rights which belong to freeborn citizens. That this was true in England of women is a point made by Wollstonecraft in *Maria,* where the heroine has no redress in "the laws of her country—if women have a country." [244–45]

The core of Kirkham's argument, however, is that Austen with craft, and craftily, included all of these elements in order to test her readers, and that her vision in *Mansfield Park* is as ironic as in her other novels:

Mansfield Park remains a puzzling novel, partly, I think, because Jane Austen enjoyed puzzles and thought it both amusing and instructive to solve them. She asks a great deal of her readers—sound moral attitudes, derived from rational reflection upon experience; quick-wittedness and ingenuity in making connections; and a belief in the wholesomeness of laughter. [247]

I would like to be able to believe in Austen's consciously ironic art in *Mansfield Park* to the extent that Kirkham does: that Austen plotted out what amounts to a cunning trap for the inattentive reader. And indeed, I find every one of Kirkham's arguments relevant to reading the novel. The only problem is that I cannot *feel* the high comedy that Kirkham detects, nor can I free myself of the sense that Fanny, even granting that she is more a victim than the "monster" Auerbach considers her, is sanctimonious and fundamentally unattractive, even frightening in the moral righteousness that Kirkham deems clear-sighted rational thought. Part of my motivation for saying this may be that Kirkham has threatened my neat formula of *Emma* as dealing with ego-development while *Mansfield Park* deals with phantasies rooted in the id and superego. But I do believe as well that Kirkham's argument for the ironic feminism of the novel derives from her own wish to find in it an extensive analogue of her own feminist values; and in so doing she makes Austen virtually a Joyce in the depth and interconnectedness of her allusions, which form, as Kirkham describes the novel, a consciously planned network of details that should lead the reader who reads *correctly* to understand the novel as Kirkham does. Like all other readings, it is inevitably selective and largely excludes any feeling of the contrast between the vivacity of Mary Crawford and the dullness of Fanny Price.

All of these readings open up areas that seem somehow to be contained within the novel, as constraints upon the reader; but the extraordinary range of styles of reading (that is, the principles upon which constraints are selected) discernible in *Mansfield Park* criticism, including my own, makes only one conclusion possible for me: that there is something about *Mansfield Park* itself that causes it to exceed any one reader's attempt to grasp it as a whole, or even to grasp his or her entire response to it. There are few nineteenth-century novels that, having received so much critical attention, still feel to me quite so much like permanently "open" texts.

IV · LITERARY INFLUENCE
AND THE READER'S
UNDERSTANDING

10 · Sexual Realism and Phantasy in Hardy and Lawrence

In this chapter and the next I turn to the question of how another "extrinsic" factor functions in reading: the reader's awareness or inference of literary influence and its effect upon literary understanding. These two chapters stem from my efforts to come to terms with works that I have found compelling and yet frustrating because of the difficulty of knowing how to regard certain crucial features. In each of the three cases, my becoming aware of specific influences gave me a framework through which to understand the text in a new way.

Considered as an aspect of reading, perceived influence need not be objectively ascertainable, for if the process of working towards understanding is subjective, then actual influence has the same status in the process as does influence constructed entirely by inference from the text: both actual and inferred influence (like actual or inferred authorial intention) become part of the reader's understanding only by becoming embodied in that reader's sense of the text. However, with most of the examples I shall be using there is in fact strong evidence of direct influence, and the knowledge that such an influence is likely a fact rather than just an inference does make stronger the effect of the awareness of influence in the reading process.[1] Further, the factor of perceived influence in readers' understandings of texts cannot be separated from the conceptualization of an author by the reader.

Of all the possible ways of characterizing narrative, mimesis is probably today the most discredited by those theorists and critics who take language in itself as a self-reflexive, in effect transcendent, system. Mimesis, as the representation or imitation of, or reference to, the "real world" outside of language seems outmoded and old-fashioned as a primary aesthetic value or critical concern. Among practicing critics, Bernard J. Paris has been for years one of the most devoted advocates for the ability of great novelists and dramatists to present the reader with insights into human behavior and internal human conflict as being the greatest strength of such authors; and he, like any champion of mimesis, may also seem naive from the point of view of those who see the world as constituted by language. In 1968 Paris argued that formalistic analysis, as well as the insistence—which he attributes mainly to Wayne Booth—that novels be clear, coherent, and moral in their propositional meaning, had obscured the actual nature of nineteenth-century realistic fiction, in which form and theme are rarely if ever fully integrated with mimesis ("Form, Theme, and Imitation"). Subsequently, using the psychological insights of Karen Horney, Paris has attempted to demonstrate how the true achievement of realistic novelists is the way they vividly concretize neurotic conflicts and patterns of behavior in their characters. A possible objection is that in depending upon Horneyan psychology, itself constituted in language, Paris is really only using one particular language system to explain another and can never reach the "real world"; but this would be equally true of Freudian or any other psychology used in the same manner.

Whatever the epistemological or therapeutic value of Horneyan psychology, Paris's analyses of characters often seem to me searching and complex enough to transcend any possible limitations of that particular psychological system. I mention his work at this point because it carries an important message: that what I and many others respond to most strongly in so-called realistic fiction is indeed the apparent rightness of its portrayal of fictional character, its seeming truth to life, within propositional structures that may seem self-contradictory or incoherent.[2] Yet I do not find it enough to understand character as the vivid re-presentation of what already exists in something called "reality," because I have found that characters are created by authors at least in part for their own emotional purposes, and in part from the texts of other authors, and thus that characters are never built up solely from either direct observation or introspection. I reached these conclusions initially not by deduction from theoretical principles, but through my puzzlement with one particular character in Victorian fiction who seems vividly real, and yet who also seems to be an authorial and possibly also a cultural phantasy: Hardy's Sue Bridehead.

I first attempted to work out a psychological understanding of Sue two decades ago, motivated by a strong feeling that while superficially she did not seem psychologically consistent, she was nonetheless a wholly believable character. The explanations offered by critics of the character as being torn between a theory of living that was more advanced than her practice could be in the historical context, or torn between the desires of the flesh and the demands of the spirit (or convention, or the superego), seemed inadequate to explain *my* Sue, perhaps because they were really only restatements of what is apparent on the novel's surface. At the time, I wrote that

it is an oversimplification to see Sue as a mental libertarian without the emotional conviction of her beliefs. There is something in her that longs for the man (as Lawrence says), just as there is something in her that recoils from sex. This has the curious effect of making her seem at once sexual and sexless to both the reader and Jude. Neither Jude nor the narrator ever formulates this explicitly as a contradiction in Sue; instead we find Jude making variously contradictory statements: he designates Sue as several kinds of spiritual being—ghost, sprite, fairy, sylph, spirit—and at a climactic moment accuses himself of being selfish in having "spoilt one of the highest and purest loves that ever existed between man and woman" (VI.iii, 373) by having insisted on a sexual relationship with Sue. Yet he has, just previously, angrily accused her of being passionless, "a fay, a sprite, not a woman!"— and Sue has replied that in fact she captivated him because of an "inborn craving" to *be* loved, and yet, possibly because of jealousy of Arabella, "I got to love you, Jude" (372). If this is not complicated enough, one may cite an earlier passage in which, in response to her newly found desire to "mortify the flesh—the terrible flesh," Jude says to Sue, " . . . there's no evil woman in you. Your natural instincts are perfectly healthy; not quite so impassioned, perhaps, as I could wish; but good and dear, and pure. And as I have often said, you are absolutely the most ethereal, least sensual woman I ever knew to exist without inhuman sexlessness" (VI.iii, 363–64). At least part of the confusion stems from Jude's attempt to argue two logically incompatible positions simultaneously—that there is nothing evil about "natural instincts" and that Sue isn't evil because these instincts are so weak in her. But at the same time, there is a clear ambiguity in Sue's sexuality in regard to both her own desires (she says that women can live without sex, and yet, "I got to love you, Jude") and the effect she has on Jude. ["Sue Bridehead," 262][3]

"Clear ambiguity" is a neat oxymoron that seems to mime the way I was trying to explain my own sense of *Jude the Obscure,* and of Sue in particular. I did note that if Jude was confused about Sue, not only were there possible cultural explanations, but Hardy seemed to share rather than to be clear-sighted about some of Jude's confusions:

[Jude's] attraction to her is dual, for he finds her sexually attractive and yet is drawn to an asexuality he senses in her, which represents an escape from the burden of sexual guilt . . . that he feels about his lust for Arabella. His passivity in the face of Sue's treatment of him, his acceptance of the mock-ceremony Sue makes him go through before her wedding with Phillotson, and his lengthy term of accepting Sue's insistence on their living together in chasteness can all be related to a pattern of passivity in other Victorian heroes . . . which has some relation to the tendency of Victorian men to idealize women and feel far beneath them. But a problem may arise when the author himself shares his character's confusions, as there is some evidence Hardy did: "there is nothing perverted or depraved in Sue's nature. The abnormalism consists in disproportion, not in inversion, her sexual instinct being healthy as far as it goes, but unusually weak and fastidious" [letter to Edmund Gosse, quoted in Florence Emily Hardy, *The Life of Thomas Hardy*, 272]. This is essentially what Jude has said, and Hardy's identification with his hero is suggested still further by his admission in the same letter that "Sue is a type of woman which has always had an attraction for me, but the difficulty of drawing the type has kept me from attempting it till now." The question we must ask . . . is whether Hardy's own ambivalence between idealizing Sue (rationalizing that she is in some sense sexually "healthy") and seeing her as a destructive type vitiates his portrayal of her—or whether he wrought better than he knew. ["Sue Bridehead," 263]

The rest of my essay, however, largely drops the question of Hardy's ambivalence for an attempt to affirm Sue's psychological reality. How she could be "at once sexual and sexless, at once flirtatious and withdrawn" (265) I attempt to explain by using Wilhelm Reich's description of a type of neurotic he calls the "hysterical character"—a person of rapidly changeable behavior and attitudes, who "has strong and unsatisfied genital strivings which are inhibited by . . . genital anxiety," and whose "sexual behavior . . . serves the purpose of finding out whether and from where the expected dangers will realize" (*Character-Analysis*, 191). In other words, such a person's sexual behavior—in Sue, her coquetry—functions, paradoxically, as a defense against sexual anxiety, and sex itself.

Recognizing that there are inherent problems in the analysis of a literary character's unconscious as though he or she were a real person, I try to get around this by claiming that I actually am posing the question, "What might be the psychic or defensive function of a character's puzzling behavior if this were a person encountered in real life?" And I go no further with this claim than to assert that Hardy had created a "coherent character whose pattern of behavior is clini-cally familiar and rationally explicable, and . . . was not simply projecting his own confusions about women" (266). Even by the time the article was published I had severe doubts about that last clause; for given Hardy's own confused statements about his attitude to the "type" of woman Sue is, and his previous baldly inconsistent comments as narrator about the naturalness or the evil of the seduction of Tess Durbeyfield,[4] it seemed clear that Hardy was in some sense "in" his novels as something more than an objective observer or psychologist of character. If there were confusions in Sue (and Jude), they seemed in part to be a veiled representation of Hardy's own confusions. So, although he may not have been simply projecting his phantasies and ambivalences upon the characters, his ability to present them convincingly may have depended in part on such a projection. Yet to go this much further than I did in my 1968 essay is not to go very far; it still limits the focus to Hardy and two or three of his characters and seems to have no broader implications for the problems of reading character or reading the author in his text. And my use of Reich had no stronger claims to clinical accuracy than might any analysis of a character's unconscious through some other version of depth psychology.[5] Only with my recognition that Hardy's Sue, and his Jude and Arabella, have a component of intertextuality, in that significant analogues exist in texts by other authors, could I move beyond that narrow focus; and only with my troubled recognition that Sue must have some special significance for me can I bring the whole question into the realm of the individuality (as well as the potential intersubjectivity) of literary understanding. My major concern here will be with Sue Bridehead and two of her literary analogues, but because of the peculiar status of the three "intertexts" I must also consider the relevance of those analogues in the lives of the three authors; and because I see the critic's motivations as an inescapable aspect of his readings, I shall also have to consider certain autobiographical bases of my fascination with Sue Bridehead over two decades or more.

When Mr. Phillotson describes to his skeptical friend Gillingham the affinity of the wife he is about to give up with her cousin Jude, it is as "Shelleyan" rather than "Platonic" (Gillingham's initial suggestion), and he specifies that they remind him of Laon and Cythna, the protagonists of Shelley's *The Revolt of Islam* (*Jude,* book IV, chap. 4, 243); in so doing, he is as much Hardy's mouthpiece as he is Phillotson the schoolmaster. The allusion, and the relevance of the more general Shelleyan notion of soul-union, have been previously noted: Phyllis Bartlett sees Sue as "Hardy's full-length, mature study of the Shelleyan woman . . . as he imagined she would disintegrate under the stress of child-bearing, poverty and social custom," and Jude's story as the "tragedy of a man captivated by so visionary a creature" (" 'Seraph of Heaven,' " 632).[6] Bartlett also discusses the way in which Shelley's successive dreams of spiritual union with a series of women are mirrored in Hardy. From one perspective Hardy's last novel is a bitter parody of Shelley's early try at an allegorical revolutionary epic, as certain episodes versified exultantly by the poet are reduced to supposedly real-life, sometimes tawdry, prose counterparts. But at the same time, if Hardy in *Jude the Obscure* cannot accept the young Shelley's optimism, the two authors share certain conscious and, I think, unconscious attitudes. A good proportion of the language in which Sue Bridehead is described early and late in the novel—in particular those expressions that allude to her lightness, ethereality, and vibrancy—can be shown to resemble the language of *Epipsychidion* (a poem Sue actually quotes as a description of herself later on); but the structure of the novel is closer to that of *The Revolt of Islam*.

Originally titled *Laon and Cythna; or, The Revolution of the Golden City: A Vision of the Nineteenth Century,* Shelley's poem like Hardy's novel centers on a beautiful visionary city to which the male protagonist comes in search of a certain woman with whom he believes himself to have a special affinity. In both works the couple leave the city together and unite sexually, the woman's only previous sexual experience having been one of "loathsome agony" (*Revolt,* canto VII, line 2875) as the "loveless victim" (canto VII, line 2870) of a man who is subsequently defeated, at least temporarily, by her passionate arguments against this kind of enslavement (the descriptive terms are Shelley's, but would seem to apply equally well to the sexual aspect of Sue's marriage to Phillotson). Eventually both couples return to the holy city and meet a sort of death: Laon and Cythna upon a pyre, Jude through pneumonia, and Sue a death-in-life through her remarriage to Phillotson and consequent sexual immolation. As others have noted, the earlier relationship of Laon and Cythna— before she is abducted by the tyrant's soldiers—and the later hint of incest between the two (although the incest was explicit in the cancelled first edition) are mirrored in the fact that Jude and Sue are cousins, a blood relationship that carries both the promise of a special affinity and the threat of something forbidden—both the danger of marriage for cousins in general and for the members of their family in particular. And though Sue is not, like Cythna, an activist in the cause of women's liberation, there is a parallel between her liberal-agnostic thinking and her insistence that legal marriage is a form of bondage, and Cythna's early vision of "the servitude / In which the half of humankind is mewed / Victims of lust and hate, the slave of slaves" (II, 985-87), which develops into her mission to liberate her sex and thus humanity, according to her mentor's vision: "Never will peace and human nature meet / Till free and equal man and woman greet / Domestic peace" (II, 994–96).

Shelley's heroine is self-reliant and courageous, dominant over Laon, and if anything she has welcomed her abduction as an opportunity to begin her mission of liberation. Thus it is she who becomes a famous apostle of freedom, she who rescues Laon when, upon his first voyage to the Golden City, the tyrant's armies regain control and threaten his life, and she who voluntarily joins Laon upon his pyre. And earlier Cythna has no hestitation about sexual love with Laon, despite the "loathsome agony" of her rape by the tyrant which had led to a long period of madness for her; indeed their first sexual union is so intense that it ends only when Laon notices that she is weak and suddenly realizes that she has not eaten anything for two days.[7] Yet despite Sue's lack of most of Cythna's heroic qualities, there are broad similarities between the two relationships: both couples go through extended periods of suffering apart from one another before they unite, and in both cases there is a further separation followed by the occurrence, in Shelley's poem, and the expression of the idea, in Hardy's novel, of an ultimate union only in death. (In *Jude the Obscure* I have in mind Arabella's final statement, " 'She's never found peace since she left his arms, and never will again till she's as he is now!' " [book VI, chap. 6, 431], but I must admit that it is difficult to know whether Hardy himself takes this pronouncement straight, or, given Arabella's destructive role in the novel, is presenting it ironically.) The implication is also clear in both poem and novel that the protagonists are far in advance of their own time, particularly in their ability to live by their own moral code. In *The Revolt of Islam* the sexual union is preceded by the exculpatory phrase, "To the pure all things are pure!" (canto VI, line 2596), while Sue and Jude are constantly reminding one another that they need not be bound by society's sexual codes and customs. It is of course a crucial distinction that while Laon and Cythna affirm that "Spring comes, though we must pass, who made / the promise of its birth" (canto IX, lines 3688–89), the corresponding belief for Jude and Sue is that " 'in fifty, a hundred, years, the descendants of these two [a couple going through the marriage ceremony with no qualms] will act and feel worse than we' " about getting married (book V, chap 4, 301).

Since the central area in which the Shelleyan and Hardyean sensibilities run together and diverge is in the treatment of the female protagonist, we should look more closely at Cythna and Sue, and at Laon's and Jude's visions of them. For both heroes the woman is a higher form of being to be worshipped and emulated as well as loved. Upon his arrival at the Golden City, Laon sees the veiled Cythna as

> A Form most like the imagined habitant
> Of silver exhalations sprung from dawn,
> By winds which feed on sunrise woven, to enchant
> The faiths of men [canto V, lines 2107–10]

while she refers to herself as the "Priestess of this holiest rite" (canto V, line 2146) and to Laon as "our first votary here" (canto V, line 2137). Jude at first sees Sue as a "half-visionary form" (book II, chap. 2, 91) and later considers himself her pupil, the disciple of her agnostic teachings. But perhaps his most exalted description of Sue occurs when she has fallen into religious fanaticism out of guilt for the death of her children: Jude refers to her as having been "a woman-poet, a woman-seer, a woman whose soul shone like a diamond—whom all the wise of the world would have been proud of" (book VI, chap. 3, 369). For Laon the sexual union with Cythna is a development of his affinity with her, a visionary act that blends "two restless frames in one reposing soul" (VI, 2658), a view shared by Cythna, but held by Jude about himself and Sue with considerable equivocation, and ultimately rejected by Sue.

The coquettishness typical of Sue, the vacillation between openly passionate response and anxious flight, are wholly lacking in Cythna, and there is nothing resembling Sue's frequent reiteration of the belief that men are coarser than women and that she could have remained chaste had it not been for Jude's importuning and her own jealousy of Arabella. One could say that this is the difference between Shelley's poetic and sexual idealism and Hardy's novelistic realism—that Cythna is pure wish-fulfillment phantasy while Sue is an instance of psychological truth. But this does not dispose of the significant residue of Shelleyan phantasy in *Jude the Obscure*. Even without the knowledge that Hardy told Edmund Gosse that Sue was "a type of woman which has always had an attraction for" him, we may feel that there is something unresolved in his treatment of the character. The descriptions of Sue (seen through Jude's eyes) as being all "nervous motion," "mobile, living," with "liquid, untranslatable eyes" (book II, chap. 2, 90), and "so vibrant that everything she did seemed to have its source in feeling" (book II, chap. 4, 104), identify her as a special female type, seeming to promise much more than the sensual but stolid Arabella—more, that is, by combining sexuality with a mental and emotional responsiveness. Such an ideal of a heterosexual relationship more advanced than those marriages that result in mutual bondage is at the heart of both Shelley's poem and Hardy's novel, but it is given two quite different developments.

Cythna is one in a whole series of Shelley's "dream women," as Phyllis Bartlett has also called a series of Hardy's female characters—creatures sometimes literally sexual, such as Cythna, or imagined as beings whose love would transcend the physical, such as the woman addressed in "Epipsychidion" (though the matter of transcending sex with the addressee of that poem is, to say the least, ambiguous). Jude, after his disappointment that Sue, though eloping with him, " 'didn't mean that!' "—i.e., sex (book IV, chap. 5, 250)—rationalizes the situation to himself by saying, "So that I am near you. I am comparatively happy. It is more than this earthly wretch called Me deserves—you spirit, you disembodied creature, you dear, sweet, tantalizing phantom—hardly flesh at all; so that when I put my arms round you I almost expect them to pass through you as through air! Forgive me for being gross." Significantly, Sue supplies the source of the allusion that he has already unknowingly made:

"Say those pretty lines, then, from Shelley's 'Epipsychidion' as if they meant me!" she solicited, slanting up closer to him as they stood. "Don't you know them?"

"I know hardly any poetry," he replied mournfully.

"Don't you? These are some of them:
    "There was a Being whom my spirit oft
    Met on its visioned wanderings far aloft.
    . . . .
    A seraph of Heaven, too gentle to be human,
    Veiling beneath that radiant form of
    woman. . . .' "

"O it is too flattering, so I won't go on! But say it's me—say it's me!"

"It *is* you, dear; exactly like you."

"Now I forgive you! And you shall kiss me just once there—not very long." She put the tip of her finger gingerly to her cheek; and he did as commanded. "You do care for me very much, don't you, in spite of my not—you know?"

"Yes, sweet," he said with a sigh, and bade her good night. [book IV, chap. 5, 257–58]

This dialogue not only tells us something about Sue's consciously Shelleyan image of herself, but brings out the extent of her coquettishness and of Jude's frustration (despite his attempted rationalization).

At this point I find that two questions become pressing: Is it really necessary to try to explain Sue, and if necessary, how is it possible? As to the first, I can only say that I find it necessary every time I read *Jude the Obscure* to reflect upon Sue's possible relation to some kind of human reality (the possible personal motivation for such a need I shall discuss briefly at the end of this chapter). The attempt to explain the literary character through the concept of a psychoneurotic "type," such as Reich's hysterical character, is unsatisfactory because we are thereby reading her as a real person, with unconscious motivations and implicitly an infancy, childhood, and adolescence. Rosemary Sumner, herself taking Sue virtually as a real person, argues that her apparent sexual aversion is due to very strong sexual desire that is equally strongly repressed: "Hardy's treatment of the story suggests 'the repressed and repudiated demands of sexuality' [a quotation from Freud], and also that this repudiation is not prompted by the straightforward distaste which she [Sue] claims, since she follows each successful repudiation by seeking to establish a new set-up where a sexual relationship will become a possibility again" (182). But I do not know how we can tell this any better than we can that Sue is a Reichian "hysterical character." Both approaches treat Sue as a real person, but if some literary works give us something approaching a full case history, in the case of Sue, *Jude the Obscure* does not.

In using an approach that deals with emotions and "response," it seems logical to consider what functions Sue fulfills for her author; but initially one might consider what functions she fulfills for Jude, the closest thing to an autobiographical representative of Hardy in this novel. Although Jude recognizes early on that his feelings for Sue, even before he meets her, "are unmistakably of a sexual kind" (book II, chap. 4, 98), he immediately "excuse[s] himself" by considering that " 'it is not altogether an erotolepsy that is the matter with me, as at that first time. I can see that she is exceptionally bright; and it is partly a wish for intellectual sympathy, and a craving for loving-kindness in my solitude.' " The narrator then wryly remarks, "Thus he went on adoring her, fearing to realize that it was human perversity. For whatever Sue's virtues, talents, or ecclesiastical saturation, it was certain that those items were not at all the cause of his affection for her" (book II, chap. 4, 99). Can we identify the narrator with Hardy in this instance? I find no difficulty in doing so, specifically in a cynical mood about the attraction of men to women ever being anything other than sexual. Yet Sue's attractions are certainly different from Arabella's, and for Jude she is a contrast to the heavy, earthbound pig-farmer's daughter, who soon after marriage comes to

seem for Jude the warder of his prison, however much she has contributed to the liberation of his hitherto dormant sensual nature.

Sue's physical lightness and mobility, her extreme sensitivity and
capacity for emotion, linked with what Jude believes to be her intellectual breadth and fearlessness, are very close to Shelley's conception
of Cythna. But in placing a version of the Shelleyan female ideal into
history, rather than the visionary world of *The Revolt of Islam*,
Hardy acknowledges the impingement of history and society, in Sue's
inability to live up to her "advanced" theories, and in the active
hostility of her and Jude's society to the temporary and intermittent
union they do manage to establish. History and genre (realistic novel
as contrasted with visionary epic) will not, however, by themselves
account for the differences. In saying that "Sue is a type of woman
which has always had an attraction" for him, *after* specifying in the
same letter that her withholding herself even when they are living
together has kept Jude's "passion as hot at the end as at the beginning" and has helped "to break his heart" because "he has never really
possessed her as freely as he desired," Hardy seems to me to be
unconsciously hinting that the ultimate attraction and fascination of
the "type" for him lies not so much in the sexuality itself, as in its
equivocal quality. It is as if the "epicene," the "ethereal," the nearly
but-not-quite sexless, and the ability to keep a man's passion "hot"
are what form the main links of the chain that binds Jude (and
Hardy) to Sue.[8]

The first two of Freud's "Contributions to the Psychology of Love"
("A Special Type of Choice of Object Made by Men," and "On the
Universal Tendency to Debasement in the Sphere of Love") seem to
throw some light on the psychological and possibly the cultural
meaning of Jude's relationship to Sue. But because that relationship
is concrete and specific, it does not coincide perfectly with Freud's
general models of the man who needs to be jealous before he can feel
truly passionate towards a woman, or the tendency to be impotent
with one's wife but not with a "loose woman" or a prostitute. Both
conditions Freud relates to an unresolved Oedipus complex: in the
first, the man repeatedly reenacts the scene of love for the mother
and jealousy of the father, with a concomitant phantasy of rescuing
the woman (mother), while in the second the "purity" of the wife
(who is unconsciously seen as a mother) makes her a taboo sexual
object. And we do see Jude fleeing from a highly erotic marriage with
a woman whom the narrator clearly wishes us to see as debased, and
then being attracted to a seemingly sexless woman—a woman who is
soon married, but who recoils from her marital "duties" (as the

"pure" mother should in Oedipal phantasy). And surely enough, Jude becomes her rescuer, specifically from this sexual degradation, just as, in a different context, Laon has been Cythna's. The operative phantasy in *Jude the Obscure* is, I think, that of Sue's ability to arouse men's desires for her simultaneously because of her sexuality and because of her purity—to provide the attraction of incest (in Jude's case, partly because she is his cousin) along with the exculpation of the woman's (the mother's?) phantasied permanent chasteness. And I would suggest that this is mimetic not so much of the neurotic patterns described by Freud, as of a society in which men's phantasies somehow lead to the actual presence of women who (however unsatisfactorily) fulfill them. In other words, if Hardy is creating Sue out of his own phantasies, he is at the same time writing mimetically because Jude appears, in his reported feelings about Sue, to be governed by the same kinds of phantasies in his sexual life, and because types like Sue seem to develop in societies where such phantasies are dominant and such women are idealized.[9]

Shelley becomes a key to understanding Hardy in this instance because Shelley's phantasies were not dissimilar: that Cythna makes love enthusiastically even when famished for food is the kind of event that can take place only in a work that does not claim to portray the real world—in pornography, or in an allegorical revolutionary epic such as *The Revolt of Islam*. Shelley's repeatedly falling in love with "seraphs of heaven," while leaving Mary to deal with the physical details of motherhood, the births and deaths of their children, suggests a pattern that is a distorted analogue of Jude's attitudes, respectively, to the seraphic Sue and the physical Arabella. As for the questions of Sue's actual enjoyment of sex, or of the repression of her strong sexual desires, these seem to me virtually unanswerable, for her sexuality exists in the mind of her author and in that of his fictional surrogate, Jude, and both men are trying to reconcile conflicting attitudes toward female sexuality. Penny Boumelha makes the point that "Sue's consciousness is opaque, filtered as it is through the interpretations of Jude, with all their attendant incomprehensions and distortions; it is that that makes of her actions impulses, of her confused and complex emotions flirtation, and of her motives 'one lovely conundrum' " (147–48). But we are at least given hints of Sue's consciousness through her behavior, and mimesis might be said to be present in the representation of what Jude and Sue appear to *believe* about their own and each other's sexuality; we can go no further than to observe that Jude is, on the evidence of his own statements, as perplexed as his author as to whether Sue has true, pure, healthy sexual instincts, or has a morbid dislike, even fear, of sex. Nor does Sue herself know; for sexual desire and sexual anxiety, a need to be "feminine" and live up to the male's ideal, a need to be loved, and a need to control the male are so intermixed that there is no way for Sue, Jude, Hardy, or the reader to sort them out. Ann Z. Mickelson remarks that "the reader must sort out answers to whether she is frigid, afraid of sex, afraid of inadequate sexual performance, or afraid of not being loved enough. The answers to all these questions appear to be yes. For fears have a way of being interrelated" (141). But I would suggest that any attempt at conclusive "sorting out," like my Reichian analysis, will inevitably be based on what the reader wishes to believe about Sue, conceptualized as a real person.

It should be said of Shelley's poetic idealization of sexual union in *The Revolt of Islam* that the drift of that poem is *away* from both individual sexuality and political revolution and toward the sublimations of a *Liebestod* and a reunion of souls on another plane of existence. For if the sexual union of Laon and Cythna is a temporary respite from revolution, revolution itself is preliminary to the trip, after their death by fire, in a supernatural boat to the "Temple of the Spirit." Shelley's main thrust is toward a spiritualizing of sexual passion into the idea of a total union impossible in the temporal and material realm. And while the genre in which Shelley is working allows him to avoid psychological complexities while expressing his own phantasies relatively directly, the demands of realism, constraining Hardy to do without supernatural solutions, enable, indeed require, him to think through and dramatize the consequences of such phantasies in actual human life. So the kind of breakthrough Hardy achieves in *Jude the Obscure* is that it is perhaps the first English novel to employ the author's own phantasies and confusions for the purpose of realistic psychological insight, without his imposing a limiting, conventional morality—in contrast to Dickens, for example, who does the latter as the defensive corollary of his startling insights into the underside of the human psyche, or to George Eliot in her own secularly spiritual way when she causes some of her most interesting and passionate characters to learn the necessity of an overpowering sense of duty.

The last point, and my use of Shelley in the discussion of *Jude the Obscure,* illustrate how I have conceptualized that work so as to come to personal terms with what are for me its difficulties. Reading a work through its source, setting it in an intertextual position, is not fundamentally different from the way one takes into account the "intentions" of authors; for these kinds of understanding can only be constructed mentally, not proven, although as my writing of this book affirms, I believe that such constructs can be communicated to and absorbed by other readers. What may above seem to be confident psychological interpretation should really be read as a series of expressions of the distance I feel I have come in struggling with the problems with my responses as a reader of *Jude the Obscure*. I turn now to a novel that also has presented me with increasing difficulties in my history of reading it. I find the use D. H. Lawrence likely makes of *Jude the Obscure* in *Sons and Lovers* helpful in regard to the general problem of male views of women as embodied in novels written by men, and more specifically in regard to some of the difficulties I have had with Lawrence's treatment of women characters in his novels.

Although *Sons and Lovers* is, so far as we can tell, much more directly autobiographical than *Jude the Obscure*,[10] Lawrence's novel can without much forcing be read as a version, or an inversion, of Hardy's—as Lawrence's attempt to go beyond what he saw as the limitations of that novel. It would seem that the polarity for Paul Morel of the two women he loves, Miriam and Clara, however much they are based on Lawrence's personal experiences, are also seen through the lens of Lawrence's special understanding of Hardy. As Miriam's function for Paul is to bring into flower his mind and art, so for Jude—according to Lawrence—Sue's role is to bring him to a "mental clarity," by "rousing him, by drawing from him his turgid vitality, made thick and heavy and physical with Arabella" (*Study of Thomas Hardy*, 499). But while Jude turns from the heavily sensual Arabella to the mentally vivifying Sue, Paul escapes from the increasing desperation of trying to love Miriam physically to the passionate release of his love affair with Clara Dawes. And there is a (perhaps unintentionally) ironic Hardyean twist in the fact that Clara returns to her husband, having insisted to Paul several times that she "belongs" to Baxter Dawes, as Sue in her guilt-inspired fanaticism insists that Phillotson is her real husband, despite her long-term relationship to Jude. Clara's return to Dawes even has something of the aura of self-sacrifice that characterizes Sue's return to Phillotson.

Lawrence in his *Study of Thomas Hardy* finds that Hardy has created an oversimple polarity in Arabella and Sue; but whether or not one considers him to be correct, Lawrence's way of resolving that part of his own plot which has to do with the physical, sensual woman suggests that Lawrence has created his own phantasied polarity between the two young women of *Sons and Lovers*. And while

Lawrence's description of Sue as essentially spiritual and bodiless suggests to me a simpler character than the one I find in *Jude the Obscure,* Lawrence's Miriam is to me more complex than what some-one (Lawrence, the narrator, Paul?) seems to be saying about her. The particular technique Lawrence employs to present Miriam is crucial to the way I read her: for she is the one character in the novel about whom I feel I can say that the narrator's interpretations of her are inseparable from Paul Morel's own attempts at understanding her, as Hardy's are perhaps inseparable from Jude's attempts to un-derstand Sue. This has been noted by Carol Dix, who comments that "much of the generally accepted view of Miriam is a mistaken one, because it is Paul's interpretation of her: and as such that of the young man trying to come to terms with a young woman, not this time his own projection, but a person in her own right. . . . As for her famous sentiments, that show her to be sexually sterile, Miriam can be seen simply as a girl trying to come to terms with female sexuality" (30–31). Although I think Dix describes accurately the way in which Miriam is seen only through Paul's (or Lawrence's) con-sciousness, I have some problem with as definite an assertion as Dix's that Paul's (and thus most readers') view is "mistaken." But then what can one legitimately say about Miriam?

The problem of Miriam as seen only through Paul was noted by a contemporary reviewer, who complained that Paul's point of view was limited, causing the reader to feel, " 'Yes, this is how Miriam seemed to Paul, but this is not what Miriam was.' "[11] This is, of course, a response, not a fact, but the basis of my own similar response can be found in Lawrence's typical narrative technique in regard to Miriam and illustrated by quoting two contiguous para-graphs near the end of *Sons and Lovers,* when Miriam and Paul are having their final meeting:

She turned her face aside; then, raising herself with dignity, she took his head to her bosom, and rocked him softly. She was not to have him, then! So she could comfort him. She put her fingers through his hair. For her, the an-guished sweetness of self-sacrifice. For him, the hate and misery of another failure. He could not bear it—that breast which was warm and which cradled him without taking the burden of him. So much he wanted to rest on her that the feint of rest only tortured him. He drew away. . . .
. . . It was the end then between them. She could not take him and relieve him of the responsibility of himself. She could only sacrifice herself to him— sacrifice herself every day, gladly. And he did not want that. He wanted her to hold him and say, with joy and authority: "Stop all this restlessness and beating against death. You are mine for a mate." She had not the strength.

Or was it a mate she wanted? or did she want a Christ in him? [chap. 15, 418]

There are other passages like these, in which it is virtually impossible to tell whether we are reading an omniscient narrator's interpretation of the characters, a direct presentation of Paul's and Miriam's thoughts, or Paul's attempts to understand her and his own feelings toward her. Certainly somebody, here and elsewhere, seems to be condemning Miriam as essentially frigid, abnormally spiritual, and responsible for the failure of the relationship: she is judged to be the sexually deficient one, who wishes only to possess Paul's soul. But in such passages we can never be sure that we are hearing Miriam's thoughts when they seem to be described—as likely, it is Paul's *version* of Miriam's thoughts (or Lawrence's of Jessie Chambers'). And note that Paul has the same complaint about Clara wanting to possess his soul that he does about Miriam, which suggests a more general fear of women's power, rather than something peculiar to Miriam.[12]

It is apparent that Jude's attraction to Sue has a sexual component almost from the outset of his knowledge of her existence, but it is somewhat less noted that Miriam, whatever her tendencies toward neurotic religiosity, is depicted as capable of intense physical feeling; although the "hot wave of fear" that goes "down into her bowels" when Paul pushes her on the swing (chap. 7, 151) reflects anxiety, it also suggests a strong capacity for physical and emotional response, as does the "naked ecstasy" in her eyes, which is so intense that it frightens Paul (154). One might say that both Lawrence and Paul are continually trying to understand Miriam, and that Lawrence sometimes draws directly on Hardy for aid in depicting her, as in the flower-smelling scenes that have a counterpart in *Jude the Obscure,* and as when Paul accuses Miriam of an "eternal and abnormal craving to be loved" (chap. 9, 218), which is almost exactly the way Sue describes her own behavior, but which may or may not be fair when applied by Paul in this accusatory way to Miriam. What I feel Lawrence has accomplished with Miriam, despite the heavy tone of condemnation, hard to separate from the author, is to portray a character whose powerful sexual feelings—more powerful than we are allowed to believe Sue Bridehead's are—are mixed up with religiosity and prevented from being fulfilled by anxiety, guilt, and shame— and, one might want to say, by the incapacity of her lover. On the one hand she is, like Sue, the embodiment of a male phantasy-ideal to which Lawrence and Paul are drawn and want to reject, but on the other hand, also like Sue, she is a psychologically realistic portrait of a woman who, given her culture and the tendency of her lover to idealize her, cannot come to terms with her own strong desires.

Jessie Chambers, the original of Miriam, would not have agreed with what I have just written, and indeed she prevailed upon Lawrence to change a passage in the original manuscript in which Miriam is credited with consciously passionate feelings that threaten the intensely virginal Paul. Jessie objected that the purity had been equal on both sides, and that Lawrence was falsifying reality (Moore, 41–46). While Lawrence accepted her emendations, this does not mean that he accepted her version of his feelings, although he may indeed have been frightened by the passion he saw (or imagined?) in her; nor does it mean that he accepted her version of her own feelings. While accepting the objection that she had had no *conscious* sexual feelings, he retains throughout the revised text an undercurrent of unconscious but strongly manifested desire in Miriam and leaves open, for some readers at least, the question of whose sexual incapacity is primarily at fault for the failed love relationship.

If there is a value in looking at *Jude the Obscure* with *The Revolt of Islam* in mind and trying to see Hardy's novel and *Sons and Lovers* as significantly connected, it lies in the way such comparisons provide a view of three different attempts by male writers to confront in narrative the split between sexuality and spirituality in (their own thoughts about) women. In Shelley the conflict can be given a fantasy (as well as a phantasy) resolution that makes it less obvious that there is any conflict in the first place, and it is significant that while there is a perfect sexual union, the resolution is on the side of spirituality, allowing the poet to have it both ways. Hardy's and Lawrence's realistic purposes require an accommodation to the possible, which leads them to present the complexity of male and female sexual psychology in a way that seems to transcend these authors' personal investments in the dramas they have consciously conceptualized (but see my qualification, below). Such a "source" study also reveals that there can be no wholly mimetic literature—directly representing reality—because what an author says or shows us must have some roots in his own emotional needs, in other texts, and in his culture. Seeing *Jude the Obscure* as in part a parody of *The Revolt of Islam* allows me as reader (and perhaps Hardy as writer) some ironic distance from the odyssey of Jude and Sue, while knowledge of the extent to which Hardy assigned his own phantasies to Jude underlines how brilliantly he has achieved a portrayal of the confusions inherent at least in men's view of women, and perhaps more broadly in modern sexual life. Taking *Sons and Lovers* in turn as a variation on *Jude the Obscure* makes clearer both the dependence of a writer's vision on his reading and the continuity of problems with men's images of women into the twentieth century.

I must now offer a personal qualification of the certainty with which I have written, particularly about Miriam's capacity for sexual feeling. To some extent this is my own phantasy, though spurred by a strong sense of Paul's (and Lawrence's) confusions, and carefully selected details about Miriam in Lawrence's text. Like Carol Dix (I suspect), I *want* to believe in Paul's incapacity and Miriam's potential sexuality, although I would guess that Dix's motivations are a matter of feminist anger at the way Lawrence treats his women characters, while my own are a mixture of distrusting such a neurotic protagonist as Paul and a participation in a male phantasy about women that I see as a part of our culture. When I was a teen-ager in the early 1950s, it was perhaps more common than it is today for adolescents to know boys who held to the difference between the girl you "lay" and the girl you marry—in those days the commonest expression among my contemporaries of the belief in a dichotomy between whore and virgin, and implicitly, body and spirit. But the problem of men's image of women, and (though I cannot speak on this with direct authority) women's of men, remains with us today. Although in an allegorical epic Shelley and his persona, Laon, can have an untroubled sexual relationship, Jude Fawley and Paul Morel both prefigure today's widespread ethos of sex-as-performance, in that both of them impose their sexual will upon young women who are clearly not ready, and in so doing reveal their own inability to re-spond to those women as individuals with individual needs. Yet the nature of Jude's self-condemnation when Sue descends into religious fanaticism seems as misguided as Paul's condemnation of Miriam's failure to respond as he would have wished.

But I feel obliged to say something more about my emotional stake in all of this, even if the main purpose of this chapter is to demon-strate the interconnection between literary influence and a reader's experience. At the age of fifty-one I find that stake difficult to de-scribe except as a matter of perplexity. Despite my "progressive" and enlightened upbringing and my avowal from childhood that I consid-ered women as equals and as individuals, and moreover that I re-jected the sexual/spiritual or the whore/virgin dichotomy, I cannot really claim to be free from the cultural peculiarities of my sex in relation to women. In adolescence I let myself be led a not-so-merry chase by a series of young women who resembled Sue Bridehead at least in their coquettishness and inconsistency; but in part, I now realize that they were resisting my attempts (like Jude's and Paul's) to force a sexual relationship on them; and on the other hand in my early teens I pulled out of a relationship quite soon because it threatened to become too seriously passionate (indeed, the frightening look of "naked ecstasy" is, I suddenly realize, all too familiar). I also married very young, motivated by love but also by a need for emotional security. But in my phantasies of desire about women I know I am still attracted more to the Sues than the Arabellas, the Miriams than the Claras—if such dichotomies really are fair to these characters or to any real woman; probably they are not, and, as I have said, I am to some extent myself trapped in both cultural images and a form of psychological intertextuality. But to pursue this further would require another book.

11 · Coming to Terms with
Outside Over There

Living testimony of the artist's view of the picture book as a "beautiful, poetic form." . . . The more it is enjoyed, the more the book yields up its secrets.
—Ethel L. Heins

. . . drearily nostalgic and sentimental.
—Donnarae MacCann and Olga Richard

Every serious reader . . . must bring to the book his own interpretation. . . . The pictures are quite simply magnificent.
—Elaine Moss

Too much is left unexplained.
—Susan Hankla

I had waited a long time to be taken out of kiddy-book land and allowed to join the artists of America.
—Maurice Sendak, as quoted by Lanes

The range of reactions to *Outside Over There* expressed in the first four of my epigraphs suggests only a small proportion of the problems that adult readers of Maurice Sendak's most recent book of original text and illustrations have found themselves faced with—problems of understanding, affect, and aesthetic judgment. Furthermore, Sendak's book evokes a range of larger questions: of the role of intentions stated explicitly by the author, or inferred by the reader; the relevance of biographical knowledge to reading; and central to my discussion, the role of literary and artistic influence in the process of reading and coming to an understanding of a text. In addition,

Sendak's own comment (the fifth epigraph) indicates that the very status of *Outside Over There* is problematic: Is it a children's or adults' book, or somehow both? The author/artist seemed confident a year or two before the book was published that he had made a breakthrough into the world of "real" art and literature, but except perhaps in the largest bookstores in the largest cities, his expectation that *Outside Over There* would be displayed in both adults' and children's sections does not seem to have been fulfilled; and in libraries it is classified only as a picture-book or a book for young children.

I am less concerned here with the status of what Sendak considers his magnum opus as children's or adults' book than with the problems other adults and I have had in reading it.[1] My attaining some confidence about understanding *Outside Over There* was made possible by my sudden recognition that it almost certainly had a very definite source in a Victorian "children's book," a recognition that provided me with a new lens through which to view Sendak's book as coherent and meaningful. Before detailing the process of my coming to terms with the book, and in particular the role of my new awareness of influence, I must go into some detail about my (and others') difficulties with it, about some peculiarities in its process of composition and publication, and about the content of the book itself. It is worth noting first that Elaine Moss, in her review for the *Times Literary Supplement,* implicitly affirms the subjective nature of reading; she does this while at the same time insisting that a reader who brings "to the book his own interpretation" would, if he wants the book to "live," do best to ignore Selma Lanes's account of Sendak's personal emotional conflicts that led to the book's creation.

I find Moss's position on the use of biography to understand an author's work in one way attractive, because it would free the reader from having to work through a mass of fragmentary and ambiguous extrinsic evidence and allow him or her to construct from the text a coherence that must be born out of the reading experience. Moss herself offers a coherent interpretation based only on Sendak's text;[2] and if my students could afford to buy *Outside Over There* and I could thus make it a required rather than a recommended text, I would have them each write individual interpretations based upon their responses to the text alone. But, having myself absorbed much extrinsic information, and having hit upon what I believe to be the major influence on Sendak's text, I find that I cannot perform such a decontextualized and personal reading even though my own subjectivity remains a, perhaps the, central factor in the way I read *Outside Over There.*

Before proceeding to discuss the range of public responses to Sendak's book and telling my own story of reading it, I shall briefly place the book in the context of Sendak's other works and offer an account of the story-line, since not all readers will have a prior acquaintance with it. Sendak initially conceived of, or came to regard, *Outside Over There* as the third volume in his "trilogy": like *Where the Wild Things Are* (1963) and *In the Night Kitchen* (1970), it involves its child protagonist in what is apparently a dream and a return to reality (although there is no explicit moment of falling asleep or waking up),[3] a dream that moreover is related to some of the phantasies, the anxieties, and the internal and external conflicts of waking life. Ida, in *Outside Over There,* is the one child-protagonist in the trilogy who is a girl, something that is important to the nature of her story.

At about nine years of age, Ida has most of the responsibility for taking care of her little sister, while her mother seems to be in a depressed and withdrawn state because "Papa was away at sea." In their house, with the baby in a cradle, Ida turns her back on her sister while playing her "wonder horn," and as a result "the goblins" come through the window by means of a ladder and steal the baby, putting in her place a changeling made of ice. At first Ida does not realize that it is a changeling, but when it melts she knows that her sister has been stolen, " 'To be a nasty goblin's bride!' " Dressing in her mother's yellow raincoat and taking the horn, she "made a serious mistake. She climbed backwards out her window into outside over there"—floating in the air looking for her sister, but apparently unable to find her because of her foolishness in going out backwards. Yet she then hears her father's voice telling her, "If Ida backwards in the rain / would only turn around again / and catch those goblins with a tune / she'd spoil their kidnap honeymoon." So, tumbling "right side round," she finds herself in a cave—"smack in the middle of a wedding"—among the five goblins, who turn out to be "just babies like her sister!" By playing her horn, she causes the goblins to dance uncontrollably, faster and faster, until "they quick churned into a dancing stream"—the double-page spread here showing the goblins sinking and dissolving into the ocean, which has come into the cave. But one baby is left, sitting "cozy in an eggshell," and that turns out to be Ida's sister. Ida carries her back along a stream and up the hill to their mother, who holds out a letter from their father which says, " 'I'll be home one day, / and my brave, bright little Ida / must watch the baby and her Mama / for her Papa, who loves her always.' " And on the last page, which reads, "Which is just what Ida did," we see Ida willingly helping her sister to learn to walk, in contrast to the book's second double-page spread, in which Ida is holding a squalling baby while her mother's back is turned on them both.

It turns out that this attempt to summarize Sendak's story neutrally has been frustrating, in part because it seems impossible to do without many of Sendak's own words, and in part because it is incomplete and leaves out many details, especially those in the illustrations, thus giving a distorted sense of the experience of the text. But above all it is frustrating because it is impossible to do such a summary without beginning to interpret.

One of the unusual things about this capstone to Sendak's trilogy is that, unlike the first two books, it received at least a five-year buildup in various media, from Jonathan Cott's 1976 *Rolling Stone* interview to Selma Lanes's *The Art of Maurice Sendak* (1980), with other interviews scattered among the intervening years. It was, we learned, going to be Sendak's major work, most impressive artistically and most important for Sendak emotionally, somehow completing what he had begun in his two other most celebrated books. This buildup is, I think, of some importance in understanding readers' reactions when the book finally was published. With such a long waiting period, admirers of Sendak's work were liable either to fall into uncritical—and sometimes rhapsodic—admiration, or to suffer various degrees of disappointment. Ethel Heins's praise unaccompanied by any attempt at interpretation is at one extreme. At the other, Donnarae MacCann and Olga Richard not only label *Outside Over There* "vacuous" (13), but claim that it, like much of Sendak's other work, has a major weakness in its adaptations of earlier artists' styles, which do not fuse into original form. They identify this eclecticism as a quality of "popular art"—art that takes few risks and relies upon "collective 20th century experience which elicit[s] a loyal following" (13). Further, they take Sendak's description of the process of creation as a response to " 'unbidden feelings' " and his conjecture that " 'children read the internal meanings of *everything*' " to be an abdication of the responsibility to achieve original form and coherent meaning (16).

It can be argued that MacCann's and Richard's judgments are based on a narrow, elitist view of fine art in relation to popular art, a view they apply to Sendak without real discussion, although what they say about Sendak's disclaimer of any responsibility to make his text coherent and his meaning apparent requires attention. But Susan Hankla's *cri de coeur* in reply to Ethel Heins's review makes a much more serious charge, for Hankla finds *Outside Over There* to be a "paranoid vision" and a "shallow, icy surrogate for a literature which will benefit humanity"; and, as my brief epigraph quoting her suggests, she also finds its meanings excessively obscure. I do not know whether Sendak's book will benefit humanity, but Hankla's response has to be taken seriously, if only to be countered. My own fascination with the book cannot be separated from my initial disappointment and ambivalence, from the controversy over Sendak's eclecticism, nor from what I discovered in the course of my struggles with *Outside Over There* about a key literary (and to a lesser extent, graphic) source of the story. Because that discovery was what enabled me to come to terms with Sendak's book, I shall treat it first in the account of my reading, thus stepping somewhat outside the chronological sequence of that process.

According to Selma Lanes, Sendak derived the "bare-bones plot" of *Outside Over There* from a brief tale, "The Goblins," which he had illustrated together with other selected Grimms' fairy tales in 1973 (Lanes, 228).[4] The connection with a story about a baby stolen by goblins is clear enough, and the artist seems to allude to his earlier illustration by providing the hooded goblins of *Outside Over There* with the same kind of staff. The other source frequently cited by Lanes, and by Sendak in interviews, is Mozart's *The Magic Flute,* which contributes the idea of the testing of personal qualities and the plot-device of using music (Ida's horn and Papageno's bells) to defeat threatening figures by causing them to dance uncontrollably. (Sendak includes the figure of Mozart playing a keyboard instrument in the pages on which Ida takes her sister back home—as if to acknowledge the influence.)[5] But no critic has identified what seems to be a more fundamental and complex source for Sendak's text, George MacDonald's *The Princess and the Goblin.* To a lesser extent there also seems to be a visual influence in Arthur Hughes's illustrations for that book and for MacDonald's *At the Back of the North Wind,* yet Sendak in interviews published between 1970 and 1980 never mentioned these works specifically as influences on the third volume of his trilogy.

He had, however, in most of those interviews referred to MacDonald, for example as a "model . . . someone I try to copy in many ways" (Haviland, 247), or to "ripping off" MacDonald, "whose fairytales . . . are for me the source book of much of my work" (Stott, 34). More specifically, in his 1970 interview with Virginia Haviland, Sendak mentioned *The Princess and the Goblin,* and Princess "Irene's travels through the cave with the goblins" as being "so strange that "they can only come out of the deepest dream stuff" (247). The special interest of the latter statement is the fact that eleven years before the publication of *Outside Over There,* its author has already in his memory transformed MacDonald's novel into something more like his as yet unwritten (and in 1970, possibly not yet planned) book than it really is: for although there *is* a goblin plot to kidnap the Princess Irene "to be a nasty goblin's bride" (Sendak's words about Ida's little sister), and she does travel through their caves, it is with the miner's son, Curdie, and she comes into the presence of goblins only once and briefly.

In *Outside Over There* Sendak was further to transform a kidnapping *plot* into an actual kidnapping, and the victim from a preadolescent girl into a baby sister in such a girl's charge. But the initial circumstances and even setting are similar. MacDonald's Irene lives in a great house halfway up a hill; her parents are absent—her "King-Papa" traveling throughout his kingdom and mother elsewhere because of a serious illness. Sendak's Ida, who also lives on a hill, must take the place of an absent-minded, seemingly depressed mother in caring for her little sister, while her father is "away at sea." The hill in Sendak's first two-page spread is similar to that in Arthur Hughes's first cut for *The Princess and the Goblin,* which also depicts a stone bridge much like that over which Sendak's goblins carry the baby.

But perhaps the most revealing indication of Sendak's debt to MacDonald is a remark in his 1976 interview with Jonathan Cott: "The only way to find something is to lose oneself: that's what George MacDonald teaches us in his stories" (Cott, *Forever Young,* 201). Although in the immediate context Sendak is referring to Gustav Mahler's "losing himself" in his *Waldhütte,* the MacDonald reference sounds as though it is to Irene's earliest adventure, when she must lose herself in order to find the magical, protective, and strangely erotic figure of her "great-great-grandmother" at the top of the mansion. MacDonald remarks that "it doesn't follow that she *was* lost, because she had lost herself" (chap. 2, 17); and Irene's inability in the next attempt to find this mysterious figure whose love she so greatly needs, when Irene *is* described as being "lost," seems to stem from her failure to "lose herself," her self-consciousness, her waking rationality (chap. 5, 32). This matter of losing oneself fits the pattern of all three works in Sendak's trilogy (as well as many of MacDonald's other works): the journey into the dream and back of *Where the Wild Things Are* and *In the Night Kitchen,* where the dream is a losing of oneself that effects a new reconciliation to one's life, and what I see as the more ambiguous experience of Ida and her sister being "lost" and restored.

The forms given to the recurrences of fictional situations from MacDonald in Sendak indicate that the latter is not merely imitating or "ripping off," but is transforming source elements. And the function of recognizing this as I read and reread is that I internalize those elements, which come to form for me a level of intertextual meaning in Sendak's text. Thus, Sendak's double-page illustration, " 'If Ida backwards in the rain . . . ,' " where I see a resemblance between Ida's floating on her back in the air trailing the yellow raincoat and Arthur Hughes's wood-engraving of the North Wind floating in the air as she prepares to take Little Diamond to his final rest, assumes for me a special resonance because the North Wind is in a sense "saving" Diamond as Ida is saving her sister (*North Wind*, chap. 37, 285). Hughes's surprisingly erotic drawing and MacDonald's text associate the beautiful North Wind, like Irene's great-great-grandmother, with spiritual goodness, a maternal love that is distinctly sensual, and a vaguely defined afterlife. Although there is no narrative parallel between the functions of the North Wind and Sendak's Ida apart from the general one of saving a small child, identifying the apparent graphic influence helped to clarify my feelings about aspects of Sendak's text: feelings of childhood loneliness, loss, and anxiety about sexuality and death, as well as the phantasy of total love from a parental figure.

The connections between *Outside Over There* and the work of George MacDonald (and, again, Arthur Hughes to some extent) thus seemed to me too obvious to be doubted. In both Sendak's picture-book and MacDonald's novel there are the neglect of a preadolescent, perhaps self-centered child (*Irene, Ida*), intended or actual kidnapping by goblins for the purpose of a wedding, and the necessity of losing oneself. Even the defeat of Sendak's goblins by music may have its ultimate source in MacDonald, whose goblins cannot bear Curdie's rhyming songs; for although Grimm, and in this latter respect Mozart, were Sendak's immediate and conscious inspiration, the story's development—and what for readers seems to be its most mysterious element, the references to a "goblin wedding," which is neither explained in the verbal text nor portrayed in the illustrations—owes more to MacDonald. Perhaps even more fundamental is the way in which in both texts danger comes ostensibly from *outside*, and from caves in the earth. One answer to Susan Hankla's question as to where "outside over there" really is would seem to be (for MacDonald and Sendak) anywhere primal dangers might lurk, outside one's own comfortable bedroom, home, and family. Yet "outside over there" is also "inside in here,"[6] both the unconscious mind and the domestic world where all the child's guilty feelings of Oedipal desire, aggression, and jealousy (sibling and other) originate; and Sendak's tale could almost be taken as a paradigm of how what is *heimlich* (domestic, private, secret, forbidden) becomes *unheimlich* (alien, threatening, strange, but also eerily familiar).

After the appearance of the first version of this chapter, Sendak confirmed that I was correct about his use of *The Princess and the Goblin* and went on to say that he had completely repressed any awareness of it during the years he was working on *Outside Over There* (only my conjecture here about the ultimate source for controlling enemies through music was not in the version that Sendak read):

And you're right. It was all Mozart & Grimm at the time—at *that* time. Had someone said MacDonald, I no doubt would have drooled like old Pavlov's dog. It is amazing (and you must truly believe me that it's the truth)—how I entirely blotted out MacDonald. And, as you know, Princess & Goblin is a great favorite—more—the text I have more than likely found myself "in." Everything you say as related to that book—is correct. Only I never *thought* of that book when I did OOT. I couldn't, obviously.[7]

It is interesting that Elaine Moss, who warns us against taking account of Sendak himself in reading *Outside Over There,* nonetheless brings to her reading a knowledge of psychoanalysis, remarks about which pervade Sendak's statements about his own work. She finds Ida to be threatened by "malign forces which may shatter the eggshell protection of childhood" and to be projecting her fears upon her baby sister, who in Ida's phantasy becomes the victim in place of the nearly adolescent Ida; Ida can then save her sister, Moss says, in a resolution as "reassuring as is Max's hot supper"—a reference to the ending of *Where the Wild Things Are.* (On eggshells, see my discussion of the reappearance of Ida's sister, below.) Sendak, too, has commented on what ties the parts of his trilogy together: "They are all variations on the same theme: how children master various feelings—anger, boredom, fear, frustration, jealousy—and manage to come to grips with the realities of their lives" (Lanes, 227). Such a scenario nicely describes the first two books, but for *Outside Over There* it seems to me less adequate, failing, like Moss's reading, to account for the ambiguity I and others have found in the ending and the complex, sometimes obscure, and definitely disturbing symbolism.

Now that I have recognized the influence of George MacDonald, my reading begins from the premise that Sendak's creative process is both autobiographical and eclectic. Such a premise allows me to integrate what I see as his main sources and what I have learned about his life into my total understanding of *Outside Over There*.[8] But I arrived at this personal understanding only with difficulty, after an initially negative response to the apparent obscurity and didacticism, and even to the new graphic style of a long anticipated book. Indeed, the possibility of my empathy with the author-illustrator's purposes was reduced, first of all, by a feeling of personal betrayal in Sendak's change of style. The flat, comic-book style of *In the Night Kitchen* (and to some extent of *Where the Wild Things Are*), which recalled the ten- or fifteen-cent tokens of love given to me, especially when I was ill, as a child, and the cross-hatching of *Higglety Pigglety Pop!*, so reminiscent of my favorite, George Cruikshank, had been supplanted by a stylistic mode that at first glance seemed to resemble, especially in the modeling of figures, the *Saturday Evening Post* commercial art familiar from my childhood, which had in my family of professional and amateur artists represented the lowest in "realistic" art.[9] Such an experience of disappointment is analogous to readers' discomfort when a favorite novelist tries something new, such as Victorian reactions to the increasing darkness of Dickens's novels, or some modern literary critics' tendency to denigrate works by an author which deviate from an approved norm, as in the supposed failure of irony in Austen's *Mansfield Park*. But worse than the shock of Sendak's new style was my feeling about the apparent message of the story: girls, if they want to be happy, content, *and* loved by their fathers, must take care of their baby sisters and their mothers. If there was any attempt to provide reassurance for the reader, it just didn't work for me.

Subsequently discovering Sendak's main source in MacDonald provided a new framework through which I could reconsider my response. If any single aspect of *The Princess and the Goblin* is dominant for me, it is the combination of Irene's virtually orphaned state with her strong and determined sense of self. This combination allows her both to find her succoring great-great-grandmother *and,* prior to that discovery, to make the all-important "mistake" (Sendak's word about how Ida goes into Outside Over There) of staying outside too long with her maid, thus putting herself in danger from the goblins' strange animals, who only come up from underground at night, and potentially from the goblins themselves (chap. 6). It is this mistake that leads to her meeting Curdie, whom she later saves from being trapped in the mine and tortured or killed by the goblins, and who in turn saves her from a "goblin wedding" (again, Sendak's expression, which may seem totally mysterious if one does not know the source in MacDonald). Because I identify most strongly with the lonely but self-possessed child, Irene, and secondarily with the older male child, Curdie, I find especially appealing MacDonald's notion that being a princess or prince depends on inner rather than contingent (genealogical) attributes. And the narrative structure in regard to both Irene and Curdie recalls childhood phantasies about myself as an orphan who attains love, power, and acceptance. Irene's great-great-grandmother (whose analogue in *Outside Over There,* if there is one, is Ida's father) is for me one of the most appealing of MacDonald's creations. Although any adult reader can easily infer a religious significance, this figure for me is primarily a quasi-erotic surrogate mother for Irene, as the North Wind is for Little Diamond.[10]

The goblins' threat to Irene has affective significance for me in three ways. There is a guilty identification with the goblins in their desire to treat sadistically and possess sexually the pure young girl. Insofar as I identify with the princess as child, however, I also feel a fear of physical violation. And for my adult consciousness an ongoing pleasure is provided by the extraordinary way in which MacDonald presents a pre-Freudian model of the human psyche, corresponding roughly to the id (the savage goblins in their deep caverns), the developing ego (Irene), the integrated ego (the miners and especially Curdie, who can work under the ground but also function rationally above ground), and, in the great-great-grandmother, a female ego-ideal that is given clear preference over the machismo of the superego "King-Papa."[11] Thus recognizing *The Princess and the Goblin* as an influence both provided some insight into Sendak's creative process and served as an external framework that, when *Outside Over There* was seen through it, made that book more coherent, and allowed me to connect it with a literary work I believed I already understood.

The published information about Sendak's childhood also helped to unblock my empathy with the phantasies behind this, his most complex book. Like Sendak, I spent long periods sick in bed; I adored comic-book and other kinds of cartoon art, especially the Disney comics of the early to mid forties, and this was related to both illness and the need for love, as I would receive gifts of extra comic-books to keep me occupied. What is probably common to this particular kind of childhood memory is a feeling of illness as something that makes one the focus of attention for a while, and brings both extra affection and extra freedom to be alone with one's thoughts. Although an only child, I did have a surrogate sister, an older girl (the "J" of chap. 3) with whom I spent much time in early years, and when she entered puberty and became less interested in her "little brother" I suffered a feeling of loss. There is nothing like this in Sendak's accounts of his sister, who was twelve rather than two years older than he, but she had a good deal of responsibility for taking care of him and his brother, and from the way he depicts Ida's neglect of her little sister I infer the possibility of similar experiences.

These connections are my own constructs, as Sendak and I in most ways had very different childhoods: he is eight years older, grew up in Brooklyn rather than Manhattan, and is a first- rather than second-generation American, with a much more definitely Jewish upbringing. But my connections further opened up the possibility that *Outside Over There* might not be so alien after all. Upon reflection it occurs to me that many of the greatest children's books, based on seemingly bizarre personal phantasies, have not only their seeming incoherences but their hints of what Leon Edel has called the "tristimania" (*Stuff of Sleep and Dreams*) of great art, the feeling, beginning in childhood, of the fundamental sadness in life. Given my experiences with late adolescent and adult students who, not having read *Alice's Adventures in Wonderland* as children, find it both disturbing and incoherent, I should not have been surprised at my own resistance to finding an emotional coherence in *Outside Over There*.

Perhaps the most seriously negative and resistant aspect of my first responses to Sendak's tale was that I saw not only the conclusion but also the initial situation as being approved of by the narrator: "When Papa was away at sea, / and Mama in the arbor . . ." Other adult readers of *Outside Over There* have conveyed to me a similar judgment (and some have said, "I wouldn't give that book to a child"), but I can see now that it is no more necessary to make such an assumption than it is to assume that MacDonald "approves" of Irene's virtually abandoned state.[12] Both of the initial two-page spreads include extremely, and I think intentionally, disturbing domestic elements: for not only are the lurking hooded goblins present in the first of these, but the mother clearly ignores Ida and her screaming baby sister, and there is a frustrated and unhappy look on Ida's face. Her sister's bonnet has just fallen on the ground, and Ida looks down at it as if hoping her mother will turn around and pick it up for her. Given this opening where things are emotionally wrong, in the second such spread, "Ida played her wonder horn to rock the baby still—but never watched," has connotations of a hostile neglect, emphasized by the visual parallel with the previous page, where Ida's mother's back is turned just as Ida's is here.

Sendak told Selma Lanes that he identified as much with Ida as with the baby, although it was he who was cared for as a child by his older sister; and it is Ida rather than the baby who is given the strong emotions, the fear, anger, and jealousy (although the baby's face is perhaps more expressive, suggesting the kind of projection that Elaine Moss has described). And Ida's unawareness of the kidnapping seems to be due to her almost hypnotic fascination with the horn, roses, and sunflowers, as her failure to recognize what the ice changeling is due to her own icy feelings towards her burdensome sister. (The flowers rising up through Ida's window from the mother's "arbor" seem to combine male sexual force in their tumescence with phallic and vaginal shapes in the leaves, possibly confirming Elaine Moss's suggestion that the main threat is that of puberty.) To say, as Susan Hankla does, that Sendak's is a "strikingly paranoid vision" that implies that without constant vigilance "the world as you know it can be replaced by one in which repulsive goblins steal real babies," apart from taking a symbolic (or, as Geraldine DeLuca argues, allegorical) tale too literally, denies a particularity to Ida's experience. It also overlooks the possibility that Ida herself is in conflict—that is, that the kidnapping and the saving of the baby, as manifestations of Ida's phantasies, represent an internal conflict between hostility and love.

The idea of psychological projection is further supported by the fact that Sendak (as I understand his use of MacDonald) changes the object of the goblins' lust and cruelty in MacDonald from the "I" (Irene, Ida) to the baby. Lanes reports that Sendak was delighted to find that the name Ida included "Id," and that the three letters were also contained, backwards (cf. "Ida backwards . . ."), in the diminutive form of his mother's name, Sadie (232–34). I am not going to claim that I know what was going on in Sendak's unconscious when he chose his protagonist's name, but given the connections with *The Princess and the Goblin* it seems likely that the choice was overdetermined and included as one source the resemblance between Irene, Ida, and "I," which is also the literal translation of Freud's "*Ich*" (ego). And to carry the parallel a bit further, although forbidden desires and hatreds may arise from Ida's "id," her story also seems one of an ego coming to terms with the external world—"out there" as distinct from "outside over there."

Ida's donning her mother's raincoat seems a symbol for her attempt to take on her mother's role—or the fact that she has *already* had to take it on; but why is it a "serious mistake" to climb "backwards out the window into outside over there"? Backwards may have various implications, including regression, but in the context of the previously turned backs of Ida and her mother it suggests to me a continuation of the unconscious neglect of her sister, whom she is now trying to save from the goblins but cannot see. It is the voice of the father (psychologically perhaps the introjected father or the superego, but also Ida's actual phantasy of the presence of the father who she feels has abandoned her) that provides Ida with the right kind of magic: his command, in effect, means "Turn around and look!" This seems to be stressed on the double-page spread in which she is hearing her father's voice by the inclusion of the figure of the neglectful—and maritally neglected—mother in her seat in the arbor, looking more glum and less aware than ever of what is going on, separated by many caves from her baby (who appears to be quite frightened), with the baby's bonnet still not picked up by the mother. And thus Ida, in the sequential order of events in the book, manages to accept her responsibility for her sister before their mother does.

The revelation to Ida that the goblins are "just babies like her sister!" may have a double edge. While, if one takes Elaine Moss's tack, it could be seen as a defense against the threats that seem to loom in puberty, it also might imply that for Ida her sister has indeed been something of a goblin—screaming and making ugly faces when Ida wants to talk to her mother, or interfering when Ida wants to play her horn. Of interest, too, is the ambiguous gender of the goblins: all are naked, and the only sex revealed, in two of them, is female. And although Sendak has said that everyone in the book is female, including the goblins (Cott, *Pipers*, 78), I see no way of telling about three of them; and further, there are two emphatically masculine sailor boys and a shepherd boy depicted on the pages with the text that begins, "If Ida backwards. . . ." Undoubtedly Sendak *thought* of the goblins as all female, and this raises again the question of whether we can take an author's word for what is not evident in his text.[13]

There is also a phrase that may connect the scene of the goblins' defeat to what Sendak has called his "invalidized" childhood (Stott, 37): "We're dancing sick and must to bed." Does this mean that Maurice himself is one of those troublemaking goblins in his memories about his childhood? Again, in the "dancing sick" scene, there is a reference to the hornpipe making "sailors wild," which recalls Ida's father the sailor and makes me think of a girl's ambivalence about her father's sexuality, for both "hornpipe" and "wild" may be sexually loaded words. In this same connection the eggshell in which Ida finds her sister seems to be a symbol of both the protective shell of childhood mentioned by Moss, and a child's belief that chickens come from eggs and babies from mothers without any role for the father— although here it could also be a denial of the mother's (or the father's?) role in parturition, for it is *only* after being (apparently) born from the egg that Ida's sister is "crooning and clapping as a baby should," quite different behavior from that at the book's opening, when the mother is present. Sendak gave a different explanation of the eggshells to Cott: "The reason the eggshells appear in *Outside Over There* is mostly in homage to the original source" (*Pipers,* 72), that is, the Grimms' tale "The Goblins," where eggshells are used to test whether a baby is a changeling or not. But the use of the eggshell in the scene where Ida finds her sister seems to be overdetermined and go beyond such "homage"—and among other possible allusions is William Blake's engraving No. 6 in *For the Sexes: The Gates of Paradise*: "At length for hatching ripe he breaks the shell."

A problem for some readers, and one of the main obstacles to my taking *Outside Over There* seriously at first, is the apparent didacticism of the conclusion, when, returning with her sister to their mother, Ida finds that a letter has come from her father which instructs her to "watch the baby and her Mama for her Papa, who loves her always." Sendak told Cott that a friend found this disturbing, in the way it "dumps everything on Ida," and thus eliminates a "happy ending"; and Sendak replied, "But who said it was a happy ending?" (*Pipers,* 77). Though not committing himself to the meaning of the ending, he also has said, "At the moment Ida takes over for the mother, but that doesn't mean that that's a permanent state of being" (*Pipers,* 78). Elaine Moss, apparently feeling a need for closure, construes the ending as reassuring, while I think my reaction and that of Sendak's friend (and of Geraldine DeLuca, who comments on the lack of "release," and being "left . . . with too much pain" [22]) indicates a similar wish for closure but an inability to find it. It now seems to me more helpful to take a clue from Sendak's demurrer about happy endings and consider the conclusion as a step reached in a process of emotional development for Ida (and perhaps for her mother as well). To venture a loosely Freudian reading: the symbolic meaning of the father's absence and his letter, for Ida, is that the female child must come to recognize that she cannot have her father all to herself and need not regard her mother as a rival. But because of the double configuration of the Oedipus complex as experienced by girls, the conclusion, and indeed the entire plot, of *Outside Over There* can also signify that the *mother* is not exclusively one's own, in the context of a sibling rivalry as well as the Oedipus complex.[14] Ida is, surely, accepting some of the functions of a mother in relation to her baby sister, yet it is a step, not a completed process with a stereotyped outcome (Ida as simply taking on the permanent role of a mother); DeLuca is interesting on this matter, expressing gratitude to Sendak for recognizing the conflict in young girls between self-achievement and serving others (15).

Sendak's stated view of his own work, and *Outside Over There* in particular, might be called "intertextual," in that he is constantly aware of—or, in the case of *The Princess and the Goblin* and *Outside Over There,* unconsciously creating his art in relation to—other verbal and graphic texts. I want for a moment to take up again the intertextual aspect of my own response, turning once more to MacDonald's novel. Irene's losses at the end are greater than Ida's, for not only is her father by and large absent, but it becomes clear that her mother has died. Yet Irene too has moved at least one step in her development: by taking the initiative to enter the mine and rescue Curdie, she has made possible the eventual routing of the goblins, whom I take as symbols of (among other things) male sexuality conceived of as dirty, violent, and demeaning. She thus clears the way for a mature relationship with Curdie, who will eventually (in *The Princess and Curdie*) replace Irene's King-Papa as her main love object after he goes through his own process of testing. *The Princess and the Goblin,* its sequel, *Outside Over There,* and Sendak's favorite opera, *The Magic Flute,* are all stories of the testing and development of individuals. Viewing Sendak through the framework of MacDonald has shown me the danger of reading their tales either too literally or too much as strict allegories, and the necessity of letting one's response and understanding of narrative flow from a contact with one's child self, insofar as that can be recovered (MacDonald, incidentally, was very firm that his books were not to be read as allegories). My suspicion about *Outside Over There* is that Sendak is essentially correct about child-readers: most of them will take from the book whatever is meaningful to them, without conceptualizing it, though this does not mean that they will be motivated to understand every detail. My experience tells me that many adolescents and adults will either admire the book for its surface beauties, dismiss it as incomprehensible or worse ("It would be frightening to children" is one complaint I have often heard), or have to spend a good deal of time finding its coherence for themselves—as they might indeed with any problematic text, such as *Alice's Adventures in Wonderland, The Princess and the Goblin, Bleak House,* or *Ulysses.* I become more and more convinced that the line between adults and children as between adults' books and children's books, is a very fine one, that may essentially be ignored in many contexts of reading.

Any aspects of the preceding discussion which may read as if they were an objective "interpretation" of Sendak's text are, of course, constructs and conceptualizations that I have created for the purpose of filling out gaps in the coherence of my response to and understanding of *Outside Over There.* Taking all the hints about Sendak's childhood and the sources of the story in MacDonald, as well as my sense of limited but definite parallels between Sendak's childhood and mine, I have tried to demonstrate how it is possible to discuss a difficult text by treating the individual reading experience as a palimpsest of the reader's own responses and associations, extrinsic evidence (sources and biography), and direct interpretation based on conventions of literary criticism—all three interacting in the reader's thoughts and feelings to produce, not "truth," but a way of coming to grips with the text. My prior knowledge and love of *The Princess and the Goblin,* in particular, directed me to a coherent way of reading Sendak's book, and the affective side of my responses helped me to construct, if not objectively discover, an emotional structure as well as a cognitive one. Undoubtedly this resembles, after all, Elaine Moss's notion of each reader bringing an interpretation to the text, but my intention has been to show that more may be involved in such a process than the mere contemplation of the text alone. I should be be less than fully honest, however, if I failed to acknowledge that Sendak's confirmation of the importance of his source in MacDonald has given the interpretation that I "bring" to the text a special kind of certainty for me in at least that one respect; but it may well not provide that kind of certainty for another reader.

Placed as they are in an introductory chapter and in this final chapter, the discussions of works by Maurice Sendak have turned out to be more important for the purpose of demonstrating a methodology of the use of individual response and extrinsic knowledge in interpretation than I had intended when planning this book. One contingent reason for this is that I have been teaching a course in children's literature nearly every year for the past ten years and have in the process become fascinated not only with Sendak's work, but with the difficulties my students and I have had in dealing with it. There also turn out to be aspects of Sendak's "children's" books that make them especially suitable as subjects for the kind of demonstration I have been carrying out. First of all, because they belong to a composite genre, his picture-books are unfamiliar as a type of object for interpretation to those trained to analyze literature formalistically or historically. For adult readers they are imbued with a degree of the mysterious and thus are a challenge to normal processes of reading and understanding, and they rarely fail to provoke strong reactions, whether positive or negative. Further, any extended acquaintance with Sendak's work leads one to realize that he makes considerable use of autobiographical material—not straightforwardly, but poetically; and so there are in a sense mysteries of the author beyond the mysteries of his texts. And while those texts may through their very unfamiliarity and uncertainty of discursive meaning motivate some readers to try to arrive at conclusive interpretations, a reading that accounts for everything in a Sendak work is ultimately unattainable.

Yet except for the matter of composite genre, I should argue that in most respects *Higglety Pigglety Pop!* and *Outside Over There* are not really substantially different as objects of the attempt to understand simultaneously one's response to a text and that text as "other" from the works I have discussed by Austen, Emily Brontë, Lewis Carroll, Kenneth Grahame, Dickens, Hardy, or Lawrence; the strangeness and the connections to the extrinsic have only become more evident in Sendak, not greater in degree. But these picture-books have also turned up here contrary to my original design because of a personal motivation of which I was not fully aware until I had completed the bulk of this chapter. I grew up in a family of which I may have been the only member without any degree of competence in visual art. Both of my parents, two of my grandparents, and two of my uncles and their wives have been either professional or talented amateur artists; and today, the four who are still artistically active have been joined by two of my cousins, one a professional "high realist" painter, the other a noted jazz musician who also does splendid murals as well as cartoons for his album-covers. My mentioning this may sound like family pride, but it is really envy. And it is thus no accident that my first major research project after graduate school was on Phiz's illustrations to Dickens's novels, and that I have also written on George Cruikshank and Arthur Rackham. It is as though I had to prove that even if I could not draw a recognizable person, horse, or dog, I could still have something to do professionally with visual art, and have illustrations (even if not my own) included in my writings. My attraction to the act of writing about Sendak's works and my desire to know something about them that no one else knew have a similar motivation, although such motivations are always overdetermined; and as it turned out, it was a kind of lucky chance that I detected something that I could tell Sendak about his own work which he did not know.

I have given this account of motivations because after making a point of insisting that interpretation—and thus implicitly, the form it takes in a given instance—is always motivated (chap. 2), I felt that I should reveal some of the more personal impulses I have detected in myself for writing this book. If Norman Holland is right about the function of the individual "identity theme" in how we read, my own identity theme is something like, "I *can* do it too." This applies not only to my incompetence at visual art, but equally to the fact that my father was for a time a successful writer of fiction, something I have never felt I could be. So again, in writing criticism, mostly about fiction, I do something analogous to one of my father's creative activities and help to still the feelings of inadequacy retained from childhood.

Many of my attempts here at a theory that connects interpretation and response have been developed either in the process of teaching, or in contemplating the problems of teaching; indeed, there is no literary work discussed here which I have not at some time taught, with the exception of "1887" and *The Revolt of Islam*. Thus, having to lecture about *The Wind in the Willows* in a course that I shared with David Bleich brought to me a number of shocks of recognition regarding a book about which I had become complacent; and the questions from some graduate students as to what one could "do" with reader response prompted me to try to put those recognitions into coherent language. As for Sue in *Jude the Obscure* or Miriam in *Sons and Lovers,* it was students' disturbed responses as well as my own that led me to the exploration of source and influence, and a rethinking of my understanding, and the same thing is true of my searching in Hardy's textual changes for a new understanding of the "pizzle" section of *Jude.* Even my pervasive concern with the relation between the intrinsic (textual), the extrinsic, and the subjective has its origin in my perception that students by and large wanted more than the text—not because of wishing to avoid close reading, but rather because texts had, in the way they were typically taught, come to feel decontextualized. Some attention might be given to historical "background," but in general students were discouraged from attempting to read the texts as the utterance of a real person, or as representing a world whose very nature depended on what they themselves brought to the text. (I include my own past "objective" teaching as one source of this process of decontextualization.)

In the course of writing these studies, I have recognized that my original but discarded goal of reinstating the extrinsic, especially author and source, without giving up my convictions about the subjective and affective motives for interpretation, would have been a logically impossible task. To reconcile the subjectivist and intentionalist positions, to have Hirsch sit down with Bleich, is an unattainable goal. Thus I have instead attempted to demonstrate the value of a method that treats the subjective and the communication of response and association as paths to "understanding" the text—or perhaps that should read, understanding "the text"—and the extrinsic as something that is incorporated in the experience of reading.

Some degree of unsupported assertion is inevitably present in every work of literary theory or criticism that I have ever read or written, and I no doubt make my own such assertions here, although I have tried to be as clear as possible that I am always talking about ways of thinking about literature and reading that I find rewarding (whether they are my ways or others'). That our perceptions are always mediated by our sensory apparatus, by language, and by our individual emotional makeups and experiences does not seem to me a difficult fact to accept, though it is often difficult to keep it in mind from moment to moment when one is engaged in interpretation. I find myself left with the realization that although I can know in any conclusive sense neither the meanings of literary texts nor the intentions of their authors, I must endlessly attempt to conceptualize authors and meanings, to seek for the personal sources of my response, and to learn about other readers' responses and associations. What I hope I have accomplished here is to demonstrate that a variety of forms of interrelation can be seen to exist between meaning, the text, the extrinsic, the individual reader, and the communication of individual understandings in a social group.

Notes

Introduction

1. The classic New Critical text is W. K. Wimsatt, Jr., and Monroe C. Beardsley, "The Intentional Fallacy" (1946), but Beardsley's 1958 treatment of the same issue seems more cogent (see chap. 2).

2. "Do Readers Make Meaning?" is the title of an essay by Robert Crosman. His answer to the question is "yes."

3. Hirsch's dictum that the ultimate test of an interpretation is how it sorts with the author's "original meaning" does not inevitably follow from the insistence on shared meaning. That is, while meanings are assumed to be "sharable" on the basis of a common language and culture, the author can be considered a construct employed to give authority to a particular interpretation. It is not clear that Hirsch makes any such distinction, but see *Validity in Interpretation,* especially chapter 1, "In Defense of the Author," and my discussion of the author-as-construct in chapter 2 and elsewhere.

4. One cannot simply by assertion impose a chosen meaning on a word, but my use of the word *understanding* in context should lend it the signification I intend. Defenders of "correct" reading have used the same word for their own purposes—not only Brooks and Warren, but Stein Haugom Olsen in *The Structure of Literary Understanding.*

5. This fifth premise, and its consequences in practice, are, I think, the closest I come to David Bleich's concept of "negotiation" among readers.

6. I shall throughout be using the spelling *phantasy* to denote individuals' (and cultures') imaginings about themselves or others, their ways of coping with desires, fears, anxieties, and feelings of inadequacy. *Fantasy,* on the other hand, is used to refer to a specific subgenre of narrative, represented in this study by *Alice's Adventures in Wonderland, The Wind in the Willows,* and *Outside Over There,* among others. Although this distinction via spelling is not now generally used by literary critics, it clears up a possible confusion and is still used as a standard distinction by psychoanalytic writers.

Chapter 1. Theories of Reading: An End to Interpretation?

1. This model of individual readers "selecting" constraints may be analogous to the way in which scientists are "constrained" by so-called empirical reality. The model of inductive reasoning based on empirical facts has been questioned by philosophers and historians of science, who suggest that instead, the range of facts that a particular scientist chooses is determined by its usefulness in proving the hypothesis he has already formulated. And such an hypothesis may itself be based on the particular (unacknowledged) philosophical and social position of the scientist, his values and beliefs. See, for example, Rudwick on the Devonian controversy: "Many of the more innocently 'factual' observations can be seen from their context to have been sought, selected, and recorded in order to reinforce the observer's interpretation and to undermine the plausibility of that of his opponents" (431–32). I am grateful to Eric Steig for pointing out this parallel. See also Raskin and Bernstein, *New Ways of Knowing.*

2. Miller has long since discarded his earlier belief in the possibility of a "unified consciousness" that was the basis of his book on Hardy (*Fiction,* 18–19).

3. See especially *Self-Consuming Artifacts,* and its appendix, "Literature in the Reader: Affective Stylistics," which is reprinted in *Is There a Text in This Class?* with retrospective commentary (21–67).

4. On the problems with Holland's approach see also Bleich, *Subjective Criticism,* 111–22.

5. The way Iser conceives of the text itself dominating the nature of the process through which the reader constructs the text's meaning is demonstrated most clearly in his chapter on *Vanity Fair* in *The Implied Reader.*

6. Cf. the title of Jane Tompkins's anthology, which covers a wide range of methodologies, "from Formalism to Post-Structuralism."

7. E. D. Hirsch has insisted on a strict distinction between the two, claiming that interpretation has to do only with "verbal meaning," while criticism has to do with "significance," the relation of verbal meaning to other concerns. This is a distinction that I don't think can be maintained, as I explain in chapters 2 and 8. (See *Validity in Interpretation,* 140ff.)

8. Holland had first made this point earlier, in chapter 10 of *Psychoanalysis and Shakespeare.*

9. Holland describes this conversion in "A Letter to Leonard."

10. The term *response classroom* is David Bleich's.

11. It is also true that the kind of response-generated literary insights that I discuss here could be considered valuable by someone who does not accept the principle of meaning-in-the-reader; and this fact may seem to suggest that creation of such insights through a reader-response approach cannot validate my theoretical position. While a critic's ability to accept one or another kind of critical insight is, indeed, not wholly dependent on his theoretical premises, nonetheless literary insights through individual response and association do not normally arise in classrooms in which such processes are not encour-

aged, nor do they appear in the interpretive work of critics who are not to some extent committed to the subjective basis of meaning. And although it is possible to persuade colleagues who do not share such premises that some of the insights thus produced are of relevance to literary study, it takes a considerable effort to effect such a persuasion, usually involving the setting out of the whole context of the response classroom. To the extent that such insights are conceded to be of value, those persuaded have entered into sympathy with both the method and its premises.

12. One direct result of these seminar discussions was my writing and publishing the first version of what is here chapter 5, on *The Wind in the Willows*.

13. Of course in a sense the teacher always does have the last word, and few students forget that; but keeping a watch over oneself to make sure one avoids *giving* the last word makes a considerable difference to the way students feel about what is going on in the classroom. In chapter 3 I discuss the ways in which I may possibly delimit my students' writing by the examples of my own response papers, and the expectations I make them aware of.

14. It has to be said that many students, particularly those who are timid, and those who think they have to have things definite, are initially uncomfortable in a response classroom, and such students sometimes do not produce very interesting work, although the degree to which initially resistant students eventually come up with at least one genuine response paper is surprisingly high. Because of the divergent ways in which students react to the whole approach, I am careful to make the matter of grading as unthreatening as possible. Thus I normally give at least a "B" to every student who does all the work and attends class regularly. This is not wholly satisfactory, because those who get a "B" or a "B+" are often disappointed. I am not concerned that I may "inflate" the department's average grades, but simply to give each student an "A" would result in many problems. The ideal practice would be a "Pass/No Credit" arrangement, but few universities are enlightened enough to grant this on faculty request. (On grading, see Bleich, *Readings*, 105–10.)

15. Bleich's treatment of Louise Rosenblatt's concept of transaction and Norman Holland's use of the same term is much more sympathetic to the former, but he still insists that she is talking about the *illusion* of interaction with a text. See *Subjective Criticism*, 108–15.

16. Norman Holland has frequently used the analogy of the "feedback loop" to describe this process, most recently in "The Miller's Wife and the Professors."

17. *Outside Over There* is the title of Maurice Sendak's 1981 book, while "inside in here" is a phrase I formulated in trying to explain how that very puzzling book works. As it turned out, Sendak himself had given the same explanation in a 1983 interview. See Jonathan Cott, *Pipers at the Gates of Dawn*, 75, and chapter 11 below.

18. There is also posed in the novel the question, "Was she guilty?" of adultery with Lord Steyne, but it seems to me that although their assignation

has been set up, the interruption by Rawdon leaves Steyne as frustrated as any of Becky's other male admirers. But this also is ultimately ambiguous.

19. Respectively, Bernard J. Paris, "Towards a Revaluation of George Eliot's *The Mill on the Floss*" (1956); his "The Conflicts of Maggie Tulliver: A Horneyan Analysis" (1969); and my own "Anality in *The Mill on the Floss*" (1971; not my own original title). I should say that I find Paris's acknowledgment of a virtually complete change of mind about Maggie between the publication of his two articles to be a courageous act.

20. I use my own essay as an example because I am able to testify that I did, at the time I wrote it, consider the textual details to be constraints that led to my interpretation; and I use Paris's two essays because at the time he began to develop his Horneyan method of interpretation we were office-mates, and thus I was aware of the extent to which he felt constrained by the texts he was interpreting to read them in a particular way.

21. Of course this argument will fail for any reader who disagrees that there is either pervasive sexual tension or an intermittent prurience in the narrator—but I would call this, in line with my present argument, a matter of the important textual constraints being in a sense *chosen* by the reader. It is also possible that the students in Bleich's classroom were already primed by a certain amount of emphasis on sexual implications in the texts they were reading to thus talk about it in their responses to *Vanity Fair,* but one could as well say that the classroom atmosphere made the expression of such feelings acceptable and thus possible, as they might not be in another class-room. (Bleich himself claims that sex is naturally one dominant concern of young people barely, or not even, out of adolescence.) In chapter 3 I consider the question of whether I myself set up a situation in my teaching in which sexual associations are likely to arise.

Chapter 2. Response, Intention, and Motives for Interpretation

1. It might be said that interpretation does not always involve that which is not understood: for example, does one not interpret a stop sign to mean that one should stop one's car? This seems to be a matter of usage. I would not call this interpretation, although it is undoubtedly an act of reading and then construing a meaning. But in such a case the meaning is already under-stood before the act of reading and only has to be reactivated in the driver. But if I were driving in Québec, knowing French but being unaware of the ways in which the principle of French-only has been carried out, I might well have to *interpret* a sign saying *"Arrêt,"* because it is not in the second-person (and imperative) form of the verb. But again, the next time I met with such a sign, I would not need to interpret it, but only apply to my action a meaning I already knew—as virtually a reflex-action. One's relation to liter-ary works is more complex, and reinterpretation frequently may be felt necessary even with "simple" texts—that is, one does not simply absorb a meaning once, as with the stop sign.

2. Here again I do not intend to privilege difficult texts; that is, I am not saying that they are better than easier ones, but rather, that they are more likely to motivate interpretation. (By *texts* I mean semiotic structures, which include graphic as well as verbal structures; the relevance of this point will become clear.)

3. I do not mean that Hirsch is wholly typical of theorists who claim that all interpretation involves, or should involve, considering intention; indeed, his position is an extreme one, and therefore useful for my purposes.

4. Hirsch's first sortie into this field was an article, "Objective Interpretation," published in *PMLA* in 1960 and reprinted as an appendix in *Validity in Interpretation*.

5. This is also a good example of how "textual constraints" can be, and maybe always are, relative to the reader, rather than imperative.

6. Lest it be thought that these students were young and unsophisticated, and too close to their childhoods to view Jennie's gluttony as anything but "bad," I should explain that my students range in age from nineteen to sixty or older, and in one class the student who defended Sendak and Jennie so passionately that her face turned red was, at nineteen, the youngest in the group.

7. In fact they were distorting somewhat here, for Jennie is portrayed either walking on four legs, like a dog, or standing up in the temporary and inadequate manner that dogs do, except in a single illustration, where she walks downstairs carrying Baby in a satchel.

8. I don't mean to claim that there are unavoidable constraints in the text that should make the reader recognize that Jennie has died. Mary-Agnes Taylor remarks that she is glad she read Sendak's book before reading Lanes's: "Had I read first that Jennie is supposed to have died and gone to heaven instead of actually accomplishing a living, fairy tale rise to fame, that knowledge most surely would have diminished what . . . has been a rich, transactional response to this complex little piece of fiction" (142). But interestingly, Taylor does not mention the river that to me suggests *some* kind of change of state for Jennie (whether or not it is from earth to heaven). Taylor also reports that approximately half of her students have read the book as an allegory of death and an afterlife, and half more or less as she does (143).

9. David Bleich has recently reported the finding, among eight readers (seven graduate students plus himself), that in "narrative, men perceived a strong narrative voice, but women experienced the narrative as a 'world,' without a particularly strong sense that this world was narrated into existence" ("Gender Interests," 239). While his discussion of the possible reasons for this are interesting, the sample seems small, and I find that my undergraduate students, who are mostly women, are unpredictable in this matter of consciousness of narrative voice.

10. Both Susan R. Horton and Jonathan Loesberg, in an issue of *Reader* devoted to reader response and deconstruction, claim that one problem with both intentionalist and response approaches is that they each assume a dualism (subjective-objective) that deconstruction, and Derrida in particular, have

made us aware is cultural and institutional rather than "natural." Yet the decision to dispense with this dualism is no less cultural and no less motivated for the individual who makes that choice. (And I can't help wondering whether it really *is* dispensable in our thinking and discourse—although throughout this book I accept the premise that in interpretation one cannot *know* what is subjective and what objective.)

11. Jameson's hermeneutic model, as he acknowledges, derives from Freud, based as it is on the assumption that manifest content is never equivalent to the real meaning for the text's creator—the dreamer, psychoanalytic patient, or author; I would add, to this list of "creators" for whom texts have meaning, the reader. This is alien to Jameson's methodology as it has developed since 1971, but if one works on the assumption that the reader does not, and indeed cannot, just "discover" or "reveal" meaning, but participates in creating it, then one can apply the same observation about manifest and censored or forbidden (latent) meaning to that reader's experiences *as* reader.

12. Norman Holland has suggested that "Derrida . . . writes out of a need not to believe, a need to *dis*trust. Yet, as with Lacan, I feel the absence is itself a presence. Disbelief is itself a belief in disbelief." And he goes further in saying that "such disbelief I would expect to mask a disappointed need to believe" (Holland, "Re-Covering," 362). Yet one could equally say of Holland's development of the concept of the individual "identity theme" that his insistence on a discrete, continuing self may derive in part from a fear that there is no such thing. (Analogous comments could be made about the present book and its author.)

13. See, for example, Ralph W. Rader, "Fact, Theory, and Literary Explanation," which argues for historical constraints on the ways we understand Swift's Houyhnhnms. This is a different kind of historicism from Jameson's claim that one can find "the object forbidden," for Rader believes that it is possible to find definite and unambiguous historical realities, apparently without using any model of surface and latent meaning.

14. A sense of this ambivalence and conflict is given in Lloyd Osbourne's account of his relationship to Stevenson, *An Intimate Portrait of R. L. S.,* 19–21.

Chapter 3. Stories of Reading: *Wuthering Heights*

1. *Margaret,* like all the names of students in this book, is fictitious. Quotations from Margaret's and others' writing are corrected for spelling and sometimes abridged, but otherwise left as they were when written for and distributed in my classes.

2. An idea borrowed from Gilbert and Gubar [264–65] and used in a way that oversimplifies and distorts their discussion of Brontë's novel.

3. It seems likely to me that Marian, who had to get my special permission to take the overcrowded course, was especially eager to do so because the "ghost" of her childhood friend Ted had *not* yet been laid to rest in her

own mind, and though she somewhat dreaded the process of exploring her past, she also felt compelled to go through with it. I doubt that she was motivated by the feeling that she had better follow my paper as a model, although again, my paper, among others, may have helped to open the way for her. Certainly Margaret's paper earlier in the semester on *Jane Eyre* (mentioned below) was personal to a degree that may have unlocked others' inhibitions.

4. I do not think that Marian or other students have needed any encouragement (as has been suggested to me about David Bleich's *Vanity Fair* class), by means of the example of my own response paper, to go into sexual matters in discussing *Wuthering Heights,* given the nature of that novel—although again it is possible that my paper did pave the way for a less inhibited discussion of such matters.

5. In regard to the possible politics of emotion and power in reader-response teaching, it seems relevant that a student in another course who was initially very doubtful about the whole approach, by the end of the semester remarked in class that it is easier to talk about personal matters to relative strangers than to those whom you know well. If indeed I delimited the possibilities for students' papers, at the same time I made it possible for them to write in a way that most of them never had before, and in a way that they themselves considered a valuable experience.

6. In chapter 4, I describe how my own understanding of *Bleak House* was substantially transformed by my women students' responses to Esther Summerson and my subsequent reflections on how these related to (generally male) readings of the character; but I make no claim for the universality of such an understanding, nor even its necessary permanence for me.

7. Although I have suggested that self-knowledge is only a bonus in the process of teaching through reader response (and in saying that I express some nervousness that I might be accused of attempting "therapy" in my teaching), two years after taking my course Marian told me that her relationship to Ted had haunted her for years (despite the insistence in her third paragraph that she had "buried" him), but that after writing her paper for the class, rather than taking on a new burden of guilt she had felt tremendous relief—the ghost, so to speak, was gone, and she now hardly ever thinks about Ted. It would appear that simply coming to understand a previously incomprehensible situation from the past was enough in this instance to effect a freeing from it.

Chapter 4. Reading Esther Summerson: Reception, Response, Gender

1. Robert C. Holub has outlined the principles and practices of the German "reception" theorists in a way that makes me doubt that they form a definable theoretical school. I have nonetheless borrowed the term to convey a distinction between a historical and an immediate approach to readers' responses.

2. Manheim's exact words are, "a sweet, lovable old bore of a psychopathic personality" (25).

3. Ford and Monod call this an "anonymous review" (937); the identification of the author as Forster is made by Collins (290), which I find convincing as, in his biography of Dickens, Forster says something quite similar about Esther, using the word "artificial" about her tone as narrator. See Forster, *Life*, 2:113–14.

4. W. J. Harvey's comment may stand as representative of negative modern critical statements about Esther, although Kilian cites many others: "The exigencies of the narrative force [Dickens] to reveal Esther's goodness in a coy and repellent manner; she is, for instance, continually imputing to others qualities which the author transparently wishes us to transfer to her" (149).

5. Mrs. Leavis, in her and her husband's belated embrace of Dickens as a major novelist, also sees Esther as consistent and refers to her as a "case history" (156), but the concerns of her chapter on *Bleak House* are not centrally psychological.

6. Hans Robert Jauss means something different by this term: changes in the "horizon of expectations" are brought about for readers by the literary work in its *original* historical context; one example given is Baudelaire's *Fleurs du mal,* which shocked its first reviewers into labeling it obscene, but which Théophile Gauthier recognized as "a critique of its time in the medium of a pure poetry" (172). On the "horizon of expectations" see also Holub, 58–63 and passim.

7. I shall not take on Hutter's disagreement with my early article on Inspector Bucket, except to say that the fact that there are other "transformations" of characters does not change my feeling that Dickens's treatment of Bucket and his attitude toward law and authority are essentially ambivalent (see Hutter, 307, and my two articles on Bucket, the second a collaboration with F. A. C. Wilson).

8. I take Zwerdling's use of that word to be intentionally ambiguous, referring both to Esther's psychological victories in the text, and her critical rehabilitation, which he is spearheading.

9. Although all students and I take part in the process of writing and distributing response papers, we do not always all write on the same topic, so that not all of my students actually wrote on Esther Summerson; but the ones who did produced the most controversial papers on *Bleak House,* which stimulated much discussion.

10. Indeed, some of the hostility in Wanda's paper seems to have been directed at me, for my attempting to make excuses for Esther.

11. It should be said that, as I write this, dire economic conditions in British Columbia, and the lack of employment for those who, like Wanda, are qualified to teach, greatly magnify the normal late-adolescent anxieties about becoming independent.

12. Of course the kind of analysis I am doing of my students' papers is an analysis of *texts* and thus constrained by the interpreter's subjectivity. And so I am not claiming objective knowledge of unconscious meanings,

although, having had the opportunity to discuss these texts with their authors, I do think I have gained insights that are not so readily available when one is dealing with text alone. And I do not mean to imply that Diane is fundamentally a more mature or better adjusted person than the other two students, but she does write as if she is more accepting of her own self-image.

Chapter 5. Response and Evasion in Reading *The Wind in the Willows*

1. An amusing bit of evidence of the special status accorded Grahame's book by its adult admirers is the anecdote published by Clayton Hamilton in 1933, in which he tells of having entered a bookshop on the edge of the Grand Canyon and seen *The Wind in the Willows* displayed "in the very middle of the centre table, isolated in that place of honour." The proprietor explained its presence as a means of telling "a real person by the look that comes into his eyes when he sees" the book. "I do not," she went on, "need to ask his name or anything about him; but I know at once that he is one of the elect" (quoted in E. Grahame, *First Whisper*, 23).

2. First edition, London, 1863. The frontispiece is reproduced in Gottlieb and Plumb, *Early Children's Books and Their Illustration*, 124. Considerable credibility is added to such a reading as Duffy's by the new material on Kingsley's attitudes to sexuality contained in the biography by Susan Chitty, *The Beast and the Monk*.

3. Peter Green's analysis of the phantasy and the satire, and of the advantages of Grahame's strategy in using animals to act them out, is contained in his introduction to the Oxford World's Classics edition of *The Wind in the Willows*.

4. I have quoted this passage with the original detached hyphens, which give an onomatopoetic sense of Mole's persistent sobs.

5. First published 1891, in the *National Observer*. Reprinted in Grahame's first book, *Pagan Papers* (1894), 34–38.

6. It has been suggested to me that the "mystery" in the seventh chapter represents the "primal scene"—a young child witnessing or phantasizing its parents in sexual intercourse. Though perhaps too narrow as a construction of Grahame's meaning (or my response), this is certainly plausible as an example of "things rightly kept hidden."

7. Two critics discuss *The Wind in the Willows* as childhood pastoral, and their arguments would seem to negate the erotic details I find in it. Lois R. Kuznets finds the animals' quest to be one for "felicitous space," while Geraldine D. Poss sees a presexual Arcadia in which feelings of discontent are lodged safely in the pleasures of home.

8. Green claims that the book is clearly a reference to William Morris's "beautifully illustrated medieval folios" (*Kenneth Grahame*, 262).

9. Grahame wrote to Theodore Roosevelt, a great admirer of *The Golden Age* and *Dream Days*, that *The Wind in the Willows'* "qualities, if any, are

mostly negative—*i.e.,*—no problems, no sex, no second meaning" (quoted by Green, *Kenneth Grahame,* 274).

10. Eric Partridge in his *Dictionary of Slang* gives "to coït" as the only meaning (928).

11. "Fly merry News among the Crews" is the first line of a song with the repeated refrain, "Up-tails all," included in Thomas D'Urfey's *Wit and Mirth: or Pills to Purge Melancholy* (1719), 4:177–78. But the song is much older: the Fitzwilliam Virginal Book (a collection copied out, c. 1609) contains variations by Giles Farnaby on "Up tails all" (Abraham, 293).

12. *The Cambridge Book of Poetry for Children* (1916). See Green, *Kenneth Grahame,* 319–20.

13. Duffy on the same page identifies Pan as "indistinguishable in appearance from the devil or naked hairy lust," which, if from my point of view an oversimplification because it does not take into account the elements of defense and denial, or the motherliness of the Pan-figure, is not to be dismissed.

14. Peter Green has an interesting theory that Grahame associated Mr. Toad, his misbehavior, and his imprisonment, with Oscar Wilde (*Kenneth Grahame,* 284). This is plausible to me only if I assume that the author completely separates Toad from what I have been calling the erotic atmosphere of certain chapters in order to *deny* that any of his own rebellious temptations were to homosexual activities; but this is a rather tortured way to make Green's theory plausible and does not fully convince me.

15. One possible autobiographical transformation Green does not mention is that of Kenneth's son, Alistair, into Mole. Apart from the fact that Alistair's nickname was "Mouse" during his early years, and that the genesis of Grahame's novel was in a series of bedtime stories about a mole, Alistair was blind in one eye and had poor vision in the other, which is suggestive when one considers that the character of Mole, an animal that in real life is virtually blind, seems to have no trouble with his vision. This connection cannot be confirmed, but considering that Green makes it clear that the Grahames attempted to deny to themselves and to Alistair, throughout his short life, that he was in any way abnormal, giving sight to a fictional mole certainly sounds like a symbolic form of the same denial.

16. Robert Pattison suggests that without the child's innocent point of view *What Maisie Knew* would be virtual pornography (*Child Figure,* 133–34). Something similar might be said about James's *The Awkward Age,* except that here the "innocent" is the elderly Mr. Longdon.

Chapter 6. Alice as Self and Other(s)

1. This is not quite true, as I had published a rebuttal (" 'The Ambivalent Status of Texts': Some Comments") of another critic's article, and it may be significant that my only writing on *Alice* was, so to speak, an act of aggression.

2. Professor Kincaid tells me that he no longer holds the views expressed in his article.

3. I have in mind the work of such psychoanalysts as A. M. E. Goldschmidt, Paul Schilder, John Skinner, Martin Grotjahn, and Géza Róheim, whose studies of the Alice books are excerpted in Phillips, ed., *Aspects of Alice*. Best known, of course, is William Empson's 1935 essay.

4. My differing with Kincaid's readings is not meant to suggest that he should read *my* way; but his attitude toward Alice does seem to be rooted in affects never described, with personal sources that are never hinted at.

5. On Carroll and Kafka, see Elizabeth Sewell, "The Nonsense System in Lewis Carroll's Work and in Today's World," 62–63.

6. He was, in fact, writing to Mrs. Hargreaves to ask that she temporarily lend him the original manuscript of *Alice's Adventures Underground* so that a facsimile could be made, printed, and marketed, and so this is not a pure love letter; yet a solely mercenary request could have been written without this profession of a kind of permanent love and idealization.

7. Carroll's recent male biographers are extraordinarily defensive in regard both to the claims of Freudian critics and the accusation (if such it be) that there was something sexual in his feelings for young girls. Derek Hudson devotes the first ten paragraphs of his preface to the second edition of his biography of Carroll to refuting the psychoanalysts, and John Pudney ties himself in knots by attempting simultaneously to admit and deny the erotic component in Carroll's "love affairs with maidens" (67–69).

8. The photograph is reproduced in *Lewis Carroll: Victorian Photographer*, edited by Helmut Gernsheim, 63, on the book's front cover, and in *The Letters of Lewis Carroll* 1: f.p. 92.

9. The photograph is reproduced in Pudney, 70, and Hudson, 169.

Chapter 7. *David Copperfield's* Plots against the Reader

1. Margaret Kirkham suggests that Austen as narrator is setting a puzzle or trap for the reader in regard to the true nature of Fanny Price in *Mansfield Park* (see chap. 9).

2. Robert Kiely suggests that Hogg had an "abstract" fascination with "narrative techniques"; he is here distinguishing Hogg, as well as Scott, from Emily Brontë (236).

3. See Roman Ingarden, *The Cognition of the Literary Work of Art*, 241–45, 288–93, 389–92; Wolfgang Iser, *The Implied Reader*; and Iser, *The Act of Reading*, 180–231.

4. See John Carey's introduction to his edition, xii.

5. The fact that some of the "secrets" in *A Justified Sinner* are, so to speak, secrets of the parental bedroom undoubtedly gives a special kind of edge to both my curiosity and my hostility.

6. For the critical position that takes David's "undisciplined heart" as the central theme, see especially Miller, *Charles Dickens: The World of His*

Novels, 150–59, and Needham, "The Undisciplined Heart of David Copperfield."

7. I discuss the various significances of this etching in detail in *Dickens and Phiz,* 115–17.

8. It is perhaps a coincidence, but in the parable of Nathan, God's messenger to David, Bathsheba is compared to a lamb taken from a poor man (a symbol for Uriah the Hittite); and it is ultimately David who takes the lamb—Agnes—from her doting "owner," her father, as well as from Uriah.

9. The grotesque in Uriah's case can also be said to represent distorted energy, as his fishy writhings seem to be a physical expression of such energy, the twitchings of barely repressed aggressive and sexual drives—presenting the kind of appearance no would-be gentleman such as David could allow in himself.

10. Chesterton, *Appreciations,* 132–35; Kincaid, *Dickens,* 163–64; and Gilmour. My own contribution to this negative view of Agnes is in *Dickens and Phiz,* throughout chapter 5. See also John Forster, Dickens's friend and first biographer, who remarks that "the spoilt foolishness and tenderness of the loving little child-wife, Dora, is more attractive than the too unfailing wisdom and self-sacrificing goodness of the angel-wife, Dora" (*Life,* 2:109). On the memorandum, see Butt and Tillotson, 128.

11. Richter is referring specifically to what he considers the failure of such teachers in their attempt to promote a "progressive" kind of critical reading informed by socialist values.

12. It is in making such a claim that I apparently part company with Louise Rosenblatt, who, although she denies that we can directly know "the poem itself," takes as conditions for "acceptable" readings, that "the reader's interpretation not be contradicted by any element of the text, and that nothing be projected for which there is no verbal basis" (115). In my suggestion that there is a "real" Agnes whom Dickens failed to present in the novel, I seem to be contradicting at least the second of these principles.

Chapter 8. The Intentional Phallus in Dickens and Hardy

1. These readings include, among others on *The Old Curiosity Shop,* those of Mark Spilka, Gabriel Pearson, and Steven Marcus, and one might add G. K. Chesterton, who wrote in 1911 that "when we come to Swiveller and Sampson Brass and Quilp and Mrs. Jarley, then Fred and Nell and the grandfather simply do not exist. There are no such people in the story" (55).

2. I believe I was the first critic to argue this seriously in print ("*Martin Chuzzlewit:* Pinch and Pecksniff"), although other readers had noticed it previously.

3. That Dickens considered Tom's organ-playing—I shall not say his *organ*—a central trope can also be inferred from the fact that he gave his illustrator, Hablot K. Browne ("Phiz") specific instructions for making Tom at the organ the center of the partly allegorical and partly recapitulating

frontispiece, originally published with the final monthly part of the novel. See *Dickens and Phiz*, 79–82.

4. For a discussion of Tom Pinch and other Dickens characters as wise or holy fools, see Robert M. McCarron, "Folly and Wisdom: Three Dickensian Wise Fools."

5. That an undergraduate today might not know that Dickens was a Victorian is not all that improbable—a quite bright student once asked me whether the Romantic poets or D. H. Lawrence came first.

6. I do believe that when Monroe Beardsley tries to refute Hirsch's insistence that meaning does not change, by citing Akenside's use of the word *plastic* in "he rais'd his plastic arm," and asserting that it has "acquired a new meaning in the twentieth century," and that therefore there is a difference between "textual meaning" and "authorial meaning," he is simply quibbling, and not responding to Hirsch's general argument that one must understand the meanings of words in their historical, and thus authorial contexts. See Beardsley, "Textual Meaning and Authorial Meaning," 175.

7. The first book edition, published in London by Osgood, McIlvaine and in New York by Harper, is dated 1896 but was actually published near the end of 1895.

8. F. R. Southerington has been the Hardy critic most insistent that the 1895 version represents Hardy's true intentions, and he retains these passages (but no others from the early editions) unrevised in his own textbook edition of *Jude the Obscure*. See also Robert C. Slack, "The Text of Hardy's *Jude the Obscure*."

Chapter 9. Making *Mansfield Park* Feel Right

1. Jan Mukařovský claims that "we must not forget that unintentionality appears to be a disturbing factor only from the standpoint of a certain conception of art which evolved during the Renaissance and reached its peak in the nineteenth century, a conception whereby semantic unification is the basic criterion for evaluating the work of art" ("Intentionality," 124).

2. Bernard J. Paris's chapter on *Mansfield Park*, in his book on Austen, gives a detailed and, within his own approach through the psychological theories of Karen Horney, quite convincing analysis of Fanny. But to consider this in detail would take me too far from the central questions of this chapter.

3. Fleishman also identifies the plot as a Cinderella story, but he makes a different use of this observation than I shall do: "To see Fanny Price's story as a Cinderella story is to assign *Mansfield Park* a position among the immortal literary legends" (71).

4. The term *family romance* has in recent years been misused, especially by literary critics, who have often expanded it to refer to the entire triangular Oedipal relationship in the nuclear family. This seems to be owing to a confusion between *Roman* (story) in Freud's German text, and the literary-

historical (or the Hollywood?) use of *romance*. There seem to me good reasons for preserving the term for the very specific phantasy—a particular *aspect* of the Oedipus complex—as defined by Freud. Perhaps *family story* would be a more appropriate term for what these writers are referring to, although as it is a more accurate translation of Freud's term, this might be confusing.

5. According to Fleishman, "to see [*Mansfield Park*'s] central position in English fiction we must recognize it as a *Bildungsroman*" (71). Obviously I do not see it that way, especially in contrast to *Emma*.

6. In addition to Fleishman, a critic who has discussed (at greater length) the incest-taboo and the "return of the repressed" in Fanny is D. A. Miller (*Narrative*, 57–61); but neither makes the connection with Mrs. Norris's opening remarks.

7. The late John Odmark calls the author's meaning the "*real point of view*" (his emphasis), and he explores certain sets and oppositional pairs of words in order to determine this. It is an interesting attempt, but still depends on the critic's selection of *which* words he will claim demonstrate how Austen uses words. See Odmark, chapters 4 and 5.

8. The supreme, bitter irony is that the inscription placed by Austen's family on her tombstone in Winchester Cathedral mentions only her Christian and domestic virtues, giving no hint at all that she was a novelist.

Chapter 10. Sexual Realism and Phantasy in Hardy and Lawrence

1. The possible exception to such certainty is the direct influence of *Jude the Obscure* on the writing of *Sons and Lovers*, but I shall suggest that there are direct parallels. The broader influence of Hardy on Lawrence cannot be doubted.

2. See also Paris's *A Psychological Approach to Fiction* and *Character and Conflict in Jane Austen's Novels*. Charles Altieri in *Act and Quality* makes an elaborate case for the humanistic value of what he calls the "dramatistic" in literature.

3. Quotations from my 1968 article are slightly revised for purposes of clarity.

4. On the matter of Hardy's inconsistency in this regard, see Bernard J. Paris's 1969 article on *Tess of the D'Urbervilles*, especially 62–65.

5. There does not seem to be much connection between Reich's "hysterical character" and the psychiatric definition of hysteria; there is probably more, in the repression of and concomitant preoccupation with sexual feelings, with the case histories of the "hysterics" out of which Freudian psychoanalysis developed.

6. See also Phyllis Bartlett, "Hardy's Shelley." For an approach to Shelley in *Jude the Obscure* quite different from mine, see Hassett, "Compromised Romanticism in *Jude the Obscure*."

7. The humor we may find in such an earnest poem as *The Revolt of Islam* is almost surely unintended, but Hardy seems to be more conscious of sexual ironies—unless I am misreading the tone, in narrative context, of Sue's refusal of sex: " 'Why are you so gross! *I* jumped out of the window!' " (book IV, chap. 5, 255).

8. That remark of Hardy's about Jude's passion being kept hot by Sue's only infrequent (and presumably unpredictable) allowing of sex is in itself an interesting comment on Hardy's—and perhaps our own (male) culture's—thoughts about what is attractive in women: Is it that eager sexuality in a woman is ultimately seen by many men (and women?) as repulsive, while coquettishness is sexually exciting?

9. Whether Freud's discussion of the tendency to "debasement" can be taken as throwing any light on Jude's return to Arabella after Sue remarries Phillotson is something I cannot judge; such an explanation certainly does not seem necessary, and a more interesting question might be whether Freud, in his belief that there is a "universal" tendency to debasement in love, is speaking personally as much as he is clinically, and to this extent sharing Hardy's confusions about women and sexual love.

10. If those who have seen Sue Bridehead as a fictional portrayal of Hardy's "lost prize," his cousin Tryphena Sparks, are correct, then *Jude the Obscure* would have to be considered nearly as autobiographical as *Sons and Lovers.* This is a debate I prefer not to take a side in.

11. *Athenaeum* review, 21 June 1913; rpt. in *Sons and Lovers,* Viking Critical Library Edition, 423.

12. Mark Spilka is certain that Miriam is "frigid" and responsible for the failure of the relationship (*Love Ethic,* 63–68), and he may be right so far as Lawrence's fully conscious intentions are concerned. On the other hand, an interpretation of Paul's relationships to women far more damning of Paul than is either mine or Carol Dix's is that by Faith Pullin, who suggests that he is not only sexually inept but sadistic.

Chapter 11. Coming to Terms with *Outside Over There*

1. *Magnum opus* is perhaps too solemn a term. Sendak has referred privately to *Outside Over There* as "that poor, darling baby/favorite book" (letter to present author)—"poor," presumably because of the number of readers who have either disliked it or found its meanings obscure.

2. Here, as in the discussion of *Higglety Pigglety Pop!* in chapter 2, when I refer to Sendak's "text" I intend both words and pictures, for the latter are not merely illustrations supplementing the words, but carry, or evoke in the reader, a good deal of the book's meaning.

3. In contrast, while Carroll provides no distinct moment of Alice's falling asleep in the Alice books, in both novels he does describe a definite scene of awakening from the dream.

4. Sendak's illustration for "The Goblins" appears as the frontispiece to the first volume of *The Juniper Tree and Other Tales from Grimm.*

5. The importance and significance of "The Goblins" and *The Magic Flute* are more fully explained by Sendak in Jonathan Cott's 1983 expansion of his 1976 interview (*Pipers*, 70–75).

6. As I mention in chapter 2, I came to this conclusion before I saw Cott's 1983 book, in which Sendak is quoted as making precisely the same statement (75).

7. Letter from Maurice Sendak to the author, 30 December 1985; quoted by permission. (I should say that Sendak is very definite that while I am right about how he has used *The Princess and the Goblin,* he is not sure about any other aspect of my reading.)

8. Lest there be any doubt at this point, I do not claim that the reading that follows is in any sense a correct or objective interpretation. It is presented, rather, in order to describe one reader's process of coming to what he thinks is an understanding of a troubling text. That to some extent I use methods quite common in conventional literary criticism does not contradict my claim that this reading is subjective; such methods are normal to those in the profession of literary criticism, and I would have found it difficult to express a coherent, communicable interpretation without them.

9. My reaction to Sendak's new style was caused partly by my unfamiliarity with the German Romantic painter, Philipp Otto Runge, whom Sendak has cited as his main graphic influence in *Outside Over There.* Having now seen some reproductions of Runge, I must say that I much prefer Sendak's portrayal of children in this new style to Runge's glassy-eyed, schizoid-looking tots.

10. Something quite idiosyncratic crops up in my associations: the long stairway Irene must climb to reach her great-great-grandmother recalls the stairway to my Uncle Bill's attic studio in his country house on the property we shared with him in Connecticut, a stairway I would as a young child always climb with great anticipation of the marvels produced on his drawing-easel. As Irene's great-great-grandmother does for her by offering her love and protection but also giving her new responsibilities, so being invited at age eight to do a drawing for the cover of *Small Fry* was rather like having a new kind of status conferred on me, since I already had considerable doubts about my artistic abilities.

11. On MacDonald as pre-Freudian, see Richard H. Reis, *George MacDonald,* especially the section titled "Psychology: Freudian before Freud," 41–45.

12. It does seem evident from *Sir Gibbie,* and to some extent from *The Princess and the Goblin,* that MacDonald believed that being on your own and thus being required to shape your own life (though *not* a lack of love) promotes self-reliance and strength of character. Is something like this behind Sendak's story?

13. Critics so far have seemed unable to acknowledge the sexual ambiguity in some of Sendak's works. Thus, presumably because the depiction of her is based on a photograph of Sendak as an infant, both De Luca (9) and Lanes (162) refer to Baby in *Higglety Pigglety Pop!* as "he," even though

Sendak throughout uses feminine pronouns in referring to Baby and ultimately has her turn into Mother Goose (the name that Jennie speaks).

14. A recent article by Michael D. Reed interprets *Outside Over There* systematically in terms of a girl's Oedipal phase; but Sendak's book seems too overdetermined for as reductive a reading as this.

Works Cited

Primary Texts

Austen, Jane. *Mansfield Park*. 1814. Edited by James Kinsley and John Lucas. Oxford: Oxford University Press, 1980.

Carroll, Lewis. *Alice's Adventures in Wonderland* and *Through the Looking-Glass*. 1865; 1871. Edited by Roger Lancelyn Green. Oxford: Oxford University Press, 1982.

———. *Alice's Adventures in Wonderland*. Illustrated by Arthur Rackham. London: Heinemann, 1907.

Crabbe, George. *Poetical Works*. Edited by A. J. and R. M. Carlyle. Oxford: Oxford University Press, 1914.

Dickens, Charles. *Bleak House*. 1853. Edited by George Ford and Sylvère Monod. New York: Norton, 1977.

———. *David Copperfield*. 1850. Edited by Trevor Blount. Harmondsworth: Penguin, 1966.

———. *Martin Chuzzlewit*. 1844. Edited by Margaret Cardwell. Oxford: Oxford University Press, 1984.

———. *The Old Curiosity Shop*. 1841. Edited by Angus Easson. Harmondsworth: Penguin, 1972.

Grahame, Kenneth. *Dream Days*. 1898. London: John Lane, 1930.

———. *The Golden Age*. 1895. London: John Lane, 1928.

———. "The Rural Pan." 1891. *Pagan Papers,* pp. 34–38. London: Elkin Mathews and John Lane, 1894.

———. *The Wind in the Willows*. 1908. Edited by Peter Green. Oxford: Oxford University Press, 1983.

Grimm, Brothers. *The Juniper Tree and Other Tales from Grimm*. Translated by Lore Segal and Randall Jarrell. Illustrated by Maurice Sendak. 2 vols. New York: Farrar, Straus, & Giroux, 1973.

Hardy, Thomas. *Jude the Obscure*. 1912. Edited by Patricia Ingham. Oxford: Oxford University Press, 1985.

————. *Jude the Obscure*. London: Osgood, McIlvaine; New York: Harper, 1896 [1895].

Herrick, Robert. *The Poems of Robert Herrick*. 1648. Oxford: Oxford University Press, 1951.

Hogg, James. *The Private Memoirs and Confessions of a Justified Sinner; Written by Himself; With a Detail of Curious Traditionary Facts and Other Evidence by the Editor*. 1824. Edited by John Carey. London: Oxford University Press, 1969.

Kingsley, Charles. *The Water-Babies*. London: Macmillan, 1863.

Lawrence, D. H. *Sons and Lovers*. 1913. Edited by Julian Moynahan, Viking Critical Library Edition. New York: Viking, 1968.

MacDonald, George. *At the Back of the North Wind*. 1870. Illustrated by Arthur Hughes (with *The Princess and the Goblin* and *The Princess and Curdie*). London: Octopus Books, 1979.

————. *The Princess and the Goblin*. 1871. Harmondsworth: Penguin, 1964.

Sendak, Maurice. *Higglety Pigglety Pop! or There Must Be More to Life*. Illustrated by Maurice Sendak. New York: Harper & Row, 1967.

————. *In the Night Kitchen*. Illustrated by Maurice Sendak. New York: Harper & Row, 1970.

————. *Outside Over There*. Illustrated by Maurice Sendak. New York: Harper & Row, 1981.

————. *Where the Wild Things Are*. Illustrated by Maurice Sendak. New York: Harper & Row, 1963.

Shelley, Percy Bysshe. *The Complete Poetical Works*. Edited by Thomas Hutchinson. London: Oxford University Press, 1904.

Stevenson, Robert Louis. *Treasure Island*. 1883. Harmondsworth: Penguin, 1977.

Secondary Sources

Abraham, Gerald. *The Concise Oxford History of Music*. London: Oxford University Press, 1979.

Adams, Robert Martin. *Strains of Discord: Studies in Literary Openness*. Ithaca: Cornell University Press, 1958.

Allott, Miriam, ed. *The Brontës: The Critical Heritage*. London: Routledge, 1974.

Altieri, Charles. *Act and Quality: A Theory of Literary Meaning and Humanistic Understanding*. Ithaca: Cornell University Press, 1981.

Auerbach, Nina. "Jane Austen's Dangerous Charm: Feeling as One Ought about Fanny Price." In *Jane Austen: New Perspectives*, edited by Janet Todd, pp. 208–21.

Bartlett, Phyllis. "Hardy's Shelley," *Keats-Shelley Journal* 4 (winter 1955): 15–23.

————. "'Seraph of Heaven': A Shelleyan Dream in Hardy's Fiction," *PMLA* 70 (1955): 624–35.

Beardsley, Monroe C. *Aesthetics: Problems in the Philosophy of Criticism.* New York: Harcourt, 1958.

———. "Textual Meaning and Authorial Meaning," *Genre* 1 (1968): 169–81.

Bleich, David. "Gender Interests in Reading and Language." In *Gender and Reading: Essays on Readers, Texts, and Contexts,* edited by Elizabeth A. Flynn and Patrocinio P. Schweickart, pp. 234–66. Baltimore: Johns Hopkins University Press, 1986.

———. "Intersubjective Reading," *New Literary History* 17 (1986): 401–21.

———. *Readings and Feelings: An Introduction to Subjective Criticism.* Urbana, Illinois: National Council of Teachers of English, 1975.

———. *Subjective Criticism.* Baltimore: Johns Hopkins University Press, 1978.

Boumelha, Penny. *Thomas Hardy and Women.* Brighton: Harvester, 1982.

Butt, John, and Kathleen Tillotson. *Dickens at Work.* London: Methuen, 1957.

Carey, John. Introduction to *The Private Memoirs and Confessions of a Justified Sinner,* by James Hogg. London: Oxford University Press, 1969.

Carroll, Lewis. *The Letters of Lewis Carroll,* edited by Morton N. Cohen. 2 vols. New York: Oxford University Press, 1979.

Chalmers, Patrick R. *Kenneth Grahame: Life, Letters, and Unpublished Work.* London: Methuen, 1933.

Chesterton, G. K. *Appreciations and Criticisms of the Works of Charles Dickens.* London: Dent, 1911.

Chitty, Susan. *The Beast and the Monk: A Life of Charles Kingsley.* London: Hodder & Stoughton, 1974.

Cioffi, Frank. "Intention and Interpretation in Criticism." 1964. Reprinted in *On Literary Intention,* edited by David Newton-de Molina, pp. 55–73.

Collins, Philip, ed. *Dickens: The Critical Heritage.* London: Routledge, 1971.

Cott, Jonathan. Interview with Maurice Sendak. 1976. Reprinted in *Forever Young,* pp. 89–219. New York: Random House/Rolling Stone, 1977.

———. *Pipers at the Gates of Dawn: The Wisdom of Children's Literature.* New York: Random House, 1983.

Crosman, Robert. "Do Readers Make Meaning?" In *The Reader in the Text,* edited by Susan R. Suleiman and Inge Crosman, pp. 149–64.

Culler, Jonathan. *On Deconstruction: Theory and Criticism after Structuralism.* Ithaca: Cornell University Press, 1982.

———. "Prolegomena to a Theory of Reading." In *The Reader in the Text,* edited by Susan R. Suleiman and Inge Crosman, pp. 46–66.

DeLuca, Geraldine. "Exploring the Levels of Childhood: The Allegorical Sensibility of Maurice Sendak," *Children's Literature* 12 (1984): 3–24.

Dix, Carol. *D. H. Lawrence and Women.* London: Macmillan, 1980.

Duckworth, Alistair M. *The Improvement of the Estate: A Study of Jane Austen's Novels.* Baltimore: Johns Hopkins University Press, 1972.

Duffy, Maureen. *The Erotic World of Faery.* London: Hodder & Stoughton, 1972.

D'Urfey, Thomas, ed. *Wit and Mirth: or Pills to Purge Melancholy*. 1719. 6 vols. New York: Folklore Library Publishers, 1959.

Dyson, A. E. *The Inimitable Dickens*. London: Macmillan, 1970.

Edel, Leon. *Stuff of Sleep and Dreams: Experiments in Literary Psychology*. New York: Harper & Row, 1982.

Empson, William. "Alice in Wonderland: The Child as Swain." *Some Versions of Pastoral*, pp. 253–94. London: Chatto, 1935.

Fish, Stanley E. "Interpreting the Variorum," *Critical Inquiry* 2 (1976): 465–85.

———. *Is There a Text in This Class? The Authority of Interpretive Communities*. Cambridge: Harvard University Press, 1980.

———. *Self-Consuming Artifacts: The Experience of Seventeenth-Century Literature*. Berkeley and Los Angeles: University of California Press, 1972.

Fleishman, Avrom. *A Reading of* Mansfield Park: *An Essay in Critical Synthesis*. Minneapolis: University of Minnesota Press, 1967.

Forster, John. *The Life of Charles Dickens*. 1872–74. Edited by A. J. Hoppé. 2 vols. London: Dent, 1966.

Foucault, Michel. "What is an Author?" In *Textual Strategies: Perspectives in Post-Structuralist Criticism*, edited by Josué V. Harari, pp. 141–60. Ithaca: Cornell University Press, 1979.

Freud, Sigmund. *The Complete Psychological Works* (standard edition). Edited by James Strachey. 24 vols. London: Hogarth, 1955–74.

———. "A Special Type of Object Choice Made by Men." 1910. In *Complete Works* 11:163–75.

———. "Family Romances." 1909. In *Complete Works* 9:237–41

———. "On the Universal Tendency to Debasement in the Sphere of Love." 1912. In *Complete Works* 11:179–90.

———. "The 'Uncanny.'" 1919. In *Complete Works* 17:219–56.

Frye, Northrop. *Anatomy of Criticism*. Princeton: Princeton University Press, 1957.

Garrett, Peter K. *The Victorian Multiplot Novel: Studies in Dialogical Form*. New Haven: Yale University Press, 1980.

Gattégno, Jean. *Lewis Carroll: Fragments of a Looking-Glass*. Translated by Rosemary Sheed. New York: Crowell, 1976.

Gernsheim, Helmut, ed. *Lewis Carroll: Victorian Photographer*. London: Phaidon, 1980.

Gilbert, Sandra M., and Gubar, Susan. *The Madwoman in the Attic: The Woman Writer and the Nineteenth-Century Literary Imagination*. New Haven: Yale University Press, 1979.

Gilmour, Robin. "Memory in *David Copperfield*," *Dickensian* 71 (1975): 30–42.

Gottlieb, Gerald, and Plumb, J. H. *Early Children's Books and Their Illustration*. New York: Pierpont Morgan Library, 1975.

Grahame, Elspeth. *First Whisper of "The Wind in the Willows."* London: Methuen, 1944.

Grahame, Kenneth, ed. *The Cambridge Book of Poetry for Children.* 2 vols. Cambridge: Cambridge University Press, 1916.

Green, Peter. Introduction to *The Wind in the Willows,* by Kenneth Grahame, pp. vii–xx. Oxford: Oxford University Press, 1983.

———. *Kenneth Grahame 1859–1932: A Study of his Life, Work, and Times.* London: John Murray, 1959.

Gross, John, and Pearson, Gabriel, eds. *Dickens and the Twentieth Century.* London: Routledge, 1962.

Guiliano, Edward, ed. *Lewis Carroll Observed: A Collection of Unpublished Photographs, Drawings, Poetry, and New Essays.* New York: Clarkson Potter, 1976.

Hankla, Susan. Letter to *Horn Book* 58 (June 1982): 347.

Hardy, Florence Emily. *The Life of Thomas Hardy.* 2 vols., 1928, 1930. London: Macmillan, 1962.

Hardy, Thomas. *Jude the Obscure,* edited by F. R. Southerington. Indianapolis: Bobbs-Merrill, 1972.

Harvey, W. J. "Chance and Design in Bleak House." In *Dickens and the Twentieth Century,* edited by John Gross and Gabriel Pearson, pp. 145–57.

Hassett, Michael E. "Compromised Romanticism in *Jude the Obscure,*" *Nineteenth-Century Fiction* 25 (1971): 432–43.

Heins, Ethel L. Review of Maurice Sendak, *Outside Over There. Horn Book* 57 (June 1981): 288.

Hirsch, E. D., Jr. *The Aims of Interpretation.* Chicago: Chicago University Press, 1976.

———. *Validity in Interpretation.* New Haven: Yale University Press, 1967.

Hirsch, Gordon D. "The Mysteries in *Bleak House*: A Psychoanalytic Study," *Dickens Studies Annual* 4 (1975): 132–52.

Holland, Norman N. *Five Readers Reading.* New Haven: Yale University Press, 1975.

———. *The Dynamics of Literary Response.* New York: Oxford University Press, 1968.

———. "A Letter to Leonard," *Hartford Studies in Literature* 5 (1973): 9–30.

———. "The Miller's Wife and the Professors: Questions about the Transactive Theory of Reading," *New Literary History* 17 (1986): 423–47.

———. "Re-Covering 'The Purloined Letter': Reading as a Personal Transaction." In *The Reader in the Text,* edited by Susan R. Suleiman and Inge Crosman, pp. 350-70.

Holub, Robert C. *Reception Theory: A Critical Introduction.* London: Methuen, 1984.

Horton, Susan R. *Interpreting Interpreting: Interpreting Dickens's Dombey.* Baltimore: Johns Hopkins University Press, 1979.

———. "Reader? / Response? / Text? / Self?" *Reader* 12 (Fall 1984): 11–20.

Hudson, Derek. *Lewis Carroll: An Illustrated Biography.* 2d ed. London: Constable, 1976.

Hutter, Albert D. "The High Tower of His Mind: Psychoanalysis and the Reader of 'Bleak House,'" *Criticism* 19 (1977): 296–316.

Ingarden, Roman. *The Cognition of the Literary Work of Art.* Translated by Ruth Ann Crowley and Kenneth R. Olson. Evanston, Illinois: Northwestern University Press, 1973.

Iser, Wolfgang. *The Act of Reading: A Theory of Aesthetic Response.* 1976. Translated by author. Baltimore: Johns Hopkins University Press, 1978.

———. *The Implied Reader.* 1972. Translated by author. Baltimore: Johns Hopkins University Press, 1974.

Jameson, Fredric. "Metacommentary," *PMLA* 86 (1971): 9–18.

———. *The Political Unconscious.* Ithaca: Cornell University Press, 1981.

Jauss, Hans Robert. *Toward an Aesthetic of Reception.* Translated by Timothy Bathi. Minneapolis: Minnesota University Press, 1984.

Kiely, Robert. *The Romantic Novel in England.* Cambridge: Harvard University Press, 1972.

Kilian, Crawford. "In Defence of Esther Summerson," *Dalhousie Review* 54 (1974): 318–28.

Kincaid, James R. "Alice's Invasion of Wonderland," *PMLA* 88 (1973): 92–99.

———. *Dickens and the Rhetoric of Laughter.* Oxford: Clarendon, 1971.

Kirkham, Margaret. "Feminist Irony and the Priceless Heroine of *Mansfield Park.*" In *Jane Austen: New Perspectives,* edited by Janet Todd, pp. 231–47.

Krieger, Murray. *Theory of Criticism: A Tradition and Its System.* Baltimore: Johns Hopkins University Press, 1976.

Kuznets, Lois R. "Toad Hall Revisited," *Children's Literature* 7 (1978): 115–28.

Lanes, Selma G. *The Art of Maurice Sendak.* New York: Abrams, 1980.

Lawrence, D. H. *Study of Thomas Hardy.* C. 1914. In *Phoenix: The Posthumous Papers of D. H. Lawrence,* edited by Edward D. MacDonald, pp. 398–516. London: Heinemann, 1936.

Leavis, F. R. and Leavis, Q. D. *Dickens the Novelist.* London: Chatto, 1970.

Lewis, Naomi. Review of Peter Green, *Kenneth Grahame. Victorian Studies* 4 (1960): 173.

Loesberg, Jonathan. "Intentionalism, Reader-Response, and the Place of Deconstruction," *Reader* 12 (Fall 1984): 21–37.

MacCann, Donnarae, and Richard, Olga. Review of Selma Lanes, *The Art of Maurice Sendak. Children's Literature Association Quarterly* 6 (Winter 1981–82): 11–17.

Mailloux, Steven. *Interpretive Conventions: The Reader in the Study of American Fiction.* Ithaca: Cornell University Press, 1982.

Manheim, Leonard F. "The Personal History of David Copperfield," *American Imago* 9 (1952): 21–43.

Marcus, Steven. *Dickens: From Pickwick to Dombey.* New York: Basic Books, 1965.

McCarron, Robert M. "Folly and Wisdom: Three Dickensian Wise Fools," *Dickens Studies Annual* 6 (1977): 40–56.

Meyersohn, Marylea. "What Fanny Knew: A Quiet Auditor of the Whole." In *Jane Austen: New Perspectives,* edited by Janet Todd, pp. 224–30.

Mickelson, Anne Z. *Thomas Hardy's Women and Men: The Defeat of Nature.* Metuchen, N.J.: Scarecrow Press, 1976.

Miller, D. A. *Narrative and Its Discontents: Problems of Closure in the Traditional Novel.* Princeton: Princeton University Press, 1981.

Miller, J. Hillis. *Charles Dickens: The World of His Novels.* Cambridge: Harvard University Press, 1958.

———. *Fiction and Repetition.* Cambridge: Harvard University Press, 1982.

———. *Thomas Hardy: Distance and Desire.* Cambridge: Harvard University Press, Belknap Press, 1970.

Milne, A. A. Introduction to *The Wind in the Willows,* by Kenneth Grahame, pp. vii–x. New York: Limited Editions Club, 1940.

Moore, Harry T. *The Intelligent Heart: The Story of D. H. Lawrence.* New York: Farrar, Straus, & Giroux, 1954.

Moss, Elaine. Review of Maurice Sendak, *Outside Over There. Times Literary Supplement,* 24 July 1981, p. 841.

Mudrick, Marvin. *Jane Austen: Irony as Defense and Discovery.* Princeton: Princeton University Press, 1952.

Mukařovský, Jan. "Intentionality and Unintentionality in Art." 1943. In *Structure, Sign, and Function,* translated and edited by John Burbank and Peter Steiner, pp. 89–128. Yale Russian and East European Studies, 14. New Haven: Yale University Press, 1978.

———. "The Individual and Literary Development." 1943–45. In *The Word and Verbal Art: Selected Essays by Jan Mukařovský,* Translated and edited by John Burbank and Peter Steiner, pp. 161–79. New Haven: Yale University Press, 1977.

Needham, Gwendolyn B. "The Undisciplined Heart of David Copperfield," *Nineteenth-Century Fiction* 9 (1954): 81–107.

Newton-de Molina, David, ed. *On Literary Intention: Critical Essays.* Edinburgh: Edinburgh University Press, 1976.

Odmark, John. *An Understanding of Jane Austen's Novels.* Oxford: Blackwell, 1981.

Olsen, Stein Haugom. *The Structure of Literary Understanding.* Cambridge: Cambridge University Press, 1978.

Osbourne, Lloyd. *An Intimate Portrait of R. L. S.* New York: Scribner's, 1924.

Paris, Bernard J. *Character and Conflict in Jane Austen's Novels: A Psychological Approach.* Detroit: Wayne State University Press, 1978.

———. "'A Confusion of Many Standards'": Conflicting Value Systems in *Tess of the D'Urbervilles,*" *Nineteenth-Century Fiction* 24 (1969): 57–79.

———. "Form, Theme, and Imitation in Realistic Fiction," *Novel* 1 (1968): 140–49.

———. "The Inner Conflicts of Maggie Tulliver: A Horneyan Analysis," *Centennial Review* 13 (1969): 166–99.

———. *A Psychological Approach to Fiction: Studies in Thackeray, Stendhal, George Eliot, Dostoevsky, and Conrad*. Bloomington: Indiana University Press, 1974.

———. "Towards a Revaluation of George Eliot's *The Mill on the Floss*," *Nineteenth-Century Fiction* 11 (1956): 18–31.

Partridge, Eric. *A Dictionary of Slang and Unconventional English*. 5th ed. New York: Macmillan, 1961.

Pattison, Robert. *The Child Figure in English Literature*. Athens: University of Georgia Press, 1978.

Pearson, Gabriel. "The Old Curiosity Shop." In *Dickens and the Twentieth Century*, edited by John Gross and Gabriel Pearson, pp. 77–90.

Peckham, Morse. "The Intentional? Fallacy?" 1969. Reprinted in *On Literary Intention*, edited by David Newton-de Molina, pp. 139–57.

Peller, Lili. "Daydreams and Children's Favorite Books: Psychoanalytic Comments," *Psychoanalytic Study of the Child* 14 (1959): 414–33.

Phillips, Robert, ed. *Aspects of Alice*. New York: Vanguard, 1971.

Pope-Hennessy, James. *Robert Louis Stevenson*. London: Cape, 1974.

Poss, Geraldine D. "An Epic in Arcadia: The Pastoral World of *The Wind in the Willows*." *Children's Literature* 4 (1975): 80–90.

Pudney, John. *Lewis Carroll and His World*. London: Thames & Hudson, 1976.

Pullin, Faith. "Lawrence's Treatment of Women in *Sons and Lovers*." In *Lawrence and Women*, edited by Anne Smith, pp. 49–74. London: Vision, 1972.

Rackin, Donald. "Laughing and Grief: What's So Funny about *Alice in Wonderland?*" In *Lewis Carroll Observed*, edited by Edward Guiliano, pp. 1–19.

Rader, Ralph W. "Fact, Theory, and Literary Explanation," *Critical Inquiry* 1 (1974): 254–72.

Raskin, Marcus G., and Bernstein, Herbert J., eds. *New Ways of Knowing: The Sciences, Society, and Reconstructive Knowledge*. Totowa, N.J.: Rowman & Littlefield, 1987.

Reed, Michael D. "The Female Oedipal Complex in Maurice Sendak's *Outside Over There*," *Children's Literature Association Quarterly* 11 (1986–87): 176–79.

Reich, Wilhelm. *Character-Analysis*. 3d ed. Translated by Theodore P. Wolfe. New York: Noonday Press, 1962.

Reis, Richard H. *George MacDonald*. New York: Twayne, 1972.

Richter, Dieter. "Teachers and Readers: Reading Attitudes as a Problem in Teaching Literature." Translated by Sara Lennox. *New German Critique* 7 (1976): 21–43.

Rosenblatt, Louise M. *The Reader, the Text, the Poem: The Transactional Theory of the Literary Work.* Carbondale: Southern Illinois University Press, 1978.

Rudwick, Martin J. S. *The Great Devonian Controversy: The Shaping of Scientific Knowledge among Gentlemanly Specialists.* Chicago: University of Chicago Press, 1985.

Sale, Roger. *Fairy Tales and After: From Snow White to E. B. White.* Cambridge: Harvard University Press, 1978.

Schachtel, Ernest. *Metamorphosis: On the Development of Affect, Perception, Attention, and Memory.* New York: Basic Books, 1959.

Schorer, Mark. Introduction to *Wuthering Heights,* by Emily Brontë. 1950. Reprinted in *Wuthering Heights: Text, Sources, Criticism,* edited by Thomas Moser, pp. 183–88. New York: Harcourt, 1962.

Sewell, Elizabeth. "The Nonsense System in Lewis Carroll's Work and Today's World." In *Lewis Carroll Observed,* edited by Edward Guiliano, pp. 60–67.

Slack, Robert C. "The Text of Hardy's *Jude the Obscure.*" *Nineteenth-Century Fiction* 11 (1957): 261–75.

Spilka, Mark. *Dickens and Kafka: A Mutual Interpretation.* Bloomington: Indiana University Press, 1963.

————. "Little Nell Revisited," *Papers of the Michigan Academy of Science, Arts, and Letters* 45 (1960): 427–37.

————. *The Love Ethic of D. H. Lawrence.* Bloomington: Indiana University Press, 1955.

Steig, Michael. "'The Ambivalent Status of Texts': Some Comments," *Poetics Today* 2 (1980–81): 193–97.

————. "Anality in *The Mill on the Floss,*" *Novel* 5 (1971): 42–53.

————. *Dickens and Phiz.* Bloomington: Indiana University Press, 1978.

————. "*Martin Chuzzlewit:* Pinch and Pecksniff," *Studies in the Novel* 1 (1969): 181–88.

————. "Sue Bridehead," *Novel* 1 (1968): 260-66.

————. "The Whitewashing of Inspector Bucket: Origins and Parallels," *Papers of the Michigan Academy of Science, Arts, and Letters* 50 (1965): 575–84.

————, and Wilson, F. A. C., "Hortense vs. Bucket: The Ambiguity of Order in *Bleak House,*" *Modern Language Quarterly* 33 (1972): 289–98.

Stone, Harry. *Dickens and the Invisible World: Fairy Tales, Fantasy, and Novel-Making.* Bloomington: Indiana University Press, 1979.

Stott, John. "The Nature of Fantasy: A Conversation with Ruth Nichols, Susan Cooper, and Maurice Sendak," *The World of Children's Books* 3, no. 2 (1978): 32–43.

Suleiman, Susan R., and Crosman, Inge, eds. *The Reader in the Text.* Princeton: Princeton University Press, 1980.

Sumner, Rosemary. *Thomas Hardy: Psychological Novelist.* London: Macmillan, 1981.

Taylor, Mary-Agnes. "Which Way to Castle Yonder?" *Children's Literature Association Quarterly* 12 (1987): 142–44.

Todd, Janet, ed. *Jane Austen: New Perspectives.* Women and Literature, New Series, 3. New York: Holmes & Meier, 1983.

Tompkins, Jane P., ed. *Reader-Response Criticism from Formalism to Post-Structuralism.* Baltimore: Johns Hopkins University Press, 1980.

———. "The Reader in History." In *Reader-Response Criticism,* edited by Jane Tompkins, pp. 201–32.

Trilling, Lionel. "Mansfield Park." In *The Opposing Self,* pp. 206–30. New York: Viking, 1955.

Westburg, Barry. *The Confessional Fictions of Charles Dickens.* Dekalb: Northern Illinois University Press, 1977.

Wimsatt, William K., Jr. "Genesis: A Fallacy Revisited." 1968. Reprinted in *On Literary Intention,* edited by David Newton-de Molina, pp. 116–38.

———. *The Verbal Icon: Studies in the Meaning of Poetry.* Lexington: University of Kentucky Press, 1954.

———, and Beardsley, Monroe C. "The Affective Fallacy." 1949. Reprinted in *The Verbal Icon,* by William K. Wimsatt, Jr., pp. 21–39.

———. "The Intentional Fallacy." 1946. Reprinted in *The Verbal Icon,* by William K. Wimsatt, Jr., pp. 3–18.

Zwerdling, Alex. "Esther Summerson Rehabilitated," *PMLA* 88 (1973): 429–39.

Index

Adams, Robert Martin, on open texts, 158
Aesthetic response: "correct," 167–68; dictated by text (Krieger), 18; non-aesthetic response to literary masterpieces, 168
"Affective Fallacy, The" (Wimsatt and Beardsley), 23
Affects: in meaning, xiii; mediated by individual reader's experience, 18; as motivation to interpret, xiv; "necessary" ones in interpretation, 18; variability among readers, 22
Alice's Adventures in Wonderland (Carroll): awakening from dream in, 235n.3; biographical details as part of understanding, 123; block against writing about, 106, 230n.1; compared to *Through the Looking-Glass,* 106; difference of protagonist for male and female readers, 120–21; foreshadowing of Kafka in trial, 120, 231n.5; graphic depictions of Alice as factor in response, 120; Kincaid on narrator's hostility to Alice, 107, 115–17, 123, 230nn. 2, 4; motives for writing about, 105; obstacles to students' reading, 106, 109, 212; problematic text, 217; and psychoanalytic criticism, 107, 230n.3; Rackin on the "readers" in, 107–8; student response papers, 108–9, 110–14; student's response at different ages, 110–12. *See also* Associative reading of Carroll's *Alice;* Author, conceptualization of; Carroll, Lewis
Altieri, Charles, 234n.2

Anatomy of Criticism (Frye), as justification for critic's responses, 30
Associations: as explanation of response, 62, 112, 118; idiosyncratic, 119; problem of reconstructing, 79
Associative reading of Carroll's *Alice:* childhood associations and response, 109, 115–19, 120–21; palimpsest of accretions upon first reading, 108
Associative reading of *The Wind in the Willows:* childhood associations and response, 85–87, 91–92, 94–95; context of childhood reading, 84–85; effect of psychoanalytic concepts on adult response, 87; evasions in, 91, 93–95; motivation for writing, 223n.12. *See also* Pratt, Branwen Bailey
At the Back of the North Wind (MacDonald), 206, 208. See also *Outside Over There*
Auerbach, Nina, on *Mansfield Park,* 166, 167, 174–75, 179
Austen, Jane, 80, 104; differences from Fanny Price (character in *Mansfield Park),* 171; Odmark on, 234n.7; resemblance to Mary Crawford (character in *Mansfield Park*), 163; seeming intention to effect narrative resolutions, 158; tombstone, 234n.8. Works: *Emma,* 163, 167–69, 173, 234n.5; *Mansfield Park,* 123, 159–79, 231n.1, 233nn. 2, 3, 234nn. 5, 6; *Pride and Prejudice,* 161, 167, 177. *See also* Author, conceptualization of; Mudrick, Marvin
Author, conceptualization of, 106;